The Control Centre

UNDERSTANDING THE NATURE AND FUNCTION OF THE SUBCONSCIOUS, SO WE CAN ATTRACT THE LIFE WE WANT

SIMON GILLMORE

First published by Ultimate World Publishing 2020
Copyright © 2020 Simon Gillmore

ISBN

Paperback - 978-1-922372-16-1
Ebook - 978-1-922372-17-8

Simon Gillmore has asserted his right under the Copyright, Designs and Patents Act 1988 to be identified as the author of this work. The information in this book is based on the author's experiences and opinions. The publisher specifically disclaims responsibility for any adverse consequences, which may result from use of the information contained herein. Permission to use information has been sought by the author. Any breaches will be rectified in further editions of the book.

All rights reserved. No part of this publication may be reproduced, stored in or introduced into a retrieval system, or transmitted in any form, or by any means (electronic, mechanical, photocopying, recording or otherwise) without the prior written permission of the author. Any person who does any unauthorised act in relation to this publication may be liable to criminal prosecution and civil claims for damages. Enquiries should be made through the publisher.

Cover design: Ultimate World Publishing
Layout and typesetting: Ultimate World Publishing
Editor: James Salmon

Ultimate World Publishing
Diamond Creek,
Victoria Australia 3089
www.writeabook.com.au

Dedication

To anyone who wants to be more in control of how they feel, and what happens in their life.

Contents

Dedication iii
Introduction vii
Chapter 1: The Last Great Reformation 1
Chapter 2: Infant Download 19
Chapter 3: The Secret Agenda of Mind 41
Chapter 4: Watching the Watcher 65
Chapter 5: Meeting Our Maker 85
Chapter 6: What Makes Us Feel? 107
Chapter 7: The Miracle of Mindfulness 123
Chapter 8: Mind Spa 143
Chapter 9: Living by Accident 159
Chapter 10: Next Level Living 189
Chapter 11: How Would it Feel? 201
Chapter 12: The Return of Alchemy 223
Chapter 13: Through the Looking Glass 243
Afterword 267
About the Author 273

Introduction

After 25 plus years of interest in personal development material I became somewhat disenchanted by much of it sounding like the same old material, but in a different cover. I mean, I loved the topic but started to think there is so much in common with all of this stuff that I should write my own shortened version. I felt a lot of people don't have an interest in personal development because they don't actually know what it is. If I could make my own 'best of' version maybe more people could benefit. There certainly seemed a need – with more people suffering depression and a smorgasbord of mental health issues, there can never be too many people trying to raise awareness.

And becoming more aware that we are the cause of our experience is always the single answer – the universal cure. When we know it is us creating our experience and why, we have the power to change it. We have some control over what happens and how we feel.

But the book took a turn shortly after I began writing. I found it impossible to write about personal development without mentioning the broader implications of this process of human beings becoming more conscious. For this was truly the good news – that the ultimate outcome of this evolution of us becoming more conscious might be closer than we think. Certainly, all of the hallmarks are present that it is only a matter of time before we experience a major shift in awareness. But to look more closely we realise that it is not a matter of time but presence of mind. Becoming more conscious and intentional was an inner journey, not dependent on our position or the conditions of our life. And this wasn't just some sort of 'sci-fi' ideal of what was possible for humanity – realising how, by our intentions, we change the nature of the physical world. We can consciously change how the world seems – what it is to us.

Because that is the promise of a more conscious life – to know ourselves as the cause of what happens. And when everyone is doing it, I think the future looks far brighter than the 'shock' media would like us to believe. Where is humanity heading? More able to consciously turn the world to our liking. For it to be a choice of how we see the world and our place in it.

But to do this we have to realise the nature of the human programming. The 'big stuff' we turn over to that automated part of our lives so we can operate in relative peace. We have to give some of the parts of our experience to the 'cruise control' settings so we can 'coast'. We would be ill-equipped to cope if we were always guessing about what things meant and how we should act. These things we just know, they are not decisions we make. But that said, this book is about bringing us to the awareness that while 'what's going on' is not a choice we make, it is not unrelated to the things we have consciously declared we want. We enact the programming, by the conscious declaration we make on how things are and what we want. To change the programming we have to work on a level of the programming. By reflecting on what is important to us – by being less resistant of how we find the present, and consciously affirming how we would like our experience to be different to the one we are having now.

Because, as human beings, we are driven to want to improve the conditions of our life, but going about this from the end of changing the physical conditions is starting from the wrong place. Conditions are always a reflection of how we feel. We have to change how we

INTRODUCTION

feel, and the pattern of reactive behaviour to change the apparent circumstances of our life. We have more control over how we feel, and the consequential conditions of our life than we ordinarily exercise. This book is about explaining how we ask for the conditions of our life, so we can ask for better ones. We ask by the perception of having – how would it feel, or what is commonly referred to as the 'Law of Attraction'. Hopefully I offer a perspective that can make this make sense for people, because I believe it is in understanding this law that we can cure much of the angst most people think of as a normal experience.

Communicating this 'Law' was certainly the fundamental insight that was supposed to be offered to us through religions, and is a common theme running through all personal development work. I believe it offers the promise of curing the human condition itself. Between understanding this law, and the ideas behind the mindful experience, I believe humanity stands on the threshold of a much more awakened experience. Feeling like we want to much more of the time – inviting more favourable conditions into our life. Mindfulness is the buzz of our era because it allows us to break the perpetual cycle of habit energy that carries us away as passengers of our lives. It allows an untarnished and more favourable expectation of what is to come. And as we will soon realise, the world as we know it is an absolute replica of our unconscious expectations. We make it the way it is so we feel like we know how to deal with it. We turn everything we see into something we have experienced that seems similar to what we have seen before. And we do it for the entirety of what we experience.

I have made an attempt to simplify how we can take control of how we feel and what happens to us. Emotions are not the obstacle, they are the fuel – we just have to change the way we think, create and use them, or they will use us. When we make clear intentions of what we want our life becomes less random. This book is my attempt to demystify our programming. When we understand the how and the why, it is not rocket science but will give us more control over how our life goes. It may seem scary to some that something beyond us is running our life, but only till we know why it is there and take the reins. If we don't, all of our efforts – no matter how much harder we work and try, we will only manage to dig a deeper hole. Because we continue to resist 'what is'. When we push against a wall, the wall gets stronger.

But this book is not just about how beneficial it is to us to have a clear target, and sense of direction – it is an insight into how personal development is raising the vibration of our planet. These are simultaneously the best and the hardest times to live in. Whilst we benefit from an ever-evolving awareness of how the mind and emotions work, we are also dogged by the need to belong to an increasingly artificial world. Advertising is the business that we are not good enough, and there are more and more targeted ads than ever in history. There is an atmosphere that we are not good enough without the right products, or without being the recipients of hordes of attention. We, the consumer, are the product in this new economy - our eyeballs the prize.

What we have as we move towards more conscious, tolerant and intentional lives is control. Control over what happens and how we feel – control over what we turn the world into and the speed at which this will happen. But most of all, what we are offered is that we don't have to wait. The feeling of having will be realised as a product of mind. In an appreciation of what mind is and perception as a conscious (rather than a subconscious) function, we will change our world, and do it with grace and ease.

We are encoded in our souls with everything we need in every moment to know peace and love what is happening – to be satisfied. There are many kinds of 'music' playing on the airwaves, we just have to adjust our dial - tune into the one that resonates with what would bring us joy. It is not what we do that brings us joy, but how we do it. The sounds that tell us what we need to hear about ourselves. We, in the conscious mind, are sending instructions to something quite supernatural – something that transcends our knowing. When we sense

INTRODUCTION

this thing, we will never again feel alone, or lacking, or insignificant, no matter who we are. This is the age of the nobodies, because we are realising that we are at once 'everybody' – our status will matter far less in a truly connected and more conscious world. We will realise we are connected to something far greater than any image of self or reality we can conjure up.

Buckle up – and bring an open mind.

CHAPTER 1
The Last Great Reformation

THE CONTROL CENTRE

> "The real voyage of discovery consists not in seeking new landscapes, but in having new eyes."
>
> — Marcel Proust

Personal development is a billion dollar, and growing, industry. No matter where you look it permeates our culture – the theme of personal growth doesn't just come from the gurus and the hundreds of courses that now saturate Facebook advertising. It's not just the thousands of life coaches that are popping up everywhere. The themes of personal development – that our dreams are possible, and of becoming the best version of ourselves – ring through in more places than ever. The suggestions of personal growth populate our music, movies, entertainment – I mean they always have, but there has been an evolution of our interest in the subject that is reflected in how broadly available information of this nature has become.

The pinnacle of human intrigue has never changed – to 'know thyself' or to realise mind has always been paramount. The ultimate quest of being human and the mysteries of perception remain front and centre. We had to imagine that at some stage we would be better equipped to answer these age-old conundrums – that the work of preceding generations would come to a head with regard to awareness of mind. That we would become more conscious was a no-brainer, and I have to say it is looking more like we have arrived at this time now. This is the age of awareness we are living in – the age in which we have now been welcomed. Because of the speed at which information flows, being met by that unquenchable human thirst for selfknowing, we have arrived at a time which could quite possibly represent the cure to the human condition itself.

If there is anything that can help us deal with the pangs of the human condition better, it quickly courses through the veins of our information channels. Happy days, right – we are here. The problem, of course, is that we still experience the world through an old evolutionary model of emotions that is out of sync with the world we now live in. It is now a fast-paced and confusing world to a being that is emotionally designed to live in tribal conditions, and it is a little overwhelming to say the least. We don't understand what the subconscious mind is doing, and we don't work with it. We don't think with reference to what is listening to our thoughts.

But personal development has always been with us – it has taken many forms. No matter what you call it now – self-help, New Thought, personal growth, **Law of Attraction** – it fills the same need, that being self-awareness/self-knowing. To me personal development could be simplified into gratitude development, for it is always what we are grateful for that becomes a more dominant and prevalent part of our lives. What we 'put on the fire' gets bigger. Gratitude is how we tell the universe what we like and would love more of. Awareness is either a great gift or our enemy depending on our conscious choice to see the world in the manner we do. In this book I have summarised all manner of awareness-raising material to personal development, or just shortened it to PD, but it goes by many names.

No matter the names it goes by you will not find any of this type of material that is not anchored in becoming more aware of our programming – more conscious of what is unconscious in us. More aware that our experience is created in the subconscious mind. There is no content that is not heavily directed at altering our feeling states or what has become trendily known as the Law of Attraction. You will have to forgive me here for not explaining attraction more fully – if you've not been introduced to it, or don't believe in its effectiveness, that will change in the coming chapters. I'll fully explain what it is and how it works in a manner we can understand very soon. But for now, I just need people to understand PD to be about improving awareness of the subconscious mind and how our emotions skew our perception of the world. Reality is not what it seems.

THE CONTROL CENTRE

For it is by understanding this trend that we might become more interested in its application and relativity to our lives. That is the real intended benefit of this chapter. Much as this might seem like some crazy and 'out there' idea, all I want is for people to understand attraction and personal development as the happiness business. PD is simple, and every step we take towards awareness is rewarded with more emotional control and self-understanding. PD isn't just about becoming leaders, richer and elevating our status. It has a practical value to anyone who wants to be more in control of how they feel and what happens to them. What happens is relative to how we feel about it.

We claim our lives matter to us and then let people spoil our mood for the stupidest reasons. Our lives are no more than a pattern of reactions that build on each other until we experience something that we claim we have no idea where it came from. It came from the cumulative effect of those seemingly small and insignificant reactions that we scarcely even considered to be a part of the energy we spend our time in. It is a pattern – it comes from a program we are running that, for the most part, we have very little consciousness of, or therefore control over. We wish we could be more patient – we wish we weren't so sensitive to the opinions of others. This is the nature of PD content.

I want people to understand personal development as an insight into being human – to how this emotional substation of potential we call a body/mind works. As I have mentioned, PD has always been around and it has taken many forms – and here comes that dreaded 'R' word that is bound to make people either despise me or run to the hills, but dare I say: knowledge of the subconscious mind and the insight to the attractive nature of emotions was once the reserved domain of religions.

This type of information carries something of an inner or 'spiritual' connotation, in that it is an explanation of the effect our thoughts and emotions have on the world we experience, and the outcomes we attract. The inner world's effect on the outer world. Our thoughts have force – they are 'things' that move and affect the physical world. The stuff that is not obvious to the conscious mind, but carries with it the promise of unlocking our emotional potential. Religions have always been entrusted with our hearts. They were the first version of personal development, for a people less endowed with the ocean of information we now bask in.

Religion was about inner sight. About understanding perspective as a superpower that could turn how our world seems on a dime. That can instantly transform a hostile and hopeless place into a bright and hopeful one without anything in our conditions actually changing. We must sense our connection to something larger and more sacred than we are conscious of, as a means to developing a more satisfying, purposeful and meaningful existence. How our dreams will come true is not obvious to the lower vibrating conscious state – so we have to 'pray' to, or trust in, this greater part of the mind for deliverance of what might otherwise seem impossible.

The 'job' of religions was proper use of mind. To explain the subconscious program we were running so we could understand how to change it. We cannot change what we have no awareness of. This is what translates to, or is the modern version of, a conscious being understanding the subconscious nature of the program that runs in the background of our lives. A human into a 'spiritual' being. This process of consciousness – of humans becoming more conscious – is one in the same as the natural evolution of our species.

The explosion of the personal development industry is but a sign that we are waking up as a species to the fact that we can have more control than most people exercise over how our life goes, and can learn how to use our perspective to turn the world into something more pleasing. Human awareness has always been building – the collective human vibration is rising. This process we are engaged in has an end goal – the mass scale realisation of mind. An end to suffering as we know it. We are the living witnesses to the evolution of our own consciousness.

I'll interject here briefly for anyone reading who isn't familiar with the term vibration. I will use whatever term I think best suits the context.

THE CONTROL CENTRE

But if ever I refer to our frequency, vibration, chi, energy, or karma, I'm talking about the same thing – our state of mind or emotional state, and the magnetic qualities it embodies.

The 'trend' as it were, of personal development, represents something far more profound than an industry that we might one day lose interest in. And we are very fortunate that this is no longer, as it once was, the influence of a single person alerting us to a cryptically 'hidden' truth. The 'truth' is far more transparent than it once was, and the delivery far less cryptic. PD is not a trend – it is a wave of consciousness sweeping our world. It is not one person – no one is spearheading this change – it is the spot fires of rising awareness that are flaring up in every corner of the world. It is a new spiritual understanding that is coming from outside of religions that is easier to understand and inclusive of all peoples, and all life for that matter. And this energy is not just evident in personal development material – it permeates our art, our culture and the general feeling of our species.

We are infinitely intelligent beings and, most fortunate of all, we understand that for something to be considered 'wisdom', it must be grounded in equality – the only measure of our growth is our level of compassion. For any idea to carry, it has to meet the prerequisite of being inclusive of all life. It has to be grounded in awareness – in the knowing that at the deepest part of us we are all connected on a soul level. At a subconscious level there is a part of us that is present in all that surrounds us – we are not separate from the outside world or each other. It is this understanding that grants us the awareness that we can manipulate our physical conditions in mind. And this knowing was, above all, what was the promise of religions – that we would be more subconsciously aware beings. That there was a higher level of consciousness – an attic in our minds that, upon entry, would allow us to feel great, to heal ourselves, and attract desirable outcomes.

Again, if this seems a little 'out there', I promise it will all start to make sense soon. I am only trying to illustrate that this personal development trend represents something of a spiritual reformation – a revolution in the way we use our visual mind, and live more intentional lives. This 'reformation' in awareness – the deepening of our understanding of the self – is something that has occurred before, but never with the clarity and expansiveness we are witnessing in the modern era. All religions began with someone who had realised mind, and tried to share a simplified version of this truth to the masses. Consciousness is a process that has always been in motion and what we are now witnessing, as life on earth, is **the last great spiritual reformation of our species**. Personal development is more than just an industry – it is a movement towards us being more spiritual/conscious beings that is raising the collective awareness/vibration of life on earth.

The great reformers

Throughout our history we have witnessed many spiritual reformations, or men who changed the way we thought about self-awareness. The Buddha, the Christ were not the founders of new religions in their time – they were men who thought that the hierarchy of their mother religion had lost the essence of the message. They had become restless with the injustice that the responsibilities of the religious hierarchy were not being met, and the faithful were being oppressed to the greater truth of personal transformation.

The Buddha was a Hindu prince, who after years of searching discovered how similar the truths of his sacred Hindu texts were to other great faiths of the time. How all of the sacred knowing comes from a single unified source. He incorporated sayings from Taoism, Confucianism, and other spiritual wisdoms of the time to try to simplify what he saw as a confusing and complicated path towards truth. And the Christ, too, was obviously displeased with the scornful ways and lack of compassion of the hierarchy – they had lost the meaning of the message. Jesus was a Jew who practiced a strict allegiance to his faith. In his words, "I have not come to change the law (meaning the Jewish law) but to bring it into perfection". Both the Buddha and the Christ used elements of their 'mother' religion and incorporated it with other sacred traditions of the time to open the floodgates of humanity to a greater, more expansive truth. There are many who revealed a strong Buddhist influence in Christian teaching. All reformers 'borrowed' truths from other sacred traditions of the time.

But the Buddha and the Christ certainly weren't the only ones. Muhammad considered himself the last in the line of the great Abrahamic prophets – paying homage to the great prophets who had preceded him. He saw himself as the last of the prophets that began with Abraham, through Moses, through Jesus and ending with himself. The monotheisms that came out of the Arab nations are known today as the Abrahamic traditions, and share the belief in a single unifying supreme source of life and the virtues of family, charity, honesty and respect for others.

Every spiritual master who made sense enough to be a notable mention in our history had the same intent and for the same reason. The hierarchy had either missed the point or disguised the meaning held in a spiritual understanding to serve their power-hungry needs. The truth was being manipulated and fed to a confused population and they were trying to offer some clarity, hope and much needed healing through insight. Zoroaster, Baha'u'llah (of the Baha'i faith), Guru Nanak Dev (who founded Sikhism) and many others like them, all had the same intent – disclose the truth of our being into a simplified truth that could carry equally for all people. Our history is dotted with the great prophets who all came with the same intent – to unify humankind into a single, simplified truth.

I have no interest in providing insight into these faiths and 'proving' how similar they were. I'm not a religious scholar, and I'm certain even those who were qualified enough to make this point with in-depth research and the correct historical timelines have been systematically dismissed and discredited. I think that is real beauty of this coming from such an ordinary person. I don't care who, if anyone, believes me. My only interest is in bringing this to people's attention. I don't care for proof or to be believed – I just want to promote awareness of how similar our religions were in their agenda, and the purpose they served. I have zero concern for being 'right' – it just seems obvious to me we have entered the time of the next spiritual reformation, and more than likely, the last we will see. Humanity as a whole is evolving to a new level of consciousness and spiritual awareness.

I have no interest in 'the proof of' my claims, for what is common to all of these religions, and the 'how' and 'why' of their beginnings seems obvious enough. Every 500 years or so a great leader emerges – a reformer of religious thinking, who comes with the intent to unify people under a single, understandable system, by which all people could live more contented, tolerant, and purposeful lives. To encourage them to walk a path of uprightness, reverence and understand their lives as a sacred gift, so that they might enjoy more emotionally sound lives. Not to begin a new religion but to unify all religions. To redefine what it meant to be religious.

This reformation of religious thinking is once again happening to human consciousness – but add to it what we are discovering in the field of quantum science and the supposed field of potentiality. Add science to what was the reserved domain of 'faith', and you have the makings of a species about to be dazzled by what the mind/heart can do – how, through consciousness, we can transform our reality.

This may seem like some way off and baseless claim – I didn't want this topic to detract from the practical aspects of understanding attraction, our programming and the benefits of a more intentional life. But it seemed impossible to talk about personal development and not bring awareness of the broader implications of what it represents for our planet. This was the 'good news' – why would I leave the best part out? That there are better times, quite possibly unimaginable times coming. This 'trend' in personal development is representative of a profound shift in consciousness that will change life on earth as we know it. The Law of Attraction being understood will allow us to utilise the most underestimated aspect of our existence.

THE CONTROL CENTRE

The New Thought movement that began in the 1830's by Phineas Quinby made every attempt to bridge the gap between science and what had been cryptically hidden in scripture – to give us a more provable element to how attraction worked so we could use it to alter our outcomes. I'll expand on the explanation of the 'New Thought', sometimes called the Mind Cure movement, in the chapter on attraction, but I make the point that what was once mysterious and hard to fathom has progressively become clearer and more accessible. Our consciousness is evolving by us understanding the attractive nature of our emotions.

Humanity is waking up. Human awareness is evolving. It always has been, and we are the living witnesses who will experience this change in our lifetimes. No one person is driving it and no one can stop it. But it is a process we can be more consciously involved in by caring more about how our lives go. We can certainly assist in accelerating the process, simply by being us – our authentic selves. By operating our lives with the awareness that we clearly have a huge influence over how it goes, and giving ourselves a clear sense of direction. By raising our own vibration, we raise the vibration of our planet. I believe by doing the simple things we do daily with a new intent – by the realisation that our daily actions themselves are directly responsible in assisting the evolution of our planet – we will do the same old stuff we used to, with a new sense of responsibility and enthusiasm.

There is an old Buddhist saying, "Before enlightenment – chop wood and carry water. After enlightenment – chop wood and carry water". I promise that you will get sick of the clichés by the end of this book, because I unashamedly admit that I don't say anything that hasn't been said a million times before. These are not my ideas but a collection, a distillation if you will, of personal development principles and a unique perspective on attraction that I think often goes unconsidered. But the point of the above saying is that what we do needn't change – what changes is a new appreciation of what we do, understanding it to be a part of something grander than we were aware. In 'enlightenment' the outside doesn't change – we change, and the whole world seems different. But no matter how insignificant we feel sometimes – how small, pointless and meaningless our contribution seems – it matters, because it matters to us. At least it should.

I could not mention this spiritual reformation without giving mention to the other unifying feature of sacred texts that was put together so beautifully in 'The Power of Now' by Ekhart Tolle. Tolle encapsulates the essence of religions into this unifying theme that the more present we are, the closer we are to truth of our being. Being more present to the senses equates to being more conscious of mind. Our journey towards improving awareness is an inward dimensional one rather than a future event.

I have devoted a later chapter to mindfulness, and given my simple explanation of why and how it works. The realisation of mind is not a matter of time, and is not dependent on conditions being met, but on our value for, and willingness to embrace mindfulness. It is the opposite of time, and Tolle's book is not the only place I have seen it suggested that the single cause of human suffering is 'time bound awareness', or identification with mind, or the 'image of self' to be what we are. But it is worth mentioning here, if I'm trying to bring awareness to the common themes of religions.

The piety of the group

The ten commandments were a tribal law that enabled the group to exist in relative harmony. It is in adherence to the law that the tribe would be able to advance in size, and the quality of life of its members. The 'grandeur' of a civilisation is always proportional to the 'piety' or spirituality of its members. It is why the Roman Empire went to such lengths to ensure the spiritual unity and compliance of the society it was building. Any great society must have a foundation in a shared moral ideology. We could never build a bigger and more advanced civilisation until we are willing to embrace a sense of shared spiritual ideals – or said another way, live in relative harmony with each other. But with all of the hatred between religions, we have become the very descent into animalism religions were designed to avoid.

Spirituality is a practice that is personal, not something that we can enact on other people. By our natures, our beliefs can never be forced but must be chosen in order for them to benefit us and be adhered to. The fact remains that what enables a society to flourish to its potential is always proportional to the piety of its members. In order for this to happen we have to come to the realisation that **it is most certainly the individual who most benefits** from this choice to live in a more spiritual condition. That is, to be considerate of one's path and what we bring to the tribe.

The prosperity of the group – the size of the 'flourish' – of what we may become, is relative to the piety of the individuals in that group. I don't believe this could ever be achieved through group or organised religion. Human beings resist having our beliefs forced. We are just too fickle and self-righteous by our nature to ever conform to universal ideals on what it means to be spiritual – on what defines a pious lifestyle. It must be a personal endeavour and responsibility. Spirituality, as I refer to it here, is purely a sense of responsibility for how we feel, and for the vibrational content we add to the whole.

> "Amalgamating all of the tribes is a process that is not yet finished."
> — Jordan Peterson

System update

We get our apps updated every month or so, interest rates reviewed every three months. And time and time again our system has been re-written with the evidence of new discoveries. If it were left to the Christian Church, we would still be living on a flat earth in the centre of the universe with the sun circling around us.

Every leap we took forward that has brought us into the light of the era we now enjoy was met by often violent opposition from the Church.

Galileo couldn't have just come out and said, "Hmm, I've been staring at the sky for a while and I think the model we are working from is wrong". He would have been scolded by his colleagues and probably stoned to death by the church leaders. All of these 'updates' to our awareness had to, of course, be secretly introduced for fear of the reprisals. The suppositions of Galileo, Copernicus, Newton, and Darwin that have carried us into new frontiers of science and understanding our place in time and the universe, were all met with heavy retaliation from the Church.

The breakthroughs that now fill our textbooks, and have brought us out of the darkness of ignorance, faced severe backlash. It was only 200 short years ago we were told by the Church (still the leading authority of the time) that the earth was just 4000 years old and all of the land formations were the result of the biblical flood. Thank god for science – but who can save us now?

Personal development for dummies

If this sounds like a swipe or belittling of either religious adherents, or the people who lived in the times of limited awareness, it is not. It is certainly not my intention to lynch religions, because we have much to be thankful for in the awareness they have brought us – the human potential for transcendence. The existence of a higher condition of mind. Religions once saved us – but in a time that has long gone, and in a world that no longer exists. Before we had our current level of awareness, we certainly needed the type of guidance that may have come from the 'sacred' knowledge in these texts. Religions were once our doorway to awareness and a greater connection with mind and 'reality', but those days have passed. We are not little ignorant children in the scale of our evolution.

There is more to our minds than we are conscious of, and that is what religions reminded us. There is a grand plan for human beings and when we recognise this higher purpose it might make a lot of the activity we are currently so obsessed with seem negligible – we might choose a more conscious system. Without religions and being alerted to the existence of higher states of mind we might have never reached our peak, or pondered the reality that there is far more to our existence than we consciously consider. Religion and the cherished sacred texts added something quite extraordinary to our life on earth, but we can take it from here. The human mind is capable of far greater things than we use it for, and that awareness might never have been considered had it not been for the pointer towards truth that religion represents.

At the time when Jesus lived people's lives were shrouded in mystery and superstition. They were searching in relative darkness to understand the mind/body and emotional system of perception, and how we change the world with our intention. The insight of these wise reformers of the time was obviously much needed, influential, and healed and transformed people of the day. But these people didn't know what lay beyond the hills as far away as they could see, and they would probably not venture that far in their lifetime.

But these are not the times we live in now. We are much better informed of the body/mind connection, the principles of attraction and the way our programming becomes embedded. Honestly, I scratch my head that our times have not changed all that much to include the benefits of our 'upgraded' awareness. Religions were systems of healing, personal growth and transformation before we had any of the insight into the nature of attraction and awareness of the subconscious mind that we now do. Why do these archaic traditions persist when we live in a much more informed era? That we should be kind to people and inclusive is a 'no-brainer' – if that is the real moral value that allows religions to remain, my god we need our heads read. Can you imagine trying to explain to an alien life form what religion is and why it still exists in our world??

THE LAST GREAT REFORMATION

> "You don't need religion to have morals. If you can't determine right from wrong, you lack empathy and common sense, not religion."
>
> **Author Unknown**

What Jesus shared at the time was relevant. But it was for a different people in a different time. It was designed for and suited to a relatively ignorant people. It is far beyond its used by date. And honestly, I do understand this longing for something greater, for something sacred and 'supernatural' in our lives, but it's here – it is living within our own minds now, and there is nothing more worthy of our worship than us. Religion was designed to heal us from mental illness and the skews in perspective that lead us into anger and despair. This 'holier than thou' context we hold religions in has obscured us from the truth of what they were designed for. It was suited and apt for people that lived in a period that was very different to these ones. It was personal development and healing for a comparatively uninformed era. How could we consider this still valid to a far more informed species living in an entirely different time? Our adherence to religions is the very definition of 'blind faith'.

These archaic systems of personal transformation persist like they are above every law. These traditions may have been very 'handy' in maintaining civility and allowing our species to recognise the profound value in kindness, but they are no longer sufficient to carry us into the next phase of our evolution. One would have to bet that the only real weight these early models carry is that they resonate with the deep human instinct for empathy and treating people as equals – principles you would hardly consider to be the basis of faiths who are so strongly opposed to the rights and freedoms of other faiths to exist in harmony with their own.

All of our systems get updated when we get new, more relevant, and more efficient information to operate with – but not these ones. Religions sit above the laws of reason and stunt our further development and surely prevent us from understanding the truths that will take us into the next evolutionary step. That happens when awareness of attraction becomes accepted by the mainstream and integrated into our healing. We can't understand the operating system of a human being while we blindly adhere to these long-outdated traditions, and I think purely on the fact that they are a tradition – as in, a 'bad habit' that we don't want to give up. We shouldn't hang onto the things that harm us just because this is the way we have always done it.

Religions divide our cultures, all claiming validation by the numbers in their congregation. We must be 'right' because there's more of us. Do we all have to agree on one to be able to take us into a brighter, and inclusive future? Because this must surely be the hallmarks of a system capable of evolving to the next level – that we have something that seems to represent a shared spiritual understanding. And for the majority we know this, but what can we do?

The World Health Organisation estimates that 1 in 5 people in our modern era suffer depression, and by 2030 it will be the leading health concern on the planet. And really, I think it is because we have lost our religion. We have in effect lost the essence of what religions were designed to offer us. Compassion, purpose and the will to help others. We haven't misunderstood these virtues because of a 'lack of religion' – we don't realise what religion is. Religion got us this far – it took humanity from infancy into adolescence – but we are grown-ups now. Our religion has not been updated for thousands of years, and as a consequence we have lost what is most sacred about ourselves.

> "Our culture has accepted two huge lies. The first is that if you disagree with someone's lifestyle, you must fear or hate them. The second is that to love someone means you agree with everything they believe or do. Both are nonsense. You don't have to compromise convictions to be compassionate."
>
> Rick Warren

CHAPTER SUMMARY

- The surge in personal development, New Thought and Law of Attraction material represents a monumental shift in human awareness that is the good news our species has been waiting for.
- You will not find any personal development material that is not anchored in living more conscious and intentional lives.
- You won't find any of this type of content that is not focused on the power of the visual mind and feeling states to create real time outcomes. That our circumstances are a projection of an inner condition.
- This information becoming more and more common signals a shift in human awareness that will culminate in the mass scale realisation of mind. The shift is not a matter of time but presence of mind.
- Presence of mind and 'time-free' awareness is the common thread weaving through all religions.
- The insight offered through religions offered hope to a comparatively ignorant people, but we are now embarking on a new era of human awareness.

CHAPTER 2

Infant Download

THE CONTROL CENTRE

> "One believes things because one is conditioned to believe them."
>
> — Aldous Huxley

Human beings are run by a program. The major aspects of our life are assigned to a part of the mind that is beyond the conscious mind – the one we think with. So before we go into how this programming becomes downloaded, we need to have a basic understanding of why we need the program and how it works. Because it really isn't some great mystery – there are parts of our experience that need to be automatic. When we enter a new environment, we aren't thinking about what things mean, and how we should act – we just know. These things are assigned to the program – our sense of direction, who we are and where we are going are not things we need to 'work out'. They are supplied and instant. The main aspects of our life we don't think about consciously, but that is not to say we have no control over them. To know how to alter the program we need to have a basic understanding of the difference in the roles of the conscious and subconscious minds.

The conscious is the thinking mind, assigned to the normal day-to-day stuff that enables us to navigate our lives and perform our jobs etc. The subconscious mind runs the program. It performs many times faster than the conscious mind and presents the world as it seems. It 'makes' our reality. There has been a lot of hype over the power of the subconscious mind, and it is indeed an incredibly fast processor, but it is powerless to lead us to satisfied lives without the right input. We have to be running the right software if the subconscious mind is to work in our favour.

So this is the scenario we are left with – neither mind being powerful in its own right. The subconscious is powerless without the right instructions from the conscious mind, but the conscious isn't helpful to us unless we are aware of the nature of what we are sending instructions to. It is the synergy of these two aspects of mind that creates the desirable outcomes, or put another way, only the program has power.

When we enter any environment, we would be ill-equipped if we had to think about what everything meant. The 'big things' are not part of the thinking mind's job. They can only be accessed through contemplation. But all is not lost – we do have control over how our life goes when we regularly reflect on the 'big stuff' questions. When we contemplate what's important to me, what do I want, how do I want my experience to be different to this one, we are interacting with the program itself. We have power over these automatic decisions when we make some conscious declarations about the type of experience we want, or when we live our lives intentionally.

Now if we don't give this aspect of our life some direction, the program reverts to default settings. We trust the accuracy of our 'life conclusions' about how things are and run on auto-pilot. This is all well and good if we are happy enough with the job it is doing, but the unseen danger is that in the conscious mind we assume we are living from 'free' will, when in fact our experience comes purely from the program. If we don't choose, the program chooses for us. And if we don't like what is happening, we believe we had no part in it – but we chose by our passivity. The act of not choosing is a choice.

We have to define how we want our experience to be different to the one we are having if we are to have intentional experiences, otherwise we turn our results over to the program. On default settings our reactions repeat in a never-ending loop. We find reason for our reactions in whatever environment we enter. The subconscious mind is designed to turn whatever environment we enter into something familiar so that we assume we know where we are and how to deal with it. It turns the 'everything' (the infinite) into something definable, so we 'know' where we are. We subconsciously create the environment that causes a reaction in us. The reaction is what the mind relies on to orient our experience. The mind converts whatever surrounds us into what validates the reaction.

If this sounds a little confusing at the moment it is what will be explored more throughout the course of the book, and become clearer when we go through how our programming becomes downloaded. The point I am making is that we have far more control over our outcomes than we exercise if we aren't living our lives intentionally. That is, being clear on what defines improved conditions for us, and consciously heading towards them. We sacrifice our control unknowingly, over far more than we think, if we are not doing things on purpose – if we are not giving the mind some sense of direction as to how we want it to go. As we move towards the **centre** of our experience, we will know ourselves as the cause of what happens, rather than just the effect. To drive the program, we just need to be clear on the type of experience we want to have. We move things to our favour when we are clear on our intentions. We allow things to go our way when we ask for something specific. Once again, this idea will be explored throughout the entire book, and will be clearer as other principles are integrated.

That said, let's get into how the program first becomes embedded as an emotional pattern. The mind is designed for efficiency, and the program runs as a means of conserving energy. And it can work fine, or well enough, for years and years, but then we want something that seems beyond our ability and the struggle begins. The struggle starts and that struggle can become a lifelong pattern. No matter how 'hard' we work the groove we are in only gets deeper. To change the program, we have to have an awareness of the nature of the program and how it became downloaded.

The download process

When an infant enters the world, it comes from pure intelligence – it is a purely subconscious being, yet to develop a reasoning mind. The young infant experiences the world just as the subconscious mind does, taking in twenty million bits of sensory data per second. As you can imagine, this is quite overwhelming, and our experience needs to be chunked down into something manageable – something we can digest and understand. And we do this by starting to look for recognisable patterns in our environment. In order to orient our experience, we have to try to recognise and keep an eye out for anything that repeats so we can identify and predict some sense of where we are, and what things mean. What is dangerous, where is safety, where do I belong?

The trouble, of course, is that once we start to recognise similarities and patterns in our environment that is all we unconsciously look for. We even 'twist' evidence to suit these conclusions. We, unbeknownst to the conscious mind, turn no matter what surrounds us into these patterns of familiarity so that we know where we are, and how we should act. Even if our conditions are not quite a match, we will instinctively fill in the cognitive gaps to make our environment seem familiar and predictable. We've experienced something similar, so we plaster our judgements over what we see. The world is the way we make it. Even if this model of the world is not exactly pleasing or flattering to our 'position', it is what allows us to know who and where we are, and as such will be recreated to the letter.

No matter what surrounds us, the mind turns it into something that seems familiar – into what causes a reaction in us.

From this infant phase of infinite intelligence, the first level of an infant's learning is to absorb the emotional frequency in its environment. It 'downloads' the emotional content of its primary carer, as well as some of the vibrational energy in its environment. This is the first level of learning for the infant – a coding of what it needs to know in order to survive. It learns on a subconscious level, a vibrational level, not on a conscious repetitive level like we do in later life. It learns from the subtle emotional vibrations of the parent. This is our core programming and goes deeply into an unconscious level of mind to form the core structure of what become our beliefs. It is the blueprint containing the basis of information for what should we be scared of and how do I be liked – all very crucial to our survival.

THE CONTROL CENTRE

As the infant absorbs the emotional content of its primary carer, this translates to how the world is perceived. This is how those patterns that become familiar are able to be recognised. The infant downloads the emotional conclusions and what things mean from the parent, and this becomes our model for how to interpret the world. What we don't realise is the part that goes on beyond the conscious mind – the ability of mind to turn whatever is in front of us to suit our model. We turn the infinite into the finite so we can understand and deal with something we know. Which, as I say, is very handy until that model of what we turn it into drives us crazy. We want a different experience, but no matter how hard we toil and try the rut gets deeper.

To change how the world seems and our place in it we have to work on a level of the programming. Who we are is an invention the conscious mind likes to stick to, because of perceptions of how much us changing may disrupt group dynamics. The conscious mind is designed to try to talk us out of change, and our abilities down. It is not designed to think beyond the scope of our personal history.

When we first recognise a pattern, it is a light bulb moment for the young infant – 'I have worked out what's going on here'. This allows the infant to be able to put its experience into the context of understanding. It is able to frame what is happening – and quite rightly the infant is quite 'chuffed'. It is beginning to understand its environment – where it is and what things mean – which of course translates to 'how to get what I want'. When we recognise a pattern in our environment, we get an incredibly soul-soothing comfort in believing we can now have an effect on the world. Believing that 'if I recognise it, I can manipulate it to my will'. The trouble, of course, being that we continue using the same unconscious programming to interpret a different world. We apply the same actions, expecting to get the same result, never realising we have turned our environment into something it needn't be.

To turn the tide, we have to change what is going on inside us, not outside of us. We control the world from the inside. We can turn whatever 'is' into whatever we want it to be, not by changing the outside but the internal meaning – our way of seeing. We change the nature of the world by how we see and respond to it. All change happens inside us.

The mind makes any environment into one that causes a familiar, but not necessarily comfortable, reaction. Here lies the key issue. We assume that if this mind is such a powerful thing, why wouldn't it deliver us at least to a decent mood some of the time? If it is powerful, why does it keep dishing up this same old shit? Because we ask by our passivity – because of the instructions we are feeding it. Many times our experiences aren't entirely pleasant, but we still gain a sense of being 'home' – not out of our depth – in the familiarity of the feeling we embody. The mind does this with precision, and in what it believes to be a matter of survival. If we don't know what to do or what we are looking at, the disorientation can seem dangerous, if not life-threatening.

We don't realise it is us who made up the world as we know it, or how this reactive pattern can carry unconsciously for the entirety of our lives.

So these early days and months are the most formative of our lives. I know there will be the child psych's out there who will tell us that the development of the mind takes place over the first four years of our life or whatever, but you have to imagine that the more jelly-like and impressionable the mind, the deeper the level these first experiences sink to. An infant's mind begins to 'set' – even in utero the embryo begins to sense and absorb the mother's emotional content, and take on the subtle anxieties and tensions of the mother. The more jelly-like the infant's mind, the deeper the level these emotional conclusions sink to and the more they become embedded – emotional conclusions, otherwise known as beliefs. We inherit not just our most basic ideas of how the world is, but a reactive pattern that turns the world into the outcome of how we feel.

No matter what surrounds us we subconsciously paint our own picture, but aren't aware it was us who made it all up out of 'thin air'.

As is suggested in the theory of relativity, we alter the outcome of an experiment by what we expect to find – **by what we are looking to find, we change what we are looking at.** We change what we are looking at by what we are looking for, and therefore can only find evidence of the pattern. It seems like the 'real world', but we are not privy to the fact that it has been created by us at a deeper level of mind.

> "We don't see things as they are, we see them as we are."
>
> **The Talmud**

So, we can't change 'reality' until we understand we were the ones making it up and why – until we understand our part in its creation. Reality is a tool we use to orient ourselves, but if it is not flattering or we don't like the situation we find ourselves in, it is far more changeable than we think. When we know we created the reality we can change it, and sometimes as simply as taking a new perspective of either the situation itself or the resources we have to work with.

And what is the benefit of becoming aware of how our patterns form? It is not just that we can more easily alter the world's effect on us, but because how we are, the character traits (many of which we are not overly fond of) that make us feel like we are a prisoner to these long-running emotional patterns, **are not our fault. It is not a flaw in our character.** They are inherited – passed to us and deeply ingrained in the earliest years of our life, and continue to play out as the patterns we know of as our life. But they are no more 'us' than hand-me-down clothes. A lot harder to change but certainly not impossible, and all the more easy when we have awareness of how they formed and recognise emotions as a habit pattern rather than something we are eternally bound to.

That surge in your guts when shit is going down doesn't come from the event, and isn't some personal flaw – it is an invisible emotional pattern trying to keep itself alive with us as the unfortunate host. Like any living entity this pattern is trying to exist and our lives are the unfortunate surrogate. This pattern is much, much older than our lives – and when we see it in this light, we can not only call it out, but we can also know that the buck stops with us to not pass this on anymore to a world already swarming with unchecked and unreasoned primal fears.

> "In the eyes of a child you will see the world as it should be."
>
> Unknown

The tribal mind

This early embedded vibrational coding forms the basis of perception – the world as we know it. These conclusions are so closely associated with our survival that we powerfully cling to them like they are life itself. It is protected by a much deeper level of awareness than we are conscious of. What is happening to us seems very real – not a mind-made invention. These patterns can continue to play out without us ever being conscious they come from inside us.

This process of passing on emotional energy patterns has not changed for many thousands of years. With all of the technology we are surrounded by it is easy for us to believe that we are far beyond this primitive model for the world as we experience it. And that, of course, is a large part of the problem – we think we are more emotionally evolved than we truly are. We feel like living geniuses but emotionally we have not come as far from our cave-dwelling days as we think. I mean no one any offence when I point out that at our core we are still driven by very primal needs, and pass on a very primitive model for interpreting the world we live in. We don't live in tribal or village lives anymore but live with a very deep need to belong and be accepted.

THE CONTROL CENTRE

Physically we can survive without the tribe's blessing, but emotionally it is 'check-mate'. We long for the approval of our group.

This is definitely not my intuition speaking here either. There is an enormous amount of science to back up the fact that our evolution hasn't yet caught up with our new living conditions. It is not something I need to prove, but need to bring awareness to if we are going to understand the depth of the human predicament. We are still driven by very primitive emotional needs and patterns – the emotional requirements of beings designed to live a tribal lifestyle. Emotionally, we are out of sync with processes that craft our reality and drive our emotional lives. We have to raise awareness of how this whole process works if we are to maintain some semblance of controlling our outcomes and how the world seems, because it is breaking our hearts to adjust to this newly needed awareness, and the lack of connection we are experiencing in the modern world. Many people's hearts are burdened because we are not accustomed to how we now live.

With threats of nuclear war, overpopulation, scarcity of food, the distribution of wealth, cultural divisions, even the automation of labour, and the pressing need for us to stand out to be considered of any value – these issues are not ones we were designed to cope with. It is overwhelming to say the least to a mind designed to live in small, supportive and simpler communities. It is little wonder we are quietly frantic and our emotions are tethered. Add to this the trauma that has carried through by the cruelty that human beings have endured and been witness to, and you have a crockpot of tumultuous emotions.

Our instinct to compare ourselves to others was once an important aspect of how we found our place in the tribe – how we discovered our value, and what we could contribute to make the tribe a stronger more functional unit. This instinct to compare ourselves is not really as handy now as it was once upon a time. We live in an enormous, single, global tribe, where we struggle to find our family of like-minded people – our tribe. This instinct to compare ourselves really does a number on us now.

We once lived for the tribe – it was our heartbeat. Without the tribe and the values it had protected for thousands of years we would not survive. So we lived not for ourselves but for the good of the tribe. And the criticisms we received came from people who actually cared about us and our will to integrate with this life support system. We had a sense of belonging that we can struggle to replicate in this modern world. We are alone and our tribe is spread – they are off finding new tribes if the one they were in didn't suit them for a time. This is the curse of our era – people can't form the bonds that were once our life blood, because they just don't exist anymore.

> "Never underestimate the power of stupid people in large groups."
> **George Carlin**

And the idea of 'groupthink' is probably the most haunting of all. The idea that people in groups are able to collectively agree to delete certain types of information from coming to their awareness. Groups are sometimes able to distort the shared truth of sometimes dangerous facts, in order to maintain group harmony. An unspoken agreement to leave out any 'uncomfortable' truths. A good example was the ability not only of the Church, but its congregation, to form a silent agreement to pretend child abuse wasn't happening. Many people within the group were aware of what was happening but there was an unspoken compliance they must remain in quiet ignorance for the good name of their cherished faith. I'm not picking on the Church here, but just trying to illustrate an example of how groupthink works, and its ability to blind spot what is obvious to outsiders. The larger the group, the more expansive the shared delusion.

Groupthink – Groupthink occurs when a group values harmony and coherence over analysis and critical evaluation. It causes individual members of the group to unquestioningly follow the word of the leader and it strongly discourages any disagreement with the consensus.

The largest group

> "Anti-social behaviour is a trait of intelligence in a world full of conformists."
>
> **Nikola Tesla**

Our instincts compel us to join the largest group. There is safety in numbers. We either join the largest tribe or will probably be conquered by them. It is pretty simple math – we stand a much better chance of survival behind the fortress walls. But these fortress walls are today represented by the majority and their will to comply with an economic model that has no foreseeable goal but its own growth. This system we support does not have an end goal or the best interests of humanity in mind. It seems no one is at the wheel and we are all happily being steered of a cliff. The beat we march to is not supportive of equality or justice and is pretty obvious it has no objective of sustainability. I rest in the knowledge that there is a higher system of justice.

We work our butts off in this shared conformity to the almighty economy. Our instinct is to look for and obey an authority figure, because this represents the greater good – the good of the tribe. I don't want to get too far off track here, but hopefully it is obvious to us that the mindset we operate with is more often our foe than our friend. We are emotionally bound into life conditions that have inadvertently lured us into becoming slaves to a system that doesn't serve us.

> "If everyone is thinking alike, then someone isn't thinking."
>
> — George S. Patton

It is an unseen but very real force to comply with the norm. It is a larger risk than we consciously know to not do what everyone else is doing. We are not true to ourselves, or free to think independently, because of this unconscious will to comply. It serves a deep need within us to stand in line – to do otherwise equates to putting our own needs before the tribe. We've been blindsided by our own good natures – confusing kindness with compliance. Even though we no longer live tribal lives, our instincts unconsciously force us to do the will of the perceived greater good. And for many, we have confused this greater good to be the blind adherence to the flawed leadership of our governments. We are unconscious prisoners to our own sense of goodwill, and doing what we believe is right. We adhere to the conditions set by leaders who have little to no concern for those they lead.

We've all had moments where we've seen or heard different trends or behaviours and thought to ourselves, 'how ridiculous'. And then at some point we unconsciously find ourselves doing or believing the same thing. This 'everybody is doing it' thing is far, far more powerful than most are aware.

Our unfree will

> "Man's task is to become conscious of the contents that press upward from the unconscious."
>
> — Carl Jung

This process of becoming more conscious is one in the same with the underpinning goal of being human – **to become more conscious of**

mind. This is what Freud regarded as the aim of therapy – "to become conscious of what is unconscious". And all of the hallmarks are present that this larger-scale realisation of mind (the outcome of the process of becoming more conscious) may not be as far in the future as we may have thought. It is not some far-fetched idea when we realise this to be a dimensional shift – we arrive through presence of mind, not through learning something new, or certain outer conditions being met. It could occur to large groups of people almost immediately. It is not a matter of time that will cure the humanity of its mind-made ills, but of understanding the value of presence. The 'future' may not be as perplexing as we have led ourselves to believe, and may be far more rewarding than we imagined.

I want to agree with your objections that who we are is never set in stone, and countless numbers of people have defied the odds of the station in life they were born to. That despite being brought up in lower vibrating conditions they managed to break the cycle through conscious will and intention. We are never obliged to remain unconscious to our inherited patterns. The ones who break the mould of their conditioning are the minority, but prove the very facts that I'm suggesting here – that with intention we can turn the world into something it wasn't prior to the intention. These people were the exception to the rule, but I propose that this will soon change as we enter this new era of awareness. Whether those who broke the mould of their conditions were conscious of it or not, it was only done, and it can only be done by sending new instructions on how we want our life to go.

It reminds me of the story in which two twin boys were raised by their alcoholic father. One son followed his dad into addiction and later prison, and the other never touched a drop, and raised a loving and close family. When both were asked on separate occasion why they think their lives turned out the way they did, their answer highlights this point beautifully. They both answered identically - "With a father like mine what do you expect". One son lived from conditioning and followed unconsciously, and the other from consciousness, and saw his father's example as what he didn't want to re-experience.

We've all come across someone who, despite what they've been through or how they have been treated, have remained positive and managed to turn their life around. So the choice is ours – live as passengers of our programming, or send clear instructions of what we'd prefer, and begin to craft each moment into one of our making – each reaction to our conscious will. To be the cause rather than the effect. How do we want our experience to be different?

Any tiny change can radically alter the course of our lives when we multiply it by time.

Probably won't happen overnight

No beliefs or emotional patterns are easily changed. They have kept us safe and fed for the entirety of our lives, so like overprotective parents, stand as the gatekeepers of what we experience and how we feel about ourselves. Our emotional state has an enormous gravity and ability to perpetuate itself. And it is what we are up against. It is certainly not impossible for a transformation to occur instantly, but this is once again the exception to the rule. Believing this happens very often can open us to being bitterly frustrated and impatient to see the results – the opposite of what invites them. So it is better to understand that this change is more commonly a process. We can enjoy every step of the way, but we have to understand the subconscious mind has an enormous momentum in our lives. We have an unconsciously strong gravity towards old feeling states, and this is what we are truly up against. A mind that operates at a different level of awareness to what we are conscious of. Be patient.

We are addicted to how we feel, and it has formed a deep track in our experience. So, when we press against what seems to be happening, by exclaiming we don't like what is happening, it creates a lot of resistance or fear. But fear is rarely something we must 'face'. In most cases when what we thought was causing the resistance is brought to the surface it vanishes, or shrinks to be beyond our concern – no longer on our radar. We are rarely conscious of exactly what we are scared of and when it is called out (brought to the surface of our awareness) the 'dragon' often shrinks or turns to dust. We can put many fears to sleep just by questioning our rationale.

Our apparent 'position' is some mind-made BS, and it would do us the world of good to keep trying to peer behind the curtain – to persistently wake ourselves up to the illusion and call ourselves out. "I'm onto you mind – the jig is up." We can loosen the bindings of this mind created situation by becoming ever more focused on the senses in the present, which will be explored more deeply in the mindfulness chapter.

Too many of us have tried to change something so many times and failed that giving up just makes more sense and is far more peaceful. And ironically it is often only in giving up, in surrender that we are able to end the resistance and when it doesn't bother us anymore the solution to our troubles comes waltzing in so simply. But what we have long considered our life, the moving from scene to scene and meeting different people, is the playing out of the program. Our experience always comes from the program. We carry the same dominant emotion into each scene and have an almost identical reaction no matter where we are.

Our eccentricities, fears and habits are often part of a long, unbroken chain that can be passed on for generations. Our fear of speaking out, performing, and many of our other phobias are not the result of our choices and bad experiences, many were absorbed as a pattern in the earliest years of our life. They're not our fault, but we can change them when we make some conscious declarations of what we want to learn, and how we want our life to go.

We can stop beating ourselves up for not living up to our dreams and having our hearts broken by our apparent conditions. It is all part of the illusion that has carried for a very long time and in a lot of people. The world doesn't need one more desperate and disappointed person, it needs more awake and contented people. And that doesn't translate to more superstars – it means more healthy, healed and purposeful beings. People who can see the truth of who they are and are on the mend. And that in itself is the single best thing we can contribute – a conscious, tolerant and intentional being. All the rest of the details are up to us. Don't be another one who wants to beat on themselves for everything they are not. Our obstacles light our way home, but only a whole person can embark on such a journey. We have to align with the energy of completion.

If we are poor communicators, nervous, suffer social anxiety or even trust issues, these traits were often not choices we made, but became unconsciously embedded into our hardwiring to keep us safe. We are not free to do anything, but rather have a small repertoire of conditioned behaviors. Understanding the process of how these deep and strong emotional patterns became embedded into our character can, in itself, often give us a little bit more freedom to live outside the box and to act in spite of how we feel.

I know that when I became aware of the process of how our conditioning happens, I became **far less trusting of every shameful or guilty emotion that ever surfaced again.** Rather than just being carried off with the emotion, I began to question, "You want me to feel this way? Why? Where does this feeling stem from? Is it, in fact, something from an ancient human programming and still exists in me? Is this feeling warranted? Am I being pushed around by something that is no more real than 'Tinkerbelle'?"

Awareness was a relief that I'm not as flawed as I thought I was. I knew that much of what I was feeling came from an irrational desperation to belong. If I was ever to feel a part of something, that was always, only and ever going to be up to me and my conscious choice to see the world the way I do.

It occurred to me that my feelings weren't being forced by real situations, but by a trickery of the mind to keep a long-outdated pattern alive. I could change the program – I could have a change of heart, if I were clear about what I wanted to change to.

Self-awareness

The aim of this book is to be more conscious – to become more intimate with ourselves. Our likes and dislikes, fears and strengths, and why they live in us. When we know ourselves better, I guarantee we will find more and more reasons to like who we are. Many of us are living the versions of who other people think we are – who we have been led to believe we are – and we can't like that person. They are not even a close relative of who we are. We need to find all of those parts we may have been denying and accept them not as character flaws we have to hide, but sometimes just our quirky way. So be it, no one cares, they may even like you more for being so. One thing is for sure – you will, which is the point of self-awareness. Self-acceptance is implied.

We aren't meant to be good at everything or beat ourselves up for the things we find overly challenging. Maybe we should do them, or maybe it is telling us we are better suited to something else and to work towards your strengths. Really, no one can give us advice on these things, because they are only for us to know and answer. If a skill we find challenging continues to surface as a goal that excites us – something we would definitely like to be better at – we can learn it. Everything is learnable. The 'naturals' we see mostly weren't born that way. They have practiced until they got it right, and then they practiced until they couldn't get it wrong. Everything can be learned and accomplished when we break it into achievable steps and find the appropriate teachers. If we notice persisting problems and unwanted emotional patterns, they are there for a reason. They are pointing towards something we have a deep spiritual need to grow from and overcome. The stubborn obstacle often points the way forward.

Our 'problems' are the signposts of our glory road – they give us direction. It does us no good to ignore or keep beating ourselves up for what we are not. The mind loves to be asked questions, and it is the quality of those questions that determines the likelihood of a solution, and the quality of our experience. Better to ask, "How can I use this?" than to state, "Why does this keep happening?". As we will see in later chapters, the subconscious does not comprehend the words 'no,' 'don't' or 'stop'. If it is in our energy, the subconscious will use it to build a familiar experience. The sub-mind cannot differentiate between wanted and unwanted – it uses everything that comes to our attention as a kind of reality 'prop'. It uses it to ensure us 'things are as normal'.

It is always better to ask ourselves, "How do I do this?" than state, "I could never do this". One statement engages the mind, the other turns it off.

EXERCISE

As an exercise in better knowing ourselves, name something that continues to give us angst. Call it out. "Why are you here and what is the purpose you serve?" The mind is incredibly clever and will always provide the answer when we craft the question correctly.

As an exercise in self-awareness, pick out someone with a quality you admire and ask, "How can I integrate this trait more in myself?". We are already far more like the people we admire than we think. We can only notice these qualities if we have a little piece of what we like in them, already alive in us. If we didn't have it we wouldn't notice it. We unconsciously and naturally already mimic or model the qualities we find appealing in others. We do this unconsciously. When we do it consciously, we can certainly accelerate the process.

This isn't supposed to be some, "Oh god, I just love them so much" – it is just a conscious declaration of the type of character traits we find admirable, and melding them into the 'boiling pot' of who we are. It needn't be someone we know personally – it can be a public figure, sports star or even a movie character. Who do you like and why? We do it already but we can become more perfect modelers and this certainly goes a long way towards that self-acceptance we were talking about earlier. There really should be no higher a priority than self-awareness and our state of mind. Being interested in our own growth and intimate with who we are is the only path to being more in control of our experience – of getting to our control centre. We stand a much better chance of loving ourselves when we define what we find admirable in others.

CHAPTER SUMMARY

- Any perceived character flaws are not our fault, they are a deeply ingrained emotional pattern we inherited in the earliest years of our life – compliments of our primary carers.
- And our parents got it from their parents in a cycle that has played out for hundreds of generations.
- This pattern is our programming, or what we have subconsciously consented to as important.
- We can consciously instruct the programming by consistently reflecting on how we would like our experience to be different from the one we're having, which we can do by living with intention (clear instructions).
- If we aren't enacting on the programming it reverts to default settings – our future must mirror our past. Our experience comes from the program and our reactions exist in a recurring pattern indefinitely.
- We have an overactive sense of danger and scarcity mindset, and an exaggerated need to belong and value the opinion of others. Many of our value systems and behavioural traits have carried from a time when we lived much more primitive and tribal lives.
- Worst of all, we have limited access to the parts of ourselves where these fears formed and consequently can't acknowledge that the 'tiger' has long since vanished. The reasons for our fears no longer apply.
- Change is an ever-evolving process to which there is no end – only deeper levels of satisfaction and control over how we feel, and consequently what happens.
- We can become the cause of what happens in our life rather than the effect when we continue to reflect on 'how do I want my experience to be different?' – by living intentionally.

CHAPTER 3

The Secret Agenda of Mind

> "Educating the mind without educating the heart is no education at all."
>
> — Aristotle

The function of the subconscious mind is to **preserve our state of mind**. Our state of mind regenerates itself by projecting our vibration onto the external world, so we can only ever 'see' or perceive a world that supports/reflects how we feel. Our heart is an extremely intelligent organ. As we became aware in the last chapter, it is our emotional state that facilitates our survival, so it has devised this ingenious method by which to sustain itself. Our feelings project into the world and reflect back to us. Our emotional state operates in a self-generating loop, where we are always looking into a mirror of how we feel.

The apparent circumstances of our life are an internally projected state. Conditions reflect conditioning, so any process of change happens internally – with a mindset or perception shift. What appear as 'events' in our life are more a consequence of how this long running emotional pattern sustains itself. Our reaction is not a consequence of an 'actual' event but a mind created, or rather an emotionally created, event. Law of Attraction 101 – how we feel skews our perception of the world so that the 'way we see' serves to support the feeling state that caused our way of seeing. The manner in which we view the world provides the feeling states ongoing preservation.

Emotions exist in a powerful regenerative cycle, because this is the primary function of the most powerful part of our mind – to preserve our state of mind, or dominant vibration.

How we feel skews our way of seeing, so that the way we see things makes us feel the same. To change reality, our circumstances, how the world seems, we have to change how we feel. We have to create emotions independently of our apparent conditions. We have to imagine how it would feel to be in improved conditions.

When we have a reaction, it has much more to do with the preservation of our state of mind than an actual event. How we feel skews our perception of the world – only ever finding evidence in the world that supports how we feel. We will continue having reactions like it until we break the cycle by responding more consciously. By declaring how we would rather feel.

If we were fully aware of the ongoing consequences of our reactions, we would be far more considered in how we respond. We would be far more intentional with how we feel. The type of reaction we have is part of an unconscious pattern that will continue indefinitely until we consciously break the cycle, and go about consciously shifting our response and the type of experience we would prefer. As soon as we are aware our reactions are part of a program or pattern, we are acknowledging we have nothing more to learn from this type of experience. We get the lesson.

The cause of mental illness is that our program is running unconsciously, and we have concluded that we have a limited control over the events of our life. We control the events by controlling our response to them. We have lost faith in our ability to create a preferred experience, because we have been unconsciously led for so long. We don't realise ourselves as the cause of how we feel. Mental illness is a misunderstanding of the ongoing cycle emotions exist in. The powerful unconscious methods our emotional pattern is able to employ in order to sustain itself.

This perspective of what emotions are more truly signalling to us allows us a new freedom of interpreting them – using them instead of them using us. It allows us a more detached cognition of what is happening when we have a reaction. Essentially this awareness allows us an ability to respond more consciously. We, in our seemingly simple improved cognition of reactions, are re-programming the mind to feel better and attract more favourable circumstances. Responding more consciously is a powerful and ever-present method for shifting our mindset. We change the nature of circumstances when we change how we react to them.

The universe is in a constant state of flux, of change, right? What we aren't aware of is that the changes are all happening inside us. The universe is moving in relationship to us. It moves in accord with how we are feeling. We are the source of the dance around us. We are the cause of what makes us feel.

Attraction works

The reason why so many claim that attraction doesn't work is because of this less considered aspect of attraction: the powerful momentum of our dominant vibration. It doesn't instantly shift the moment we have some great version in our head of a preferred life. It can and does shift, but it has an enormous gravity towards the old pattern that has supported us up until now. To change our life we have to give the program clear instructions – we have to have a change of heart. Attraction works – it is a law, just like gravity – but if you claim to be practicing it but aren't seeing the results you think you should, it is because you are still looking to conditions to make you feel better. We have to see beyond them, and into how we want to feel – how we would feel if we were doing that thing we would love to.

We have to feel that way before we can see it, just as in the Wayne Dyer book titled 'You'll see it when you believe it'. When we align with the energy of having what we want, it will feel like we are there already. We will see the evidence, and 'the way' in everything we see. We can never see evidence or have an experience that is contrary to how we feel.

The subconscious is an emotional mind – it is the mind of the heart. It governs the subtle energetic frequencies that are the core of our programming. It has a powerful momentum in our life, one that often steamrolls us in its bid to keep the program running. It is the unfortunate part about this process of wanting change that these patterns are 'subconscious' – that the heart has a powerful affinity to what has got us thus far. It is tried and tested. We need not just new programming instructions, but also patience, mindfulness and an ability to imagine how it would feel to have change if we are to experience it.

Re-programming our mind - one response at a time

When we understand our circumstances and reactions as a function of mind, designed to preserve conditioning rather than real time events, it allows us a perspective that is less forced – less bound by a single unconscious way to react. It allows a new way of seeing. This awareness unfortunately doesn't make the events seem any less real, but it does allow us to be less affected – because we are now aware that in our response, we are changing the nature of circumstances, and what is attracted to us from this point forward.

In our response we are undermining the beliefs that no longer suit our needs. We can't change what happens right? But we literally do when we change how we feel about them, when we change what they mean and how we respond. This is no minor occurrence. When we respond more consciously, we aren't just changing the nature of the event in that moment, we are changing how we are affected by everything similar from this time on.

We are changing the neuroplasticity of our minds to react automatically in favour of our new program. This tactic of responding more consciously changes how we are affected by **all events** from this time on, not just those of a similar nature to our current experience. We are becoming more emotionally agile – changing our minds for the better and forever. We change the nature of the event itself when we feel differently about it. If it doesn't bother us, it never happened.

Responding more consciously is another ever-present means of living a more intentional life. The bigger and more pronounced the reaction that we challenge, the greater the change in us. But this is a trajectory of change – over time these results become accentuated and the process exponentially builds upon itself as we experience more and more of its results. As we play this game and become more skilled, we end up a completely less affected person. Things that may have once bothered us now no longer do, because we are more certain what we care about – what matters.

We have all experienced situations where we have over-reacted in the spur of the moment and later regretted it. What we are doing here is forming a new, more conscious pattern. In making our reactions more considered we are reclaiming our ability to feel the way we choose.

> "If you are willing to look at another person's behaviour towards you as a state of their relationship with themselves, rather than a statement about your value as a person, then you will, over a period of time, cease to react at all."
>
> **Yogi Bhajan**

THE CONTROL CENTRE

What we have been through

I would never say that our feelings and the events they attract aren't real. What I'm saying is that being more conscious of how we are affected is how we reclaim our power in each moment – how we re-program. I believe there is nothing more real than emotions, and we are power hubs of emotional energy. Emotions are the building blocks of the material world. I am in no way trying to trivialise the tragedies many have endured, or insinuate all of the shit we have been through in our lives is somehow our fault. I have been gifted what I consider a very fortunate life, and it would be hypocritical of me to ever claim "I know how it feels" to endure the turmoil many people have been forced to endure in their lives. I don't know how it feels, and I hope I never do.

I'm not trying to dismiss or understate anyone's hardships in any way – what I'm referring to here are methods of coping with feelings and situations that alter our programming. A way of coping with events so the effect can be diluted and dealt with more easily than if we were to be unconsciously carried off by them. In giving our power up to the situation and allowing it to dominate our experience we will always feel beaten by what has happened.

Sometimes our emotions overwhelm us – they swallow us and we are left unable to function properly. Getting back to control – to being the cause of how we feel – and into our power is what interests me, and what I am trying to share here.

It may be difficult to view your hardships as an opportunity, but if you are the one who has managed to come out the other side of tragic circumstances, you may be the only one who is in a position to authentically empathise with people who are still in the midst of similar struggles. Anthony Robins uses the motto "How can I use this?". It hasn't happened to us, it has happened for us. It's often reformed drug addicts who make the most effective drug counsellors. If we can learn to use what has happened to us, it may become a strength – the way we offer a greater level of service to those who most need it, in a way no one else can.

The most difficult part of any hardship is the loneliness we experience – we think we are the only one, and no one has ever been through this before. It is always comforting to know that someone has – they have been through something very similar and they've come out the other side. It is often the hardships we've reluctantly endured that makes us invaluable to others. There are people that need us, because of all of the things we've been through. The events haven't broken us, they have made us into the only person with whom some can relate.

I understand healing from trauma takes time, gentleness, and understanding. It can take many years and a lot of support. I know people diagnosed with clinical depression aren't helped by being told to 'snap out of it', or me trying to say that it is all 'imaginary'. I know there are many causes of depression that have nothing to do with the sufferer. What I am saying is it is impossible to see a world that is different to how you feel. If you feel terrible the evidence will begin to stack up. We always find in our environment the reasons to support our dominant feeling state. Tragic or not it is a law that governs our heart and the world we perceive. Often a shift can begin with us asking something as simple as, "What have I got to be grateful for?". It is hard to find things when we feel like shit, but it is worth trying because it can be the start of a momentum shift that leads us to seeing more things we are grateful for.

Gratitude is the spring from which all good fortune flows.

When we understand that this is also 'attraction' at work, we stand a much better chance of beginning a pattern of seeing the new – seeing the wanted – and changing our expectation of what is possible for us. We have a right to feel great, we are worthy of wellness as much as anyone who has been awarded a life. We can shift our dominant vibration by becoming more sensitive to the words we whisper in our ear – by the **language we use with ourselves**. It can be easier than we think to change the conditions of our life. It is only in our way of thinking that anything seems difficult. The mind we think with, the conscious mind, isn't designed to think beyond the scope of our personal history. Nor is it our encouraging friend – it is designed to talk us out of the thing we want, and make change seem much more difficult than it truly is.

Different rivers to the same ocean

We can only ever see evidence of what we already believe to be true. One person can see opportunity where another will only see doom – it is all relative to their state of mind, and what they are looking for confirmation of.

What is referred to as the confirmation bias, and the observer effect, are both ideas pointing to the same universal truth of attraction. In the confirmation bias it is suggested that we can only see evidence of what we believe. The observer effect states that we are only looking for what proves our theory. We affect the results of an experiment by what we are looking for. By how we measure our results we rule out opposing theories. We look for what we have a strong emotional bias towards. We always see/find what we are looking for confirmation of. We change the world by our expectation. Reality must always be a precise match to our expectation – we are the ones that made it.

Attraction really means that we see the world relative to what interests us. A mother walks into a shopping centre and sees things related to her children – to being a mother. A businessman walks in and sees things related to doing business. It really isn't rocket science, but it can dramatically shift how we see the world, or rather what we start looking for. Knowing how this works makes us players in our own game – "If I can see anything, what am I going to start looking for?".

What we are most interested in is confirming our conclusions of how the world is. That reality, or our model of the world, is accurate and working perfectly. Another part of our mind puts it up on the screen, and then we turn and say, "Well would you look at that" – like we had nothing to do with it. We always see confirmation of what we believe in everything we look at. What we think is true will be true, and we are blind to all contrary evidence. From an infinite number of possibilities, we make it what it is. We turn the 'nothing' into something, to suit our model of the world.

> "Beliefs are the sole determinant of our experience – there are no external influences."
> Dr. Joe Vitale

The confirmation bias

We effect what we observe by what we are looking for and expecting to find.

If we knew it was 'us' – a part of our own minds presenting our reality, the event wouldn't have the desired effect of pushing our emotional buttons. Part of the role of the subconscious is to ensure we never cotton on to it being us that caused the reaction. To ensure that we are never conscious our experience comes from the program. The subconscious mind constructs our experience and then stands back and exclaims, "It wasn't me". The reaction caused in us is what the subconscious assumes to be vital in maintaining our reality model.

We begin to see the car we want to buy

The confirmation bias is often explained like this – remember when you were thinking of buying a new type of car, and all of a sudden, they come out of the woodwork – it seems like they are everywhere. The fact of the matter is they were always there, we just didn't notice them because it wasn't something that interested us. We don't notice them until we are 'emotionally aligned'. And it is the same with everything we notice in our world. So if we want a change of heart – to see the things that would please us most – we have to be emotionally aligned. Our attention is subconsciously drawn towards what matches our vibration.

The subconscious mind is not designed for happiness. It is designed to keep us safe. If it has been doing that then any prescribed change to our conditions is seen as an unnecessary risk. If we want change, we have to define how we want it to be different, if it is ever able to show up. To get somewhere we want to go we have to know where that is.

If you want to change your reality you have to turn a blind eye to much of the old pattern that will continue to present itself for some time. Notice less of what we don't like, and replace it with what we'd prefer. We have to start to like what is happening, because this is confirmation, we understand it is made in mind.

This may not provide much comfort when we are completely losing our mind, but it hopefully may allow us to regain our composure quicker, and always take a somewhat more detached perspective of the dramas the conditioned mind is trying to suck us into. To be more conscious by asking ourselves, "Is this an experience I want to continue? I want more of in my life? What am I attracting by how I am thinking and feeling now?" Even just stopping long enough to ask yourself the question can be enough to distract you from emotions and therefore dilute their effect a little.

Momentary lapse of reason

In that single moment where we drew a strong and influential conclusion, we weren't able to see the longer-term implications of how this would forever affect our world view. In that moment when we were tired and something really got to us, this would become glued to our experience as one of those 'reality checkers' we spoke of in the last chapter. The things the mind uses, good or bad, to orient us that things are normal/as they should be. We drew a conclusion and it continues to become reinforced as a means of ensuring we are not out of our depth in knowing the type of world we live in.

Over time this pattern just begins to frustrate the s#*t out of us. And that frustration only further compounds the problem. "I keep seeing this thing that frustrates me" – and the answer of the subconscious mind is always the same – **"As you wish"**. The more frustrated we get, the deeper the experience becomes embedded into our 'reality'- as a means of keeping us oriented. "I see things everywhere that frustrate me – I'm surrounded by people that are out to get me – men/women are horrible and treat me like I'm nothing." These are statements of our programming that the mind is compelled to make real, in its bid to keep us in a place where we know what's going on and how to deal with it.

The events that happen in our life may seem very real at the time, and we may be completely justified in our interpretation and everyone we know "agrees with us". But what we aren't always aware of is how that justification continues to find supporting evidence of 'how things are'. How when something 'happens' it carries with it the seed of becoming a permanent part of the reality we experience. In order to reduce the effect and influence of anything unwanted we have to make a conscious effort to notice it less. "It just doesn't bother me the way it once might have." In the words of the gurus, "we must turn from what disturbs us".

> "The secret to change is to focus all of your energy not on fighting the old, but on building the new."
> **Socrates**

THE CONTROL CENTRE

In order to reduce the impact something annoying has over our lives, we have to consciously let it go, like we never even knew it was there. It is also a good idea to immediately replace it with something we would rather have in our experience. Blot it out and replace it with something preferred. Our vibrational state has a powerful momentum in our life, and it will not vanish the first time you ask nicely – it will continue to appear and show up out of habit. We are forced by our habits and changing them is not always easy. But each time something unwanted shows up, we can acknowledge it and respond with less and less resistance.

We are no longer dragged into being the victim of a situation, because we are aware of the higher reasoning of why it was created – **to keep an old conditioned pattern in place**. This perspective allows us to take the reins of how we feel, and diminish the effect of anything in our experience that has gone past its 'used by' date.

Nothing is as real as we make it in the moment – we are having the reaction. The reaction is trying to tell us something 'real' is happening – something 'real' is being lost or challenged, but it is no more than our old conditioned model of the world and we are now calling it to account. What is being lost or challenged isn't as crucial to our survival or our status as the mind is making out. It is trying to convince us our values have been compromised somehow, but they are values of a conditioned state exaggerating its importance. We have an extremely over-active sense of the importance of what is being lost.

It may well be the case that some 'bastard' is dismantling something real – a valuable part of our identity we have been building for a long time. I'm not saying this is not real, but our reactions to the conclusions we are making are often not the most efficient way of servicing the issue. I'm not implying that this is not the case that something real is being threatened in the moments when we have these reactions. But in reducing the emotional impact on us, and moving away from the type of people who perpetuate those types of experiences, we are allowing something new to enter.

People can and do steal from us, people can bad mouth us, people can inflict violence on us, but nothing can harm us as much as our own response, and our own unconsciousness to the true nature of the event. Our own unconscious willingness to allow the experience to remain in our energy, by failing to affirm this isn't what I want, and shift the feeling state towards our preference. People often move from bad relationship to bad relationship because their old conditioned mindset remains. What is embedded into their unconscious minds about what a relationship is doesn't change in the next relationship. They have a deep belief that this is how they deserve to be treated.

If we want something new in our life we have to give specifics about what you would prefer – the 'magic' is in the details as they say, which we'll delve into more in the attraction chapter. But I want to answer some of the objections here. I'm not suggesting we tolerate poor treatment because it is not 'real'. I never want it to be said that I insinuated it is ok to be walked all over, and that you should 'suck it up' because it is not 'real'. That is in no way close to what I have suggested here.

What I've tried to explain is a tool to reduce the effect of undesirable circumstances so we no longer have it unconsciously 'stuck' in our experience. We are the cause of how we feel, not the event. We can phase anything out of our lives if we reflect on its importance to us. If we don't need it, we recognise it when it comes, and it is gone, and gone forever. We have recognised at a deeper level why the experience continues to surface. Let shit go that we no longer want to experience. If we are angry at something or someone, our anger doesn't change the other person, or the situation – it just perpetuates the feeling state of anger, and draws to us situations that inspire the same reaction. Our anger does change things, but not for the better.

> "The most important spiritual growth doesn't happen when you're meditating or on a yoga mat. It happens in the midst of conflict, when you're

> frustrated, angry or scared and you're doing the same old thing, and then suddenly you realise you have a choice to do it differently."
>
> Anon

The heart isn't just a muscle

The subconscious is an emotional mind – the mind of our heart. It is a habit mind and has formed a strong groove in what we experience. Nothing can change without good reason, consciousness, and the new option being introduced. Without intention and a more effective means of serving our needs. The subconscious mind is not at all like what we may have pictured a mind to be. It may be a super-powerful processor, but the only power we are interested in is its power to deliver us a satisfied life. And if that is not our experience then it is not the fault of this 'all-powerful' mind but the program we are running. The heart is powerful but it needs a target – it needs a sense of direction. We can provide this by reflecting on:

- What's important to me?
- What do I want?

If these questions are kept in mind, we have some sense of control over how our life goes. We give this 'super powerful' brain of ours a track to run on, instead of feeling 'stuck' in a rut. We all live in a rut, but if we don't have an awareness that this is a normal part of our experience, we can work and try as hard as we like but won't feel like anything changes. We can only experience a change when we have a change of heart.

Our heart is our control centre, and is the cause of our experience. It tells us what everything 'means'. It controls **the way the world seems**. Feed it clear instructions and we'll start to feel like we have some degree of control over how our life goes. We can consciously change what things mean, what we care about and how we are affected. But if we don't know that, in our conscious thoughts, we are feeding instructions to our control centre, our lives can feel like a monotonous 'groundhog day'.

But the heart is not just a blood pumping muscle, it is a powerful neurotransmitter that emits a frequency that both attracts the events of our life and tells us how we should feel about them. The event and the feeling state are one in the same. How we feel attracted the event as a means of keeping the same emotion alive in us. **The heart, it seems, has a mind of its own.**

From an article I found on the internet by Rollin McCraty, P.H.D, Raymond Treavor Bradly, P.H.D, and Dana Tomasino, BA:

> *"Far more than a simple pump, as once believed, the heart is now recognised by scientists as a highly complex system with its own functional 'brain'.*
>
> *Compared to the electromagnetic field produced by the brain, the electrical component of the hearts field is about 60 times greater in amplitude, and permeates every cell in the body.*
>
> *The magnetic component is approximately 5000 times stronger than the brains magnetic field and can be detected several feet away from the body with sensitive magnetometers."*

It seems the same conclusions are being arrived at from science, from spirituality (old and new) and personal development. The context is different but the truth is agreed. Attraction is carried by many different rivers, but all arrive at the same ocean – the same conclusion. The heart is the most powerful organ in the body – not the mind.

We don't attract what we want, we attract what we are. Attraction is the energy we project. We attract what we believe to be true.

The secret agenda

Why do I say secret agenda? Because it is part of the mind's job to ensure that we don't recognise that our circumstances are created by another part of our consciousness. Our 'will' is not as free as we would like to believe. This idea doesn't resonate with many people because it questions both the absolute nature of their reality and the ability to believe in the freedom of will. Some are fearful of the idea that there is more to our minds than we are conscious of, because to them it insinuates a loss of control.

But to the contrary, the only way we can have control is to understand we are running a program and feed it the right instructions. We change the world around us when we live intentionally. This information is not designed to scare people into believing they are out of their depth within their own minds, but to remind them it is everyone's birthright and within their ability to control how they feel and be the cause of what happens in their life. Attracting desirable experiences is more within our power than many people think.

Energy is passed on

Humankind is in something of a frantic state, but because we have this frequency in common it has been somewhat normalised. But because we are so on edge, we have become somewhat numb to our feelings – to our internal compass. We have a mind that is conditioned to look for and find danger and threats in our environment. We are naturally poised for attack – it is little wonder much of our population has medicated itself out of being able to feel much at all.

When the caveman raced back into his home in a state of adrenaline fuelled panic, his vibration was felt by the infant in the home – passing on a very sure signal to the young that its survival hangs on a thread. Over time this fear-fuelled energetic pattern has become intensified by all of the harshness of what human beings have seen and endured.

We have witnessed people being burnt at the stake for practicing their medicine, and beheaded for speaking their truth. The brutality that man has inflicted on each other still lives in the minds and energy pattern that we sustain. That lives and breathes in us.

We still carry this energetic fear that we are much better off shutting up, especially about anything we care about deeply. Fear rises in us and we daren't open our mouths for reasons that go far beyond what we are conscious of. Because of the ancient, subtle energy we carry, we live by the unconscious conclusion that we will probably be scorned and quite possibly ostracised if we don't bow to the weight of the majority.

> "Who has fully realised that history is not contained in thick books, but lives in our very blood."
> Carl Jung

Does it give us any more of a sense of responsibility to understand that the pattern can end with us? We can stop passing this on, and stop filling the emotional 'airwaves' with a frequency we would rather doesn't continue – not in us, not in anyone. What we send out always comes back to us.

The pattern can stop with us, and it is not just our greatest pleasure to be aware of this opportunity, it is our greatest responsibility to enact. We are of course the primary beneficiaries of becoming more conscious, but everyone in our life benefits as well. Do you need a more compelling reason?

Is this 'hard' to comprehend?

That we have been convinced our value can only be validated by the opinions of the majority is what is fundamentally wrong. And yes it's cultural, but more to the point a sign that our evolution hasn't 'caught up' with the conditions in which we now live. We are still driven by very tribal emotional urges, but are now living in one huge fishbowl of a tribe. The conditions we now live in (social media and the like) have contributed to this devaluation of the 'normal' and 'ordinary' experiences that make up our life. The normal is our window but it has been devalued out of its purpose of enriching our lives. Some of the most compassionate, purposeful, and contributing people I know don't have or care for the attention of the world. Too many of us have fallen for this 'we are less than' conspiracy of our culture.

I really think we've been hoodwinked not just by our own minds and the evil programmers, but by our own compliance. By our own agreement of our worth – our agreement that it can be gauged externally. We think mental illness is a problem, but we've all willingly 'bought into' the cause.

What the seers, prophets, and gurus of old communicated to us was the internal projection of feeling states. All any of us want is to feel better, and this comes from the stuff going on inside us, not outside of us. I want to de-mystify the term 'spiritual' and how it is used. In the context in which I use it in this book, it quite simply means immaterial. That the invisible stuff of our thoughts and feelings that aren't just real and effective, they form the blueprint of the material world. Our emotions and thoughts have form, and move the physical world. We are often sadly dismissive of the 'immaterial' because we can't measure and touch it, but from a higher perspective it has a powerful effect on the material world.

The outside seems to force us to feel – let that old-world view go. Worry about who you are and what you want to do. We should never concern ourselves with how we think we are perceived, or what we think is 'going on'. The outside will eventually fall in line with how we feel, when we adjust our logic to recognise that the outside reflects how we feel.

Very often we find that fears only exist because we've never questioned them. Are there substantiated grounds for us feeling this way? When we ask why something scares us, often we come to the realisation that there is no good reason, we just never thought to question the fear. And when it doesn't 'hold up' under the spotlight of awareness the fear often just fades without us 'facing' anything.

We don't have to conquer our fears, just see them for what they are. Realise they are generated from an out of touch and overactive sense of what is dangerous. **It is very often awareness that banishes the shadows we were running from, not any noble sense of bravery.**

Benefits of realising the agenda of mind

My query is – how often are we consciously promoting our mood, and not just being the passengers of where our attention takes us. How often are we noticing the faults of others and what's wrong in our environment, rather than what we would rather experience?

We know this stuff – what we complain about gets bigger, and becomes our practice. And it is the same with what we are grateful for. Our life is a pattern, a practice, so what are you practicing? This broad field of becoming more conscious, often dubbed personal development, could really be referred to as **appreciation development**. You can read someone's 'fortune' by what they think of what they have already. Realisation of mind is really an appreciation of what it can do. When we appreciate what mind is and can do, we empower it – enabling it to turn our world around without anything in our situation changing.

The practical benefit of this awareness is that we understand how much power we wield with our attention. Notice less of what we don't like, and more of what we do. Replacing the annoying with the 'preferred' begins an entirely new pattern that can ultimately sail us into vastly different waters, when multiplied by time. Look away from what disturbs us and we shrink its effect.

THE CONTROL CENTRE

When we understand that our situations are mind-made and why – that our reactions come from an unguided program – we will feel differently about it. And it is not as if we are becoming emotionally numb to our lives and what is happening. We are forming a new habit of becoming more poised and reflective people, rather than reactive victims of the program.

The most powerful part of our mind has one job – to preserve the frequency of our heart. And it does it by how it makes the world seem. Makes the world seem the way it makes us feel.

PRACTICAL EXERCISE

The following exercises offer strategies for varying degrees of emotional reactions, with the common goal of becoming more aware and in control of how we are feeling. In becoming more sensitive to how we feel we are more in control of what is happening to us.

Ex 1 – This is when something overwhelming occurs. How we feel seems completely out of our control.

The idea is that as quickly as possible we use the perspective gained from this chapter to get back to square one – maybe not 'Buddha' calm but at least to a point where we can take a few breaths and have a handle on our thoughts. To regain the control the event seems to have over us. This exercise is designed to give us a new cognition of the events and see them more as opportunities to become more emotionally flexible. It is stated in NLP (neuro-linguistic programming) that the winner of any negotiation (which is what many of our interactions are) always goes to the one who has more emotionally agility. Often getting what we want relies on our ability to remain calm. On our egos not getting in the way of what we want.

THE SECRET AGENDA OF MIND

Of course, the idea is we are more and more conscious and willing to ask ourselves, "How am I feeling. Is this experience something I want to continue? How would I like it to be different?"

Ex 2 – These are the milder emotional reactions that will occur more regularly. The times when someone says something annoying or does something stupid, and it's mildly irritating. Things 'happen' that don't seem exactly ideal, and they make us stew a little, before we think of something better to occupy us and return to our cool, composed self. It's just an exercise in being less bothered. Ask yourself, "Does it matter? Is it important? Have I got better things to worry about, and what are they?" As much as this might seem simple and trivial, it is the core of intentional living. It is how we change our mindset, and begin a trajectory of a less bothered life.

Ex 3 – The last part of this responding more consciously exercise is when we think that we are experiencing minimal emotion. In those quiet times when nothing at all is bothering us, and we can just go into a quick meditative moment where we become even more sensitive to how we are feeling/attracting/responding. We are always vibrating and the world is always moving in relationship to how we feel, so get a little intimate with your heart in those quiet times when you are able. And it is not as if this type of practice makes us some type of super sensitive freak – to the contrary, it makes us much more aware of when we are veering from our course and how to get back there.

As much as this is the mildest of the exercises it is also the most profound. We are tuning into our control centre – the centre from which all events find their cause. When we become increasingly more sensitive to how we are responding in those quiet moments we are the ever more vigilant guardians of our peace.

THE CONTROL CENTRE

We don't wait till we get bowled over by a succession of sneaky and unnoticed events building up to become a bigger one. Our heart becomes like a peace-seeking missile – ever more wary when it even slightly veers from its course. Returning to peace is the most valuable skill of all.

CHAPTER SUMMARY

- The subconscious has one job – preserve our emotional state. It manages our emotional state by skewing our perception of the world, such that everything we see supports how we feel.
- To alter the program we have to work on a level of the program. We have to consistently reflect on what's important to us, and the ways in which our experience will be different to the one we're having.
- We have to be always navigating how we want things to go. Giving ourselves a clear sense of direction. If we are not steering, we are passengers.
- The subconscious is an emotional mind – the heart's mind. The heart is the cause of our experience. In being aware that we are creating the world the way it is, we become less affected and more accepting.
- In responding more consciously we change both the nature of the event itself, and the beliefs that no longer suit our needs.
- Becoming increasingly more sensitive to how we are feeling/attracting/responding is the single best thing we can do to alter our external experience. Everything comes from the centre.

CHAPTER 4

Watching the Watcher

> "The moment you start watching the thinker, a higher level of consciousness becomes activated."
>
> **Ekhart Tolle**

There is a profound benefit from being able to view our life remotely, as an impartial observer. We are not drawn into the emotion of a situation, buried under the weight of the certainty of our judgement. We are not tied to a single way to view our circumstance, or the emotional reaction we wouldn't choose or invite. When we are able to stand back, as if we are watching a movie with ourselves as a character, we are not tethered to the reaction – it is not happening to us. We are free to respond in the way the hero of our movie would – calmly, confidently and unstirred by the event itself. Our emotions often run away with us. We have turned the event into the single meaning that is relative to our life experience, and of course, we know how this is going to go. We know what it means – we know we have one way to react – one course of action.

THE CONTROL CENTRE

When we are the observer, another level of our awareness becomes activated, and what's happening doesn't matter as much. And just as mentioned in the last chapter, it is not as if we are becoming emotionally numb to our lives – we are free to choose the effect, because of our ability to respond. We can improve any aspect of our lives we don't appreciate when we are more awake to our response options.

When we are the 'watcher' we are not operating from our preconceived conclusions, and can wait like a sleuth for all of the evidence to form a better picture. We are not so 'close' to our events that our perception has become strongly biased – our prejudice has not yet ruined the outcome for us. What is 'happening' is not always apparent, and we have become a little more patient to find out. We know the world doesn't happen outside of us, it is our internal representation, our history that has caused the event. In knowing this, we stand back, we observe – we are poised and considerate.

Just like Sherlock Holmes attempted to point out, most detectives start to form their conclusions too early and then are directed by the prejudice of these deductions – only looking for evidence that supports their theory. Their judgement has been skewed to only look for evidence that 'proves' this early suspicion. And we, like these misled detectives, do the same with our lives, if we are not able to stand back sometimes and look at the bigger picture.

We can't see what is stopping us because it is right in front of our face, or rather, it is hidden by our 'backstory' – the solution is invisible to us because of our way of looking at it. We never recognise ourselves (or rather our program) as the enemy because "Why would we sabotage ourselves?". We often have to apply a detached and 'unemotional' logic to our situations to see the solutions.

> "In order to use your head, you have to go out of your mind."
>
> **Timothy Leary**

It would be obvious, if we weren't so emotionally invested in the 'roadblocks' we ourselves have set up, that we failed to see them. When we can view our life remotely it can often occur to us almost immediately that our reactive pattern has caused the problem.

When we listen to other people's problems, it often seems to us like the solution they seek is staring them in the face. It is almost painful to watch as they avoid making decisions that could easily put them in the position they would like to be in. We can solve other people's problems, but we can't solve ours. As a consequence, I always try to listen to other people's scenarios with a sense that something of a similar nature is going on in my own life. Something about what is happening with them is relative to my situation. The solution I form in my head for their issue often leads me to see my solution more clearly. They are inadvertently offering me the cryptic solution to my own puzzle. If I can apply my own reasoning without my 'story' getting in the way, the answer could be so much easier than I'm making it.

The mind sends us on this wild goose chase looking for the 'enemy' (the cause of our angst) in all the wrong places, because we are always looking out rather than inwards for what is going 'wrong' – for what we are up against. It may sound strange to be critiquing our own life as if we are an outsider, but it is precisely how we awaken to this higher aspect of our consciousness. An aspect that can see our problems from a perspective that is less bound by the story of 'who we are' – the self-image we have so much emotional investment in that we can't see past. Detachment is a skill – awakening a part of us that isn't bound by the impulsive reactions and conclusions that don't make as much sense as we might think. A part that can detach from the 'actual', and live in the unbiased and theoretical. Because in theory things shouldn't bother us, or be as difficult as we are making them.

When we ask something as simple as "How should this affect me?" – in that moment we are less affected by it because we have temporarily 'removed' ourselves from the emotion of the situation. We are not 'feeling' what we are wondering about. In that moment we are not being affected – we are doing something else. We are the questioning entity rather than the affected. We have disengaged the 'actual', and engaged the inquisitive.

The 'watcher' is the subconscious mind – the impartial observer of the turmoil we call our life. When we 'watch the watcher' – when we observe our thoughts and emotions more objectively – we align with that deeper part of ourselves that doesn't really understand why we are creating all the drama. We are able to contemplate paths, without the skew of emotion. To take actions that are aligned with what we want, rather than fettered by some unconscious force of habit. It's kind of like we are having a meeting with the 'boss upstairs', and he wants to know what all of the fuss is about.

The subconscious mind is always 'spying' on the conscious – watching everything that we think and pay attention to, and turning it into what we have asked to experience. When we take the position of the watcher – **of spying on the spy of our mind** – we are aligning ourselves with this higher, more conscious perspective. We are creating a union with that higher decision-making faculty – or interfacing with the program itself.

We rise above the emotion of situations. We have less emotional stake in the outcomes, and so can act with less bias or concern for what may happen. We act with regard to best case, or best action instead of being persuaded by the fear-filled antics of the conditioning that is so swayed by false scenarios, and glued to our personal history. The conscious mind cannot 'see the light'. It is not designed to think beyond the parameters of the position we currently perceive ourselves to be in. To see solutions, we have to view from above.

> "The great kick of the mystic experience, the exultant, ecstatic hit, is the sudden relief from emotional pressure."
>
> **Timothy Leary**

This is also said to be an important part of **healing from addictions** – separating behaviour from identity. We are not drug addicts – we are people who are in the habit of taking drugs. The behaviour is not 'who we are' – it is a coping mechanism we adopted because it temporarily cured us from what we were experiencing. It was a way that once worked to deal with a feeling we didn't like. But we couldn't, at that time, see the longer-term health consequences – how damaging and ineffective this strategy would become. When the behaviour is linked to our identity it is almost impossible to shift. It is very much more difficult to change 'who' we are than it is to change what we do. To change something attached to how we identify ourselves usually translates to losing something of ourselves we can't see as being 'worth' the risk. The addict will surmise, "What other aspect of myself might I also be sacrificing? I won't know myself."

It is never just the drugs we are trying to drop. We are giving up our world view – how we are seen, and the relationships of our like-minded users.

Don't let your struggle become a large part of your identity.

The ability to separate behaviour from identity is fundamental to taking the reins of our actions. Even if we don't have a drug problem, we are addicted to old circumstances, our problems and our way of thinking as fundamentally linked to our identity. We don't want our problems solved – we love them. And have much more invested in them than we realise. They are keeping the whole picture in frame – who would I be without my problems? The last thing the ego wants is to be free of the 'problems' it regards as a framework to who we are. So what happens? We carry on frustrated by those same unsolvable riddles that must remain if we are to preserve a sense of who we are. We keep scratching the same old itch.

Am I a stutterer, a struggling single dad, a broke artist – look, I think you get it. We don't have to be, and without anything in our conditions changing but the light in which we see ourselves. Someone else put in your shoes might see things very differently, and it is not beyond us to do the same. The cage we have built around us for protection that 'allows' us to avoid action always becomes our prison, and we didn't even notice as we were happily laying the blocks.

Nothing in our conditions needs to change for us to have more control over our experience. We just have to recognise ourselves as the cause.

"You mean, I don't have to feel guilty about not wanting to spend time around friends who aren't supportive?" I mean as crazy and as straightforward as that sounds, many of us are in a pattern of satisfying other people's needs at the absolute expense of our own. It is not just women who are cursed with the disease to please – many of us are 'forced' into actions we'd really rather avoid for the 'good' of the whole. Bugger the whole – get a new whole. One that isn't looking for a 'doormat'. When we watch the watcher, we wake up to the fact that many of our grinding behaviours aren't as 'compulsory' as they seem. They can be let go with ease – without guilt, or facing fears, or any fear of the imaginary consequences. They just go, and everything about the repercussions are exposed as inventions of a conditioned mind.

The subtleties of emotion

> "Are you carrying unspoken resentment towards a person close to you? Do you realise the energy you are thus emanating is so harmful you are contaminating yourself as well as those around you?"
>
> **Ekhart Tolle**

It reminds me of an anonymous quote I saw on Facebook that read something like – "You can eat all the leafy greens you like and drink nothing but Kale juice, but it won't matter a bit if you can't let go of that grudge you carry about your friend". We are nourished much more by our thoughts and feelings than we are our food. We can eat extremely healthy and exercise and sleep right, but we turn whatever we eat into toxicity in our body if we remain unaware of the effect our emotions have not just on our bodies but on the type of events we attract to ourselves.

We 'feed' on all of our input. The conversations we engage in, the shows we watch, podcasts we listen to – even the company we keep. But even more so the grudges we hold, and the righteous stance we take. To be 'healthy' we have to be conscious and considerate of all of the emotions we allow to live in our body. They too are our 'nutrition'. We can sabotage our joy simply by our willingness to maintain unflattering opinions of ourselves and others. The old adage to hear no, speak no, and see no evil, was a reminder to pay no mind to any aspect you didn't want to allow into your experience. It is turning away from the old and towards the new.

Guilt and stress do more damage to your body than chocolate cake ever will.

The idea of forgiveness being for the benefit of the perpetrator, or who we think wronged us, has for a long time puzzled me. How can we not see who is the real beneficiary is of us letting go of the apparent 'wrong' that was done to us? Forgiveness in no way carries the implication that we must spend time with people who aren't respectful of us or our time – it in no way implies that we open ourselves to similar behaviour. We dump the energy so it is no longer a part of our chi. In letting go of the event, and the dark energy surrounding it, we decrease the likelihood of any 'event repeats'. When we hang on to things, we bind them to our experience.

THE CONTROL CENTRE

> "We cannot keep bad thoughts from sometimes entering our heads, but we can prevent them from nesting in our brain."
>
> — Anon

Forgiveness has little to nothing to do with the 'forgiven' (although it indeed may have a profound effect on them). Forgiveness is about our bodies and our responsibility to maintain what goes on within them. In being the 'watcher' of our lives, we are emotionally detached – we don't even bother talking about it anymore – we've got better things to do. We have a new sense of responsibility for how we feel, and what we allow into our space. When we feel good, we do good and we attract good. We forgive people not just for our sake but for the sake of the world we all share. When we forgive we let someone out of prison, and the prisoner is us.

When you forgive you don't change the past, you change the future.

Is peace of mind a priority?

As I stated in the last chapter, it's how we look at a situation that causes the reaction, but that we have played a part in the dynamic rarely occurs to us. We can change our point of view, particularly if our perspective inspires a feeling we know we would rather not continue to experience. So often we claim we want to feel differently, we confirm to ourselves that peace is something we want more of in our lives. But then some 'dick' cuts us off in traffic and we take two hours to **let it go** – the event simmers in our thoughts spoiling many hours that could potentially be filled with something else. Is peace the priority? Or are we unconsciously letting 'the pattern' run our life, with us in the passenger seat? Are we the slave to something beyond our control, creating unnecessary misery? How often do we hold ourselves to the flame for things beyond our control?

Being our own life coach

In taking the observer role in our lives, we can become our own **life coach**. We begin to see the fictitious nature of the stories we've been telling ourselves that prevent us making the decisions that would take us forward. Coaching works because coaches can see what we are so close to that we can't see. They don't have the emotional investment in remaining 'stuck'. They throw options at us that we've never considered, and present obstacles as the opportunities they more truly represent, so they become something we really want to do rather than continue avoiding. A coach's primary role is to invite us to question our reasoning. Why is this difficult? What makes this so hard for you? To see beyond the 'fiction' of our 'back story'.

If we are able to see our life as an outsider, the issues that have remained exceptionally well-disguised get found out. That pebble in our shoe that has been bugging us becomes clear and easy to fix. "How would someone else see this problem? How would they go about solving it? How would my life look once it is no longer there?" Being able to consider this future perspective carries with it the assumption that the problem is solvable. Looking back from the future, we can often see how we did it, and it is not as hard as we thought.

A coach never assumes they can solve our problem. They have not lived our experiences so can more easily see what is getting in the way – can see what we can't. A coach can't solve our problem, they facilitate options for change, and poke holes in our reasoning. What's going on with us is a story. And when we can learn to occupy these strategies on our own, we can often forego the need for help. Tread unbiasedly into what you don't like about what seems to be going on, and the answer just may come from nowhere. The solution you never considered, was in the last place you thought to look. What do you want? What are you going to do about it? It is more often clarity on these questions that allows the problems to solve themselves, but in my experience a coach always helps. They can see what we can't. The question is, are you able to view your life remotely enough to be honest about what's important to you, and what needs to change in order to live this truth? To embody the solution as a part of your life?

When we are honest with ourselves about why we think we can't, often the reasoning starts to fall apart. When exposed to the light of awareness, the reason for the 'roadblock' that was unconscious, or unknown to us, usually just stops making any sense, and we can see clearly what needs to be done to turn the table on an issue. Our 'brick wall' becomes a house of cards when we ask better questions.

Often, when we take this observer role on our issues, we can see more clearly what we imagined was stopping us doing what we wanted to. We can sense how we are creating our own obstacles, simply by the manner in which we communicate internally – the inner language we use. We become more aware of the inner dialogue, and the story we tell ourselves about our situation that we believe to be real. We ourselves create our 'blockages' for a reason – and when we know what that reason is, we can contemplate more efficient ways to serve the need that the problem was serving. Every behaviour serves a purpose – we are getting 'something' out of everything we do.

The problem occurs because our behaviours become so forced by habit that it doesn't occur to us when our actions become out of sync with our changing needs. What we want and value changes, but we try to meet that new need from within an old behaviour pattern, an 'expired' sense of rationale, and wonder why our lives aren't working. We can never apply old logic to a new set of problems. We get frustrated because as much as we consciously want change, we are bound by the momentum of a long persisting pattern.

As an example, a smoker is never really conscious of all of the triggers that signal the need for a cigarette, or why smoking appealed in the first place. For many smoking provides an unconscious belonging to a group that are nonchalant about the rules. They have in common that they aren't one of those people who get all anal about their health. They look their own mortality in the face and laugh. For many smoking is more than just a relaxing buzz, it is a little bit of anarchy – a little bit of and 'I don't care' type attitude that pervades much deeper into their psyche than they imagine.

As suggested, these reasons go much deeper into our sense of identity than we are aware, and it takes more than willpower and determination to break the bonds that nest in our unconscious. A smoker has a mindset that smoking is 'good', and for more reasons than they are conscious. It is hard to quit smoking, or any of the emotional habits we are addicted to, but it is even harder if we are unaware of all the subconscious needs that the behaviour serves, and has been serving well for many years. For many smoking is more than just a guilty pleasure. Even admitting to anyone that you want to quit is divorcing yourself from a group you have a long history of belonging to. Smokers are a like-minded unity, and you have 'all of a sudden' turned your back on them – making them feel like they should do the same. It is not just that cool rush of smoke you will miss as it enters your throat and lungs – it is a group you no longer wish to be identified with.

This is how strong the unconscious will is – tobacco smoke is filled with poisons similar to many that come from the back of a car. They make us feel temporarily ill and a little queasy, but we bounce back ready to light up again before too long. But I don't want to pick on the smokers – I myself am just as addicted to the patterns of emotion that have shrunk my comfort zone without me knowing. It is always a case of us doing the best we can with what we know, and when we know better, we can do better. Knowing better means becoming more sensitive to our needs, and finding a better way to serve the same need. What is the need? The need is the reason you do it.

We never find clear choices difficult. What we lack is clarity, not willpower.

The storyteller

Often our stories have been running so long without being questioned, their reasoning has become so matted and tangled into our subconscious minds, we lose the sense that they no longer apply. We tell ourselves an unconscious story of the time we were humiliated as a child when we performed the crocodile rock dance in front of the school, and this pattern carries as the unconscious voice that tells us, without rhyme or reason – performing leads to humiliation.

We are deeply emotional creatures – we aren't rational ones. The stories we tell often stopped applying to us many years ago. We are different people with different skill sets, but that old story remains. They exist so deep in our nature that we can't find them to stand before us and be brought to account. The things that block us are so deep we can't find them. The idea of coaching, and I imagine a lot of therapies, is to bring these deep dwelling reasons to the surface where they can be properly scrutinized.

When unconscious reasons are shone under the light of awareness there are no shadows.

If we knew where this reasoning stemmed from, we could easily knock it over. Our only knowledge of these blockages or irrational conclusions is that pit that forms in our stomach when we want to speak our mind, or that fury that ignites in us when someone challenges our method for something trivial. We are helpless to mend what unconsciously sabotages our lives. It has to be brought to the surface of awareness with questions. Why do I feel this way? What is the benefit of this feeling? Or is what the feeling is warning me of real?

I guess being the watcher is not dissimilar to that game we play when we say to ourselves, "What would so and so do?" (Chuck Norris comes to mind). When we do this, we are taking on a less emotional and more rational stance. We are considering the problem from an outsider's perspective, a new set of eyes, and can often much more clearly see what the situation, and our peace of mind, calls for.

Seeing inside our problems

When we are watching as if we were the subconscious mind, we start to smell the BS in our story. Many times this perspective can be illuminating. We can 'all of a sudden' see the simplest solution to a problem that may have persisted for a very long time.

I had a friend who had become estranged from his children after a recent separation. After a couple of expensive battles with the courts, his former partner still failed to comply with visitation rights or any contact with his two young children. He was at his wits end and felt he had very little hope of seeing his children, and no one was sticking up for him. He felt guilty for having left, and not just as a bad parent, but as a failure as a human being. Being a father was a piece of his identity he held as his greatest privilege. He was helpless to be the influence on his kids he wanted to be.

I asked my friend if he loved his kids, an obvious question. "Would you do everything in your power to help them," I said. To set a good example for them? Again, the answers came with an objectionable scoff – "of course I do". Have you done everything in your control to show you love them and attempt to make contact? Then why do you persist in holding yourself to the fire for things that are out of your control?

In the space of the conversation that followed, my friend came to the stark realisation that in order to be the best dad he could, he needed to stop the torture he was putting himself through, as it did nothing to serve him, the kids, or the situation. If he was to be a good dad, he had to get healthy in both body and mind, and pursue anything else he got joy out of. When the occasion did arise that he would see his kids, he would meet them as the strong, compassionate and devoted man he was, rather than exhausted, beaten and bitter. Remember, we should never hold ourselves to the flame for things that are beyond our control.

What I failed to mention at the time of conversation, and I wished I had have, is that we are an influence on our children's life even when they can't see us. We are the living example of what we hope they would do when faced with the same obstacles. Being estranged is hard – really hard. But we don't make anyone's life better until we understand we are examples, even in our absence. That we can reach them in mind and nurture them in our heart – it is the part that no court room or no distance can ever take away.

The eavesdropper

The subconscious mind is always listening to the quiet, idle, unconscious chatter that is so automatic that we can hardly hear. And the subconscious mind, our powerful genie, always answers the same, **"As you wish"**. If we are saying to ourselves our life is hopeless and we can't get a break, "As you wish". If we affirm to ourselves that a problem is hard, and a mountain to overcome, the subconscious mind works to affirm our reality - making things seem much harder than they need be. Reality must always be a match to our statements. We think we are making statements about how things actually are, but the subconscious mind assumes this is how we want things to be. The subconscious mind assumes we know the deal – we know what's going on. It is hanging on our every word.

The most powerful part of our mind believes everything we tell it.

Everything we notice, everything we pay attention to gets larger. Good or bad, if it's in our attention, it will persist in our experience. The subconscious mind controls what we notice and where our attention goes, and this is the true benefit of living intentionally. We are giving clear instructions on how we would prefer it goes. Our goals focus the mind on something in particular, rather than letting it wander into something arbitrary. The subconscious mind is always pulling us around to what we have consciously claimed we want to be a more prominent part of our experience.

Benefits of a detached perspective

Often, overcoming some of the biggest issues in our life is not about anything so brave as facing fears – in awareness we often realise what we thought scared us isn't as 'real' as we were making it out to be. It existed purely as an unchallenged habit pattern we didn't realise we were holding onto for no good reason. We realise we live in a different world to what we did when the patterns formed, with a different skill set and different knowledge, and a better logic to approach challenges. The old patterns of fear no longer apply. We often cling to images of ourselves that don't do anything very flattering for us – "It's just what we've always done". And we don't recognise this old image of ourselves to be what also prevents us doing things that appeal to us (be they dreams, fears, lifestyles or whatever).

It all of a sudden occurs to us how unfounded the worries we had were. We don't have to face fear – when we turn to look at it, and it runs away. We have made mice into lions, and why? For no better reason than that we wanted to take on something as scary, and a lion seemed like a good choice. We built nothing into something, for no good reason – and we do it all the time. We call it our life.

Our problems never go away, we just choose new ones that make the old ones seem insignificant. We're often not avoiding them – the old hurdles just don't challenge us the way they once used to.

> "A clever person solves a problem. A wise person avoids it."
>
> **Albert Einstein**

THE CONTROL CENTRE

An exercise in self-coaching

Life coaching is one of the fastest growing health and wellbeing industries in the world today. A good coach can shortcut years of hard work and mistakes or unravel long persisting issues, often in a single session. The right coach can open doors and leap-frog our growth in ways that might not have occurred to us. But more than anything a coach is in our corner – they make us accountable for taking action on our solutions. Here I've compiled a list of the core coaching questions, in the hope we can better understand the process and apply it so we can coach ourselves.

A coach's skill is to continue their line of questioning without bias – without jumping to their own conclusions about what they would do in the situation because, as it is said in coaching, "the map is not the territory", meaning we haven't lived their experiences, and so can't assume we know what is best for them. We haven't lived in their shoes, so can't solve their problems from our perspective. We just want to bring all of the evidence and options to the table where they can be seen for what they are, and let the client come to a solution so they 'own' the action steps.

A skilled coach is impartial, and listens without prejudice. To act like Sherlock Holmes on a fact-finding mission, and not be led to falsely formed conclusions (the client can already do that). If the coach does this they will unconsciously begin 'leading' with their questions as to what they think the client should do, and it probably won't work for them.

Under the scrutiny of questions, our fiction begins to unravel. What is really bothering us, and what is our biggest obstacle is often not what we think, and maybe far easier to solve than we thought.

A coach does two things to help us on our journey – create a **compelling reason** (why do we want it? What's so important about it to us?), and help us to **be excited about the outcome**. It is something we'd love to see happen.

We either want something, or we want to be rid of something. Achieve a goal or overcome a problem. And here are ten commonly used questions towards getting us there.

1. What do you want? People generally focus on what they don't want rather than what they want. This needs to be re-directed to state the goal in the positive – "I want".

2. Why is this important to you? Useful for resolving conflicts of values.

3. How will you know when you've got what you want? Goals need to be measurable so we can tick a box, and reward ourselves for it. We have done something so celebrate it. This builds momentum.

4. What is getting in the way? Defines interference. What needs to change?

5. What resources have you got to support you? Show people they have more resources, both internal and external, than they're aware of at the moment.

6. When you accomplish your goal and look back on your success what will you experience? Envisioning the end point shows the desired result is possible.

7. What is the question you don't want to ask yourself right now? Gives you a chance to convey something that may be troubling you that you weren't aware of.

8. What's a way to make this really easy? Increases focus and fun.

9. What's the first step? The first step makes the shift from being the effect to becoming a cause.

10. And what else? Go beyond the immediate challenge.

THE CONTROL CENTRE

These are 10 core coaching questions taken from 'Coaching with NLP for Dummies' by Kate Burton. I am hoping that by providing this insight into the types of questions a coach would use, we can understand how the coaching process serves us to undermine the 'deadwood' of our beliefs that no longer serves us. I just thought it appropriate to install here because of how relative coaching is to us taking on the observer role of our own lives, and how we can benefit from this perspective.

But the real value in having a coach is the accountability. You have given voice to something you want and that is always the first step in the creation process. We speak it, we write it down, and then we live from the place of completion. How would it feel to have this thing we want?

Another less considered question that I like to use is, "What will you have to give up to achieve this?". What will you have to sacrifice? It is often the things we don't consider that secretly hold us back. What will you have to sacrifice when you've achieved this? Is it worth giving up? We fear success just as much as failure.

We often can't see our self-created blockages from the inside – we have to take an observer perspective. What would a life coach ask me? And even without engaging a coach, the insight might surprise you. There are always things in our life worth getting excited about – something we want that maybe we believed we couldn't have simply because we weren't asking ourselves the right questions.

CHAPTER SUMMARY

- Being the impartial observer of our lives dissociates us from being the over-emotional victims of our situations, and helps take a logic-oriented view of what is happening.
- We think more 'subconsciously' – meaning with regard to what is listening, and creating how our world seems from those thoughts. We are more conscious of the effect of what we are telling ourselves.
- We understand the fictitious nature of the stories that have become embedded in our reasoning – many of which no longer apply and unconsciously limit what we will attempt.
- When our obstacles can be seen as opportunities for maturation, we want to take them on, rather than avoid them.
- Getting what we want is easier when we are not so emotionally invested in the story we've been telling ourselves.
- The reasoning behind any obstacle cannot hold up to the light of awareness. There are no shadows when darkness is exposed to the light.

CHAPTER 5

Meeting Our Maker

THE CONTROL CENTRE

> "The reason man may become the master of his own destiny is because he has the power to influence his own subconscious mind."
>
> — Napoleon Hill

'The secret agenda of mind' was about understanding the function of the subconscious mind — this chapter is about understanding its nature. Primarily in understanding that although this amazing thing that is our subconscious mind is an incredibly fast processor, and powerful in that it builds the world as we know it, it is also very gullible. It is powerless without the right input. It has no faculty with which to dispute what we state as true in the conscious mind. It just makes it undeniably true for us. Although it is powerful in shaping the world as we know it, it is also completely submissive to our commands.

The subconscious has no 'mind' of its own. No decision-making faculty. In comparison with the conscious mind that we use and know as ourselves, there is 'no one home'. It just supplies meanings, and doesn't decide anything like the conscious mind that we understand to be who we are. When we have an awareness of the nature of the instructions we are sending and what it is we are instructing, we become ever more mindful of how we think.

There is nothing more worthy of our interest and understanding than the realisation of what our own subconscious mind is. Once we realise how it uses our statements to construct what is 'real' it will become our friend rather than our foe. As well, we begin to accept that there is a higher order at play in our lives — we trust in the process that the things we have asked for are coming, and we loosen our narrow-minded grip on how this will come to pass. Sometimes things happen that seem to be going wrong — they are not part of the plan — but with a sense of connection to the subconscious mind we start to trust in the way we are being guided towards our life's purpose.

We trust that things come in their time, and not every part of our story makes sense in the moment it happens. We trust that sometimes doors must close in order for us to be redirected. We are calmed by our sense of what we are connected to, and guided by. We trust that the universe often works in mysterious ways. Something quite beyond our imagination has it all in order.

When we understand this 'world maker' is listening, we **talk to ourselves better** – we address ourselves with a sense of reverence. And we get clear on the details – the instructions of how we would prefer things went. The type of life we would prefer to experience. We have to define the type of changes we want to see, if we are to ever begin looking for them.

We become more centred and grounded in our experience – we are not alone. We are connected by our awareness to something that would truly boggle the mind if we could calm ourselves enough to sense it. We live with more of a sense of wonder, and allow things to happen in their time. We are less jumpy about things, and the manner in which others conduct themselves, knowing that in controlling our response, we control our world. Things may not be happening in the way we expected, but we trust in the way – we stay true to our feeling state, and trust that the evidence of how we feel will soon be evident in our experience.

When we know the nature of the subconscious mind, we share in its deep sense of peace. When we understand what we are at the helm of, we realise that peace is an ever-present and accessible part of our consciousness. Understanding the nature of the subconscious mind, we come to trust in a part of us that, even though it is beyond our awareness, is deeply comforting to sense our connection to.

Our father who is in heaven

As I suggested in the opening chapter, Jesus was attempting to communicate a message of the parts of our mind we aren't conscious

THE CONTROL CENTRE

of, to an era that, purely by their place in history, were far less informed than we are today. Dare I say, they were ignorant of the aspects of mind we now refer to as the subconscious, and had no awareness of what we now understand to be our programming.

The subconscious is the parent to the conscious mind, taking care of the big business of 'reality'. It is running the program, so that in our conscious lives we can rest in the comfort of the accuracy of the auto-pilot settings. The mind is designed to conserve energy – to not have to think about what everything means and the direction of our lives. We operate from a pre-conceived notion of these larger aspects of our life. We would be unable to cope if we had to think about what things mean – is this taking me in the direction I want to go, and is this a suitable behaviour for the character I want to portray? These calculations have to be instant and automatic – they come from the program.

What I'll refer to as the 'big stuff' – the who, what and where – are the main aspects of our life. Who we are (how our character behaves), what's going on (or what things mean) and where we are going (or the direction of our lives) are handed over to the automatic part of us that doesn't think – it just 'does'. If we consciously consider these elements, we can certainly impact all of these things to be more in unison with our values. In particular, the **'who we are'**, and **'what's going on'** that many assume we have limited control over, are not unrelated to our consciousness. These elements are 'passed over' to our 'rudder', but as we become more conscious, we will understand how much impact and choice we do have over these things. Over what is happening, and how things go.

The 'big stuff' is handed over to a part of mind that doesn't think and choose, but through reflecting on what matters to us we can still have a huge say in how these things run. We can claw back some of the control we have unknowingly sacrificed to that automatic aspect of our consciousness.

MEETING OUR MAKER

The subconscious mind is what is referred to as the 'father' in scripture. It is always in a deep sense of peace or what could be regarded as 'heaven'. The subconscious mind was in effect our 'father that was in heaven', who we could 'pray' to in order to receive favourable passage. Or, as we'll come to understand, a perceptive shift that would appear to 'place' us in the conditions we were asking for.

The 'Lord's prayer' is a plea to that higher aspect of our consciousness that provides the shift in perception necessary for our dream to 'seem' realised. It cannot occur to us how all the stars will align to make something difficult for us to imagine come true. Our goal being realised is far more a shift in perception, a mindset change, than any physical conditions being met. Prayer is an appeal to the part of our mind, above the one we think with, that shifts perception to 'make' it all seem real. We imagine it being real – we feel it – and the supporting evidence begins to show up.

I made reference in the last chapter as God being the 'G' word, because I think there is a misunderstood connotation to the word. It inspires everything from visions of the almighty in the sky, to feelings of mistrust and deception from the atheist. I think you've gathered I'm certainly not the religious type but very few words are able to encapsulate the otherworldliness like 'God' does. Call it the Supreme Being, the collective unconscious, or the universal mind if that suits your ideologies better, but it is all the same to me.

The idea that there is more to our minds than we are conscious of should come from common sense – it is not any great mystery or a fairy tale. **God to me is the subconscious mind – our 'maker'.** The thing that makes the world seem the way it does. Something every bit as worthy of our respect and devotion as anything in the known world. Something that, by understanding it more fully, won't just improve our lives, but will act as what I have to perceive as the only route to humans knowing peace in themselves and consequently on earth.

The act of prayer was a surrendering to this greater part of our mind, trusting in the way it works – its ability and its willingness to help us.

There are ways it works that we are not aware of, but we should trust in the providence of this part of mind that is above us. God works in mysterious ways, as it is said. Praying was an acknowledgement that there is this other part of our minds that can make what we want seem to be true. We aren't aware of all of the ways the magic of the universe can work, we just have to trust and surrender to its presence. To trust that all that happens is the will of a higher part of us, and should be respected even when our path brings us to an unexpected fork in the road. It may not be the path we planned in our diary but we should keep faith in 'the way'.

That is how we pray. By the faith of knowing how it would feel to already have the thing we want. We no longer want it – we already feel like we have it. We live in the absolute faith of knowing how it feels to have it. Our 'genie' is not a wish-granting super being but an emotional state – the emotion of already possessing the thing we most want.

Meeting our maker

I had a fight on my hands with wanting to title this chapter as I did. My partner said, "it's what they say when you are about to die". This chapter is not about dying, but making acquaintance with the thing **that makes our world** the way it seems. The thing responsible for the world as we know it. This chapter is about understanding our connection to the thing that 'makes' our world. That what's going on is also an element of our experience we can have some choice in. When we understand this, we will know ourselves as the 'maker' – to be the absolute creators of how things seem. The power of our 'maker' itself. When we realise there are doorways in our minds that can ultimately shift our perception of how things are, what could interest us more?

We are taking a step towards a deeper sense of contentment and purpose. We are here for a reason. To find what has meaning – what we care enough about to devote our lives to – that is our purpose. And when we pursue that path, no matter what we choose it to be, we are blessed with the sense of the personal meaning of our path – that we are guided, and no matter our foes we can endure whatever challenges we face. We are in the hands of something powerful that has our very best interests at heart.

We think we are making a statement about how things are, but the subconscious mind takes this as instructions of how we want things to be. It thinks we are driving, or better said it thinks we know what we are driving and how to drive, but if we don't think with reference to the subconscious, there is quite literally no one at the wheel. Our reality must always be a match to the story our thoughts tell. To change our reality, we have to be more conscious of the stories we quietly whisper to ourselves. We have to think in terms of what is listening, and building our world as a consequence.

Our lives often seem less than desirable because of this gap between the conscious and subconscious minds. We are unconsciously asking for situations by our willingness to accept that this is just how things are. This is not how things are – it is how we have made them, and only we can change them. Our experience can never be different from our unconscious expectation – what we unconsciously believe to be true. We don't ask for it to be this way as any form of punishment, but through our ignorance of what is listening to our conscious declarations. We 'ask' by our passivity. We ask by not asking for anything to be different.

The problematic mind

We cannot get to somewhere 'better' if we are steeped in the regret for what we are doing now. If we don't forgive ourselves for where we are – if we 'hate' the apparent conditions of our life – we create resistance without any offer of a solution or alternative. We sentence ourselves to almost certainly repeating more of what we hate – the emotion is what becomes our practice. We create even stronger reasons to dislike what we are doing. You can't get to doing what you love by hating what you do now – it can't work like that. You can't create cool by adding more heat.

THE CONTROL CENTRE

We have to align with the energy we would be in if we were doing what we love. When we live in the energy of doing what we love the evidence begins to shift – 'the way' will become clear. But in already having the feeling, we can act out of inspiration and without haste. We are not impatient, because we already feel like we want to. As we choose to.

We all know what happens when we take domestic problems to work – we have a shit day, because the issues are constantly on our mind. And it is the same if we don't think we have any problems – they brew in the background and 'surprise' us in many different and unwanted ways. If we are not actively engaged in improving some aspect of our lives, the problem-seeking mind just makes its own stuff up, and tries to solve them without our conscious input – without our presence and participation. Whereas when we are engaged in resolving issues – in finding solutions – that becomes the overriding theme of our experience. We feel like we are getting somewhere of our choosing.

In a very real sense, we are defined by what we allow to be our problems – by what 'bothers' us. If it is fairly trivial, we sentence ourselves to a life of boredom and mediocrity, as judged by us. The obstacle is the way we can know ourselves better – learn something about ourselves we didn't know before. Obstacles are an exercise in self-discovery, and more rewarding than any trip we can take. We have to have a vested interest in our lives, or, like a boring movie, we will stop watching it, and probably wonder why no one else is either.

> "People with purpose, goals, and visions have no time for drama. They invest their energy in creativity and focus on living a positive life."
>
> — Anon

We are not the same people we were five or ten years ago, but the changes in us are typically incremental. Our growth is not usually a leap and bound but something that happens so slowly over time that we often neglect to realise how much we have changed. We just feel the same, even though we are far more learned and capable people. We are not conscious of how much we have grown – that is not how the conscious/thinking mind works. It is more likely to 'occupy' us with how lacking we are. It's why all of our goals need to be clear and measurable, so we know where we've come from and what we are capable of.

The conscious mind is a lower vibrating state and tends to trivialise our gifts and talents. This makes it all the more difficult to imagine how possible it is for us to learn the things we'd like to. Our goals appear as mountains before us, firstly because we haven't broken them into achievable steps, but also because of our inclination to deny how much we've grown over time – to 'normalise' our accomplishments.

We sell ourselves and our abilities short if we are not continually mindful of measuring where we are, where we've come from and where we want to be.

The changes in us are so subtle, and happen so gradually over time, it is easy for us to become hoodwinked into thinking that nothing has changed. I say 'hoodwinked' because this is often the minds twisted version of motivation – to continue to 'inspire' us with the illogical reasoning that, "We aren't good enough, and nothing we've learnt to do is very hard for anyone to do". Once we have learnt to do something – something great that we once wanted to do – our instinct is to dismiss its value. It is no longer a talent because, "Well god, if we can do it anyone can do it".

We diminish what we've learnt as ordinary and easy. And this is not really a big deal, until we realise it is because of this minimalising of our gifts and talents, we make everything we want to do larger and harder than it truly is. We inadvertently sell ourselves short, never realising how much more difficult it makes the things we want to do seem. What we want to be better at is always learnable and achievable, especially in light of the many things we have already conquered.

Everything we see other people excelling at is something they learnt and practiced. There are far less 'naturals' in the world than we think.

If we don't give the mind something to 'chew on' it will do more to annoy us than to allow us to feel anything even mildly satisfying – and then sit in the grandstand of our experience telling us we are no good, like some bored heckler.

Living by the tyranny of our false conclusions

We have all had occasions when we have jumped to the wrong conclusions about what is happening. Someone didn't call back. We didn't get the job offer or someone didn't show up for a party or dinner date and our mind races to find the cause, and we lock in a conclusion only to later realise we were wrong. We show up at a restaurant to meet someone and after an hour of sitting on our own, we go through everything from "maybe they've had an accident", to "I knew they didn't like me". And then you get home and realise we got the dates mixed up.

Seems harmless enough right? Until we realise how much of our life is lived in precisely this manner. What if everything we were so convinced to be true was little more than a misled conclusion. Many of the circumstances we find ourselves in have the potential to be a very similar false creation or interpretation of events. We call it our life, but it is more like jumping from one false conclusion to the next. Even after we realise we were wrong, we still play these stupid scenarios over in our mind the next time we get antsy about 'what's going on'. The reality of false conclusions is far too often where we live our entire lives. It is a pattern we would be doing very well to drop – drop it like it's hot. 'This' doesn't always mean 'that' – often the best thing we can do is withdraw our judgement, and wait patiently until we have more evidence.

As a perfect example of this – I have a friend who creates YouTube content. Having over 400,000 subscribers, she expects every single video to be a hit and each and every week judges the quality of her content on the number of views. I use this example because I think it is much easier for us to imagine the multitude of different reasons why a video has less views that have nothing to do with the video itself – particularly when you are talking about the fickle world of YouTube and that number of followers. But every week the stories begin in her head. Maybe it was the thumbnail, maybe it was the title, maybe people aren't interested in that or don't like my stuff anymore. How many reasons could there be that a video doesn't get watched? People were busy, watched other videos, her video didn't rise to the top of their feed. My god, how many reasons could there really be that had absolutely zero to do with the quality of her content or the story that circulated in her head?

But every week her feelings are swayed. Her angle changed, her spirits lifted or dumped because of the hundreds of reasons out of her control. We all live with these short and long stories that we tell ourselves about how the world is and why things happened. These 'stories' are what we sadly refer to as our life. They define the mood we spend our time in, and the actions we take going forward, but they're BS. It doesn't make any sense to live our lives this way. But that is precisely because we aren't reasonable creatures – we are emotional creatures. It's why salesmen have a field day with us – because they are skilled at pushing our emotional buttons.

> "Self-control is strength. Calmness is mastery. You have to get to the point where your mood doesn't shift based on the insignificant actions of someone else. Don't allow others to control the direction of your life. Don't allow your emotions to overpower your intelligence."
>
> Jazz Zo Marcellus

Monkey see, monkey do

I don't know if you are familiar with the story, but I have seen it a few times, so I'll assume it is fairly common. I don't want to digress too much but this little story does illustrate this point perfectly. It is the story of an experiment (I'm assuming was real) where a room was filled with ten or a dozen monkeys. In the middle of the room was a tall ladder, and periodically a bunch of bananas would be dangled that were accessible from the top of the ladder. However, if the monkeys tried to climb the ladder to get to the bananas, they were blasted with a fire hose – preventing them from reaching the bananas and soaking every other monkey in the room.

This scene was repeated enough times that the monkeys stopped going for the bananas, and even violently subdued any monkey in the group who approached the ladder. Over time some of the monkeys were changed out with new monkeys, who had never experienced the 'wrath' of the fire hose. But they were nevertheless subdued by the more experienced members of the group, who were saving everyone in the group from a sure soaking. The monkeys continued to be changed out in small groups to the point where none of the monkeys within the room had ever experienced the hosing, only the beating they would receive if they attempted to go for the bananas.

So, what you were left with in the room was a group of monkeys who had never experienced the reason they daren't 'go for the bananas'. They had never witnessed the hosing take place, they just complied with the behaviour of the group, without ever really knowing why. "It's just what we do."

This story of course has deeper implications about how our society operates at large. We don't question the effectiveness, or appropriateness of our traditions and the way we go about things. It's just what we've always done. Much of what we do doesn't work anymore – many of the beliefs we hold aren't valid, but they never the less hold, for no better reason than tradition. Our instinct to tear people down is often for no better reason than "that's just what we do". But this also illustrates how ineffectual our own stories are. How the reasons they began in the first place are no longer relevant. We are living by rules that don't apply. But because we are emotional creatures of habit, the rules continue to govern our experience. And it is these very rules that are our 'demons' – that block us from what we want to do. They punish and torture us and we have no idea how to stop it. We stop it by questioning our story, and of course reflecting on those go to questions – what do I care about? What do I want to do?

The terrible truth

We've all had bad days. Things just don't seem to go right – our mood slumps and we find evidence in our environment that of course feeds the reason for our mood. The very unfortunate truth is that things may not be as bad as they seemed when our mood started to form. It was just a bad day, but that 'vibe' began to shape how the world seemed at a deeper level of our awareness. On that fateful day, our world took a turn for the worse and the supporting evidence continues to stack up and rally in support of this conclusion.

Our mood supplies evidence of a fictitious world. It skews our perception of what stands before us, making it into something it's not – something that serves the purpose of preserving an unfortunate mood. But the connection is rarely made, we don't realise how much our mood skews our perception of what is 'real' – of what things mean. And so we are carried off into a falsely created hell, but the 'devil' remains disguised.

It becomes our habit to look for and find circumstances that match the disappointment we felt on that fateful day. But it is not a 'true' or 'real' world. It is a mood-created world that crept in when we weren't at our best. That fateful event changed our world view and the course of our life, and for many we remain the passengers of a bad day that got worse. A day that turned into a pattern, a story that we keep inadvertently cementing around our feet. We can no longer shift this cycle, because it comes from our program – our default settings. How unfortunate it is that we are not privy to the fact it was these seemingly innocent false conclusions that became a lifelong cycle.

We've all had bad days – don't let them unconsciously become bad years and bad lives.

Talking to ourselves more

> "As far as I can tell it is about letting the universe know what you want and working towards it, while letting go of how it comes to pass."
>
> **Jim Carrey**

Change isn't some mystical formula, or blindly wishing things were different. We have to give that part of mind that is beyond the one we think with some sense of direction. It is always about defining what we want. Being clear on the details of the type of experience we would prefer. The 'magic' is in the details as they say. And not changing our mind and talking ourselves out of what we asked for one moment before, because we were confronted by some fickle evidence of how hard it was, or someone told us we couldn't or the outcome wouldn't be that good anyway. Or whatever flimsy reason blows us off course.

The more conscious we are of thought and the mindset of who we want to become the sooner the change begins to surround us. It is never a matter of time but clarity, and our commitment to the state of having what we want. Often touted as a sign of madness, it is in talking to ourselves more that we can accelerate change. The more conscious we are of thought, the more we understand the effect of thought, and the more our thinking changes to suit the person we want to become.

We have to be ever more mindful of the squatters, the unwanted and unwelcomed ideas entering our mind space. A wandering mind is an unhappy mind and I think personal development can easily be summarised into that simple statement – "more conscious of thought". Increasingly more aware of what we are asking for and not changing it the second we get a little discouraged.

Be mindful of your self-talk. It's a conversation with the universe.

A different type of intelligence

I have met some people recently who upon hearing I was writing a book have commented to the tune of, "Gee you must know what you're talking about to be writing a book". And as flattered as I might be to accept the compliment, those who know me also know that I lack even the most basic common sense at times. The 'smarts', if you will, that I'm writing about and referring to in this context have zero to do with intellect, and are certainly within the reach of everyone to understand. If I've not made it simpler to understand what the subconscious mind is like, and that we can change our world when we talk to ourselves better – then I have failed. I'm not referring to an intelligence that is learned but one that is 'remembered'. That is sensed by going deeper into ourselves.

I fully believe that understanding this is not just much simpler than most people may have thought but an entirely different type of intelligence than the one we are accustomed to associating with being 'smart'. As will become clearer in the chapter on mindfulness, realising the 'pre-conditioned' state is childishly simple, but does require a fundamental reversal of the type of intelligence we have come to value and many people pride themselves in. An ability to suspend our judgement of the apparent situation we appear to be in. Placing our mood at the top of our priorities is a very smart thing to do when we understand all of the 'reality-shifting' implications, but peace of mind is not arrived at conditionally, and it is not learned. Realisation of mind is an ever-deepening sense of presence.

THE CONTROL CENTRE

I meet many educated and 'scientific' type people who assume the intellect is our greatest gift and operate with a very limited awareness of the program they are running, or their operating system. Their 'more personal' sources of dissatisfaction, hover so close that they can't see them. I think there is a fundamental flaw in what is considered intelligence. Many of these 'smart' people can recall, collate and discern vast amounts of learning, but the stuff of emotions is just kind of disinteresting fluff. Often the 'smarter' people are the more difficult it is to validate the type of intelligence I'm speaking of.

And that is the inner knowing that can lead us to a sense of fulfillment that doesn't come from achievement, recognition, or anything outside of us for that matter. The sense of living our lives on purpose and guided by what means something to us. I'm sure I've said it, but what could be of more interest to us than the way we think and see the world – than what leads us to peace of mind?

It is often the strength of our intellect that forbids us from validating this type of knowing as having any valid or practical use. You don't have to be learned to benefit from this type of intelligence. You just have to be willing to look inside yourself. Our soul contains all of the ingredients we already need to lead satisfied lives. We just have to be quiet enough to hear ourselves. The language that can only be heard in the stillness. What we are accustomed to equating with intelligence is learning and recall, but there is no one smarter than us, for us. No one who can take us closer to ourselves.

It is unfortunate that many of the 'intellectual' types view the conscious mind as the limit, not just to what we know, but to who we are. I know many of them who struggle emotionally, and fail in all the same ways as us 'simpler types' do to be able to communicate and express themselves. I think that is the most basic cause of emotional ill health – a failure to be able to communicate something that is important to us. And this is not usually dependent on the extent of our learning. We know the content we are talking about, but are often like unarmed warriors when it comes to sharing it, or being heard.

> "Loneliness does not come from having no people about one, but from not being able to communicate the things that seem important to oneself, or from holding certain views which others find inadmissible."
>
> — Carl Jung

Living by the belief that the conscious, or the mind we think with, is the limit to us, disconnects us from the influence and the peace of the subconscious mind. From being able to sense its profound presence in our waken life. We don't understand the importance of self-talk, or sense we are communicating with something with a godlike power to affect the 'atmosphere' of our life. How it seems is within our control when we operate with regard to what is listening – this could be heaven or this could be hell depending on how we address ourselves. What we assume are the limits of our own mind.

Hypnotic language patterns

When it comes to more conscious living there is nothing that makes this difference between the conscious and the conditioned mind more obvious than the use of hypnotic language patterns and why they work so well. We, in the conscious mind, are unable to dispute any conclusion in the programming that challenges what we believe to be true, both of the world and ourselves. We will consciously resist anything we are told that challenges what we know to be true, and how we have always felt about ourselves. We push back against any loss of personal autonomy. So, the aim of hypnotic language is to plant a suggestion in the subject that is resistance-free. To engage consciousness, or the thinking part of them to consider a more suitable, or pleasurable option to be a choice for them. To wake up out of automation, and into consciousness – into the thinking mind and a conscious choice without any need to reject or resist it.

THE CONTROL CENTRE

We can tell someone they are fabulous, and confident, and suggest anything to them we would prefer they believed, but if it challenges their 'status quo' it cannot be accepted – it will be met with resistance. It has to be said/suggested in such a manner that it by-passes the critical faculty. It has to get past what we unconsciously believe about ourselves. We have to understand it to be a choice we are making to be the way we are. We have to be woken up to our options to choose a new and better response. A choice we are free to change, but just never understood the idea of 'how we are' to be optional.

To kill any need for resistance the therapist uses language that allows the subject the freedom to choose, but at the same time plants suggestions of how different their lives might look if they took this choice – if they integrated the suggestion. The therapist will use words to the effect of, "I wouldn't tell you to…" or, "You might want to… now". There is no resistance because they are free to make the choice on their own. If they are to say, "I'm not saying you should" they are then free to implant a suggestion that we both 'think about' and offers no resistance to belief patterns. The therapist is not telling us to do anything, so we are open to hear and perhaps take on the suggestion. Particularly if we can surmise the benefit to us.

If the therapist is to say, "I don't know if this is a good thing to do?" the subject wakes in the conscious mind to the choice they are free to make. The subject begins thinking – it wakes them up from the stimulus response mode, and just reacting automatically. They consciously consider the suggestion, without a flat and unconscious refusal to believe something other than their programming.

Most of what we do is not a conscious choice we make. We are steered by the rudder of our programming. We don't think about most of what we do, we just do it. And we cannot 'be' or do what is counter to belief. A hypnotherapist helps us think about our beliefs in a resistance-free manner.

Would this be good for us? How would our life be different? These are questions that engage modes of thinking that undermine the automatic part of us that quite often sabotages large areas of our life. We unconsciously resist anything that threatens the image we hold of ourselves, because we don't realise the depths of our reasoning. But when the resistance is removed through the use of language patterns, healthier suggestions can be pondered and assimilated without us feeling anything 'real' has been threatened or disturbed. We can often feel like we are suddenly free from some imagined obstacle, because of a simple suggestion being slipped past the guard of our automatic patterns. Or we make a decision to look at the obstacle as an opportunity for maturation. Something we really want to do, rather than avoid.

People don't think – they just do.

PRACTICAL EXERCISE

Sensing the divine

In the quiet of our minds dwells a silent superpower. It is in the sights, sounds and smells of the moment we're in. Find just five minutes out of your day, preferably in the day time, to try to sense this giant within us. To acknowledge in your own mind that you know something is there, and quietly and gracefully ask for a sign. A sign that doesn't have to come immediately, but to be shown without any doubt that there is more to this universe than we are conscious. The sign is yours so only you will recognise it, and only you will know – but acknowledge it – give thanks and say, "I hear you, I see you, I recognise you".

Acknowledging that we are not alone in our struggles has a profound healing effect, making everything we want to do seem easier. Something is helping us, and every now and again, if we acknowledge this awareness as an integral part

THE CONTROL CENTRE

of our lives, it shows us the magic. It reminds us that we are in the right place, and at the right time. It reminds us that we are precisely where we should be. Something is watching over us. It wants our desires to come to pass – it wants us to sense its grace in our conscious awareness, but we have to be still in order to sense it.

CHAPTER SUMMARY

- The subconscious mind is what we understand to be 'God', for want of a better word. The thing that 'makes' our world the way it seems.
- When we understand what is listening in our minds and how it uses our statements and constructs our reality to be a match, we automatically become much more conscious of our self-talk.
- To be more conscious of thought, and clear on how we want our experience to be different is the accelerator of manifestation, and how we become the conscious drivers of the program. If we are not driving it, we are passengers to our own lives.
- This is not religion – this is self-awareness. It is the knowledge of what we are, and the parts of our experience we sacrifice to the autonomous program. We are all moving towards a greater awareness of this process.
- We often dismiss what we have learnt to do and what we are good at as 'ordinary'. We think if we can do it anyone can. This makes our challenges and what we want to learn to do all the more difficult.
- This type of intelligence, the type that can lead us to a satisfying experience and peace of mind, is not intellect but self-trust. It is not learned, it is remembered, and can only be sensed by going deeper into the quiet of our minds.

CHAPTER 6
What Makes Us Feel?

"Visualisation is daydreaming with a purpose."
Bo Bennett

I can't imagine there is anyone who has not had some introduction to visualisation – how it works and the benefits. Our ability to picture things in our mind isn't some new discovery, but it is certainly much more widely utilised and acknowledged for its effectiveness to heal, manifest, and alter our outcomes. The true impact of visualisation work is beginning to be understood, and be more and more utilised as awareness of its effectiveness grows. In fact, it is claimed to be, in many cases, even more effective in improving performance in sports as actual physical practice – because it sets up a neural expectation of a successful result. We live in an amazing time, and I think one very much defined by the awareness of the efficacy of our visualisations. If we're not using mental imagery as part of our regular routine for creating a desirable life, we are not utilising the single greatest tool in the human body, and the most pertinent discovery of our time.

Pineal activation

Visualisation in itself is not a discovery, but the absolute effectiveness in creating results and lasting change is something of a revelation. I think it represents the single greatest definable change of how we live our lives in the modern era – the heightened use of the visual mind to achieve desired results. Is the mind's eye possibly an ancient aspect of consciousness that has lain dormant and underutilised in our minds? There is little doubt that this age represents the wider spread use of the third, or mind's, eye. It is the flowering or activation of the pineal gland. The outside world responds to our energy, and our energy is created by the pictures we hold in mind.

> "If you can see it in your mind, you can hold it in your hand."
>
> **Bob Proctor**

What is happening to our species as a whole, as we more fully understand the use of this small jelly bean sized gland in our mind, is we are creating what we want faster. Time is shifting because visualisation works – it changes our state, and consequently changes our perceptions, outcomes and what is seemingly attracted to us. More light is coming in through the pineal gland, amplifying its effectiveness. Or better stated, we are realising its real-time effectiveness, and so using it more. The heart's 'frequency' is the central controlling aspect of our lives, but there is a direct correlation between what is in the mind's eye and the frequency of the heart.

There is only one thing that makes us feel, and that is the **pictures we hold in mind**. Whether they are aroused from environmental triggers, our dreams of the future, or our memories of the past, the effect is the same. The only thing that makes us feel is what presents on the 'screen' of our mind. When we think of something, anything, it is represented

WHAT MAKES US FEEL?

in the deepest part of our mind as a picture or a short-running movie. The oldest and deepest part of our mind thinks in symbols and images and has done since long before we had words. The subconscious mind doesn't understand words – all words are represented by a picture. Images are clearer and far less ambiguous than words. There is no confusion about the meaning of images.

When we have a memory or are asked to imagine what something would feel like, we run a mental movie in our minds. It is why storytelling is so effective in producing superior learning results. When we are being told a story, rather than just fed information, the visual part of our mind engages and begins to picture our own version of what is happening in the story. We are engaged in the mind rather than wandering.

If something in our environment triggers an emotional response, we run a mental movie. It is always what is going on inside us at the level of mental imagery that produces an emotional reaction in us. Some of this happens at a deeper unconscious level, where we are less aware of the pictures surfacing in mind, but it is nonetheless a very similar process to when we consciously use the visual mind to picture a desire or remember a past event. The visual mind is a deeper part of our minds and an aspect of the subconscious mind itself. It has no filter to distinguish what is past, present or future. No matter from what time or place the picture is generated it has an identical effect on us emotionally.

The most powerful part of our mind believes everything we tell it, and assumes everything we picture in mind has already happened. It makes it a part of our 'normal' experience.

We can take ourselves to a place in our past that makes us angry, makes us smile, or brings a tear to our eye, all by picturing memories. And similarly, when we need a little inspiration, we can picture ourselves in the scenes that would make us the happiest. We cannot arrive anywhere desirable without the ability to picture it in our heads. And we humans have become much more aware of this ability in the era in which we now live.

Today visualisation is used in sport, personal development, hypnosis, and all forms of healing work. It is the common link in making our wishes into a reality. The clearer we are on the pictures and the more often they enter our minds, the sooner we will live in the real evidence of the pictures. We have activated a dormant part of our consciousness by the realisation of the function and power of the third eye. Visualisations have a powerful effect on our emotional states, which in turn has a very real effect on the physiology of the body. There have been countless cases of evidence that have proved we can heal the physical body by using the visual mind. The 'belief factor' is evidenced by the proven theory of the placebo effect. What we believe about our treatment has an enormous unconscious effect on how the treatment actually works.

Visualisation in sport

> "Every second of the day I was daydreaming."
> Connor McGregor

Michael Phelps, the most decorated Olympian of all time, has been a long-time proponent of the real-time effects of visualisation. Bob Bowman, Phelps' coach, since he was a teenager, instructed Phelps to watch a mental videotape of his races before he went to sleep and when he woke up in the morning.

> *"We figured it (imagery) was best to concentrate on these tiny moments of success and build them into mental triggers. It's more like his habits had taken over. The actual race was just another step in the pattern that started earlier that day and was nothing but victories. Winning became a natural extension."*
>
> Bob Bowman, www.picksports.com,
> 'Sports Visualization - The Secret Weapon of Athletes.'

Phelps dove into the pool, expecting to win. He had been through the mental tape so many times in his head that winning just felt right – became a natural and automatic extension of the process. The picture becomes so strong in the minds of mentally prepared athletes that they even become numb to the pain of physical fatigue. And from the same article quoted above:

> *"Visualisation in sports or mental imagery is a way of conditioning your brain for successful outcomes. The more you mentally rehearse your performance, the more it becomes habituated in your mind."*

In the modern arena, an athlete who is not using visualisation as a key aspect of their training is behind the times. Visualisation has been proven to have a very real effect on the physical body, similar to if they had performed the actual physical exercise. Just through rehearsing mental tapes in their mind they actually improved their performance, oftentimes eclipsing athletes who had only done the physical practice.

And visualisation is obviously not limited to its use in sports. Anyone wanting to produce desired results has jumped on the bandwagon, and realised this mind hack – this short cut to re-programming the mind itself. To make new, familiar and successful neural pathways seem like a normal part of our experience. Visualisation means we are less forced by habit in our experience – experience comes from creation. All walks of life are utilising this time and effort-saving hack to produce more defined and desired results. From all levels of life and business, people are realising they can affect real-time outcomes by mentally playing desired pictures in their mind. Imagining outcomes affects results.

Effective visualisations

> "The subconscious mind cannot tell the difference between what's real and what's imagined."
> **Bob Proctor**

Effective visualisation relies on four main qualities: **repetition, clarity, intensity or 'realness' of the emotion, and using all of the senses**. Using all of the senses gives the unconscious mind a much clearer map of the desired experience. We have to feel like we have already actually been there. **The clearer we see it in our mind and the more frequently we replay our mini-movie, the sooner it becomes our reality.** We have to make the imagined experience seem as realistic as possible – it has really happened. Don't spare the details. What are you wearing? Who else is there? What are the sights, sounds, and 'smells' in the scene? And most importantly – how are you feeling when all this is happening? This 'created' environment has to seem just as real as the one you think you are in now. The aim is to create a complete sensory event. The clearer we are on the subtleties, the clearer the map, or experience created in the subconscious mind.

The universe is moving in relationship to us. Change how you feel and you change the nature of the physical world. The universe is in a constant state of flux, of change – but it is not moving randomly. It moves in accord with our frequency.

More real than real

Your world is fraught with illusion, but the stuff of imagination - now that is much more definite than what you are convinced is real.

The world we live in is fettered with tricks of the mind relating to how we see what we see, in order to maintain the status quo. We understand now that how things seem is a projection of how we feel. What things mean depends on if we care about it. If something bothers us our mood shifts, and our perception of what is 'happening' swings like a pendulum – sometimes dramatically. Often the slightest bit of new evidence can dramatically turn our view of 'what's going on'. If we are at the mercy of the program, the mind is often jumping from one falsely formed conclusion to another, with us getting blown around like a candle in the wind. We turn nothing into something, depending on how we feel at the

WHAT MAKES US FEEL?

time, and in the moment it happens, we have a very limited awareness of our part in the drama. We don't even know we are doing it.

What's going on in the outside world? It depends on how the mood strikes us. An event can go from terrible to not bothering us at all in the space of an hour. There are so many subtle factors affecting the reality of our situations, it is difficult to believe we are ever accurate in our interpretation. The 'real' world is so filled up with mind tricks – what's real is relative to our mood. But such is not the case with our visually created world. In the land of our visual creations, there are no such misgivings and confusion. Our visualisations come from a place of certainty and purity. This is exactly how we want it, exactly as we want to see it, and the consequent emotions are not swayed by any such 'emotionally-skewed' illusions of what is real.

The emotional state produced from our visualisations can be trusted as how we want to feel – a claim that could never be attached to an emotionally-skewed and illusion-filled world. Visualisations are chosen, whereas 'reality' is unconsciously created. We can live and bathe in the warmth of a consciously created world, and the subsequent emotions produced. From our deep visualisations we come out smiling, fresh and restored by the effects, but then we step into 'reality' and scratch our head to think, "What the hell is going on here?".

It's crazy to think that the quality of our life can be determined by how much time we spend daydreaming. One world is 'real' and the other imagined. It is a shame we have confused the two. Because when I close my eyes and imagine – I am precisely where I chose to be, and that has a marked effect on what becomes real.

When we see our visualisations as more effective and trustworthy as the outer world of conditioning and illusion, we will be halfway to feeling how we want more of the time and being much more in control of our experience. I believe it is the evolution of our being to validate the effectiveness of our visualisations and the subsequent emotional states, so we begin using them more.

I understand how crazy that might sound, but the absolute quality of our life depends on our ability to trust in the effectiveness, and implement the use of visualisations. We want to live in a more chosen and controlled emotional space? We have to believe in the power of the visual mind to produce very real emotional states. We have to believe in the gravity of imagined emotional states.

This theory of how real and effective our imaginations are is also a tool a life coach employs in trying to persuade us to use our imaginations. The reality we assume prescribes to the idea that the real world is fictious and imagination created. So imagining where we want to be is just as real and effective as the story we are so convinced is real now. Part of a coach's job is to make us realise the 'realness' of the things that are desired, but yet to enter our reality. By our desires, they merge into the real. The situation we think we are in is more creative than we might have imagined. A coach's role is to convince us how effective our imaginations are of where we want to be, and how 'imagined' the situation we think we are in. I think it is best demonstrated by the below diagram of the reality a coach encourages us to believe in.

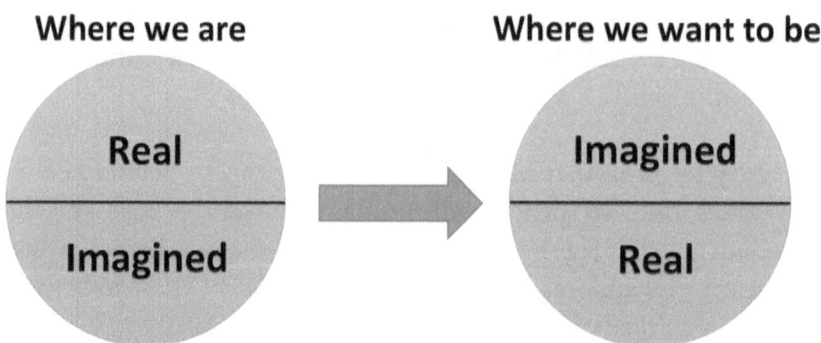

The lines between what is real and what is imagined become very blurred, and merge into one another when we understand our role in creating our perceptions of the world. There is something very real and effective about our imaginations and being able to define the details of where we want to see ourselves. We are unconscious to many of the reasons we feel the way we do. Of our 'choice' to see the world in the way we do, and the fictious nature of the story we tell ourselves. The role of a coach is to deconstruct our reasoning by questioning it. Why do we believe that? What is the benefit?

A coach's job is to help us realise we are not as far from where we want to be as we might think. Because the mind we think with doesn't know. We are often the ones unable to see with honesty where we are. A perceptive shift is often simmering just beneath the surface, and then all of a sudden it dawns on us – "Maybe I can do this – maybe I'm closer than I thought, and already have the resources I thought I lacked". We have often buried ourselves under the path of work we assumed is the only route to our goal. But a coach can show us that it is not as hard as we've made it. We often don't have to move a mountain to 'be' there – we just have to take a step.

We are never lying to ourselves about 'how things are' when we are engaged in inventing the world just as we'd like it to be. We are giving the mind a clear map – the program clear instructions. Everything is always changing, and we are just ensuring that change moves in accord with our intentions. The accelerator of change is our clarity and presence of mind – our commitment to moving towards a more conscious experience. In becoming increasingly more present and mindful of our energy, we become much more elastic, and less resistant to what appears to be happening. We start to believe we can mould our experience into the life of our choosing.

Live in your fantasy – what we imagine is real begins to surround us. Play there so much that the unwanted begins to fade away.

Metaphoric visualisations

Animations or explainer videos have become a very effective tool in being able to communicate complex ideas much more simply. Explainer videos can go outside of reality to express ideas imaginatively and metaphorically.

THE CONTROL CENTRE

We know information can spread with lightning speed nowadays via the internet. A video can go viral in a matter of minutes. We know this in our heads, but when we see an animation of the globe and information spreading across it in a matter of seconds, we get a much clearer picture of what is actually happening. Animations can communicate complex ideas simply and easily by using metaphoric moving pictures.

We can see our minds expanding, our millions of cells communicating, and get a much clearer understanding of these ideas when displayed with the help of animations. I hope you are familiar with the idea, but if you are not, just go to YouTube and watch any 'video explainer'. Animations have become a powerful way of communicating a complex message in terms our minds can more easily chunk down and understand.

In a similar fashion, we can use the idea behind animations to give our visualisations a much stronger and more marked effect over our emotions. Many guided meditations will ask you to picture light coming down through the top of your head, to see the light coming in through your lungs and darkness going out in the exhaled breath. Darkness is represented as any form of disturbance and it can leave our body much more effectively when we picture it leaving through the lungs in our out breath. Something 'very real' happens when we use our imagination in such a way. We can alleviate hours of a stressful pattern with just minutes of quiet breathing work. And when we incorporate the mental imagery of darkness leaving the body, it is much more effective than just some quiet breathing on its own.

Picturing light entering the lungs and darkness leaving the body can quickly alter a state of mind that hasn't let up for a very long time. The more concentrated our picture, the more real the effect. The point is, the effects of these creative pictures can be far greater because they are not restricted by what's 'real'.

They allow our imagination to exponentially expand the effect. We can cleanse the whole body of darkness and stress and fill it with a rejuvenated light in a matter of minutes. Visualisations that incorporate the use of these imaginative metaphors can be far more effective than pictures that are less intentional and restricted by reality-based imagery. We can picture light and health going into every cell in our body and every cell communicating with each other metaphorically to accentuate the effect of our visualisation practice.

Get creative and use animated metaphors to enhance the effect of our visualisations. Picture money raining from the skies, or our body cleaning itself from disease and unwanted contaminants. Picture our heart clean and crisp and shinning with light. Visualisations have a very real effect on the health of the physical body.

PRACTICAL EXERCISE

The Swish Pattern

This is an NLP, or neuro-linguistic programming, technique used to change old, stubborn habits into new, more favourable ones. NLP is a tool for creating change, which makes use of visualisations and the pathways and language patterns we use to store memories. It has been successfully used for many years to cure long-held phobias and deep-seated habits, simply by going into the subtleties of how we internally communicate with ourselves. What is the story we are telling ourselves, and what is the language we are using, when we are in the grip of an 'un-resourceful' state? Through NLP we are becoming more sharply aware of what is going on internally as we experience these unwanted states, so we can use more effective methods to instill desired changes.

What's going on within us on a visual, auditory, and feeling level when we recall good events, and how is that different to when we are experiencing undesirable states? What's

THE CONTROL CENTRE

happening is not going on outside of us – it is going on inside of us, and when we work from the inside out we often find difficult changes are much simpler to make. When we shine a light on these internal patterns, and become more aware of how we are communicating with ourselves, we can transpose the mind language patterns we have running for things we find easy and apply them to the things we find more challenging. We all have times where we felt on top, things we can do easily, and we can apply what's going on within us at these times to the things we find more difficult. NLP is about getting more clear and 'sensitive' to what is going on within us so we can communicate with ourselves to effect changes more efficiently.

I saw a video presentation where Richard Bandler, the co-creator of NLP, was attempting to remove a tormenting memory from a subject. Bandler is masterful in his application of NLP, and his presentations resemble something more like entertainment than therapy. His application is always dosed with a slice of light-hearted humour. He first asks his subject to give this memory a size, as in, is it a small or a large picture in your mind? Of course, the subject says, "Large, life-size - like a movie screen". Bandler retorts, "So if someone comes into your house and paints a horrible picture on your wall, you would paint over it, but you're happy to walk around with this in your mind".

Again, Bandler is challenging the subject to think differently about his issue. If he genuinely wants to be rid of the disturbing memory, he must shrink or completely remove the recurring picture he holds. Bandler is a masterful hypnotist, and quickly drops the subject into a trance state, wherein he changes the frame, size, and colour of the picture, making the picture round, shrinking it down, and flashing it from colour, to black and white and back again to colour.

WHAT MAKES US FEEL?

In manipulating the size, frame, and colour of the picture, he is also manipulating its **emotional effect**. In controlling aspects of the picture, we can control the emotional effect something has over our lives. The Swish Pattern is a commonly-used technique in NLP that works off the same principle. Firstly, we must define the change we want. How is it different from our current experience? What is the dominant experience we are having now, illustrated as a single, understandable image? And what is the new experience, the one that seems far away and maybe even beyond our abilities at present?

So, we have two pictures – one of where we are now and another of where we want to be in the future. Of course, where we are now isn't hard to imagine. It is clear, in colour and is the larger picture at the forefront of our mind. And where we want to be is a smaller, further away, maybe even a little pixelated, and black and white. In this exercise, we close our eyes and go into a state of deep relaxation. When we are calm and poised, we bring the two pictures into our minds. The current picture of how things are now in the foreground and the future picture, smaller and in the background. And then suddenly and sharply, the pictures are switched. With a swish of wind, the foreground picture is rushed to the background and vice versa.

Apparently, the swish noise is an important part of the metaphor. The old is moved and the new locked into place in our minds. Like the use of the swish noise, it is helpful to lock the new picture in place at the end of the move like we are snapping a container lid on, or fastening a clip. If we aren't familiar with this type of technique, it may seem a little silly and we would question its use and effectiveness. Those beliefs will have a marked effect on how deeply the new pattern embeds, but it will be effective nonetheless. I can assure you that NLP and the Swish Pattern has been used to help hundreds of people cure themselves from a variety of

THE CONTROL CENTRE

phobias and unwanted habits. If we want to create lasting change, we have to work on the level of the programming – with reference to the nature of how the subconscious mind works. And it works in pictures – the language of the deepest part of our mind is imagery.

> "Our souls do not speak human language. They communicate to us through symbols, metaphors, visions, poetry, deep feelings, and everyday magic."
>
> Anon

CHAPTER SUMMARY

- Whether our mental images come from memories, triggers in our environment, or dreams of the future, it is only the pictures we hold in mind that make us feel.
- Past, present and future are irrelevant to the visual mind – no matter where the picture comes from it has the same emotional and attraction effect.
- The subconscious mind cannot tell the difference between what is real and what is imaginary. No matter where the image comes from, it will have an identical effect on how we feel.
- This age represents us waking up to the use and power of the visual mind – the activation of the pineal gland.
- Visualisations have been incorporated to enhance the performance and success in business, sports, healing, and personal development. We are waking to the effectiveness of visualisations like never before in history.
- All visualisation work is effective, but the clearer we are on the details of the picture, the more physical senses we engage in the scene, and the more often we practice it, the more effective. Frequency, intensity and clarity are the main contributors to its effectiveness, but it is also more effective when done in a deeply relaxed state.
- Visualisation can change our life, cure phobias, and uproot many long-term and harmful emotional habits that may have haunted our life for many years. They can do it quickly, effectively and are the quickest route to impacting the programming to create lasting change.

CHAPTER 7

The Miracle of Mindfulness

> "All cravings are the mind seeking salvation or fulfilment in external things and in the future as a substitute for the joy of Being."
>
> — Ekhart Tolle

The shift and the promise

There was a major shift in consciousness in 1997 with the release of the book 'The Power of Now' by Ekhart Tolle. Mindfulness was an old idea, but the insight and benefits became available to a much wider audience with the release of this book. More eyes were opened and given a clear target to aim for in our pursuit of peace. Tolle gave the ideas behind presence of mind a new transparency – it was clearer and had become available to more people as a consequence. The book broke ground and introduced many to the idea that a freedom from psychological suffering wasn't just possible, but that it didn't require anything of our conditions to change.

In the book Tolle suggests that there is a single cause to human suffering, and this is also the central theme of every religion in the world. I'm not sure about you, but this alone was enough to tweak my interest. Along with the fact, of course, that nothing in my world needed to change for me to realise this. It was a natural condition of mind. The cure to the human condition itself was identical to the path of a seeker who wished to realise mind. Enlightenment, and the panacea to every human illness. Hmmm – got to be worthy of further investigation I thought, for both my own peace of mind and the farther-reaching global implications.

The implication is that peace isn't just possible – it was freely available and far simpler than we'd been making it. This is the promise of mindfulness – by concentrating our awareness on the physical senses we can hack our state of mind. Mindfulness allows a freedom from the prejudice our expectations hold over each moment we enter. It promises the freedom to step into future moments free from the weight of our conditioned past. Mindfulness is not something we have to learn – it is childishly simple – it is something we have to validate, because it forces us in the opposite direction of the mind-identified condition we have come to trust in.

Peace cannot come in the future; it can only come via a deepening sense of the present moment. The present moment is the single and only portal of entry to the dimensional shift in consciousness that would allow a pre-conditioned experience.

By becoming more present to the senses we become more conscious of mind. We are altering our state of mind and with it our outer conditions. Nothing in the outer has changed, but we have changed how it seems, simply by becoming more focused on the physical senses. We are naturally compelled to want to improve the conditions of our life, but we are conditioned to believe the only way to achieve this is by 'doing'. Mindfulness approaches the same goal from the opposite end of the spectrum. It is not in the 'doing', or what we do that changes the world, but in 'being' more present that we transform how the world seems. This is the promise of mindfulness – by an ever-deepening sense of presence, we change the perceived conditions of our life. **We don't have to wait to be more present, and it is the key to improving our sense of connection and our state of mind.**

More present to the senses equates to more conscious of mind.

This was the shift 'The Power of Now' brought us – the realisation that we were always closer than we thought to a profound sense of connection and peace of mind. It had been staring us in the face the whole time. And not just a little bit more peaceful – this was the single path of all seekers to the ultimate goal of becoming more conscious – the realisation of mind. We were looking in all the wrong places – it wasn't years of learning away from where we are now. It didn't require torturous self-denial. It wasn't the outer conditions of our life that needed to improve, it was our sense of presence. 'The Power of Now' shifted the illusion of seeking, and being able to find joy in things, or conditions. The state we all cherish most is contained within our souls now – each moment we enter holds the promise of what we've been waiting for.

We have this ill-conceived notion that it is the ones with the most money and attention that are experiencing huge quantities of joy in every moment. But life is a sensory experience and the rich and famous are experiencing it through the same crude tools we all have in common. It does not take the outside world to change for us to sense what we are connected to. This is not some fun thing to do when we are not too busy. This is paramount to the human experience, and freely available to everyone at all times. The ultimate goal of being human is one and the same technique many healers have now adopted in their treatment of an assortment of mental health issues.

A new take on an old idea

Mindfulness is an ancient spiritual practice that is fast gaining momentum in the more science-based modes of therapy, psychology, psychotherapy and the like, as the go-to practice for anchoring the mind in the present and temporarily suspending our judgement of the mind-made situations we assume are so real. It helps to shift our perspective on the unpleasant truths we had been telling ourselves that maybe weren't as true or threatening as we'd suspected. Mindfulness is effective because it takes us out of our 'situations' for a time and, when we come back to them with an improved state of mind, we seem less bothered by these previously troublesome issues. Our worries just don't seem as real. Mindfulness has become a popular healing method for the full spectrum of mental health problems – addictions, anxiety, stress and depression. It has been found to be effective in treating them all.

Mindfulness, or what is often referred to as 'grounding' in life coaching and psychology, is a practice of complete sensory immersion – our undivided attention on the data coming in from the senses. We are so focused on the physical senses that for a brief period we are separated from the psychological circumstances we thought we were in. Our situations seem less 'real' as a consequence and we are free to explore other ways of looking at them. Our situations fade, and so too does the worry, stress or the feeling of being completely out-of-control of what was happening.

How can something so childishly simple have been for so long overlooked as a mind cure? Why is it only now we are realising how effective it is as a healing therapy? Mindfulness is something so simple, and perhaps this is why it has been so overlooked as the cure-all panacea it appears to represent. It does not require any special initiation or us to identify with any group, or train for any length of time. But it does require something of a reversal of the values we have been universally conditioned by, both in that we have to 'do' in order to improve conditions, and that it is only by our self-image that we can know our value.

Why didn't it catch on as, "This is all you need to do to achieve a 'next level' peace of mind"? Because it asks us to completely reverse our understanding of what the mind gravitates towards as valuable. It is our identity that must remain intact if we are to have any cognition of what is pleasure and what is pain. And it is for this reason we are never actually able to sense the source of our pain also stems from the very identity we are sworn to trust as our 'navigator'. It is the ego itself that lies as the 'thief in the night' of our feelings and state of mind. Our most cherished 'possession' is, inadvertently, the one that throws the knives while our back is turned. The identity that we cling to with a quiet sense of desperation that goes unnoticed as the sole source of our psychological suffering.

Our identity is our protector – how can it be the same thing that also stabs us in the back, and we don't even know where it's coming from. As Tolle states it – it is like we have assigned the chief of police to catch the arsonist, when the arsonist is the chief of police. We are doing everything in our power to hide the criminal and ensure they remain undetected. The perpetrator is us – are we to imagine we must bring our take on reality itself into question?

> "You think it is other people that are making you unhappy, but I tell you it is your own mind."
>
> — Anon

The ego fears the deeply mindful state for it implies a loss of identity and with it a loss of control over us. It can no longer push our buttons. The ego assumes it is our pain that allows us to navigate life itself – where would we be without it? The ego fears we would lose our sense of who and where we are, and therefore how we should act and what we should be scared of. If the very judgements we had relied upon to orient us were to be temporarily suspended, we may tip into the void of not knowing ourselves, or be unable to manufacture familiar conditions.

In mindfulness we are in essence being 'no one' for an instant – and as we'll see, it is in being 'no one' that we become something quite boundless. We enter the blank canvass of the 'creative'. We sense ourselves as a connected part of source energy. An absolute union with the subconscious mind and the peace it knows as its natural state. For we are by birth inherently healthy, but then the mind draws conclusions that are usually far from flattering about us and concretes them as an ongoing torture, and we spend our lives praying we can be free of them.

The greatest state of all

> "There is no greater obstacle to God than time."
> — Meister Eckhart

The true beauty of the realisation of mindfulness is that it is always freely available to us. No guessing for where to look, or what we should do to 'achieve' peace. We are never too late – and no matter who we are or what we've done the entry fee is the same – our undivided attention to the senses, and a letting go of who we thought we were or had to be. Nothing in our conditions needs to change for us to realise this higher quality sensory experience. But with the inherent improvement in our state of mind, our conditions can become seemingly transformed. This portal is constantly and permanently available to us – the requirement is the temporary suspension of how we think things are.

The Buddha, the Christ, and all of the celebrated enlightened beings, were just normal people who had realised what their mind was, and were able to use it to manipulate outer conditions from the inside. Everything around us is a reflection of state of mind, so if we are able to anchor ourselves in state of mind, we can control our outer conditions. It is for this reason it would appear the enlightened masters were more interested in feelings than material possessions. We only want certain conditions to be met because of the state of mind we assume they carry with them. If we already exist in the state of having, the outside world becomes more of a beauty to behold than something that 'lacks' anything, or has any power over us.

> "To the mind that is still, the whole universe surrenders."
> — Lao Tzu

Our commitment is to surrender to however we find the current conditions – then there is no resistance, no blockage to the state of having. To surrender is to turn 'whatever is' – meaning however we find the world – into something that seems chosen.

I made the suggestion earlier that all we needed in order to change was to be excited by the result. Is this result, the promise of self-actualisation – the reality that we can sense a higher condition of mind without our circumstances changing – is that exciting enough for us to give this mindfulness stuff a go? Even just as an experiment, to sense if it has any effect on how we feel. It is a very easy practice to implement.

I believe we are the first generation that it will finally dawn on – the first time we will 'get it' on a wide scale, and start to benefit from the results on a global scale. Peace is here and now and starts with us – starts inside us, and with our ability to manipulate conditions by realising our natural state of mind. A pre-conditioned state of mind. We can improve the condition of our minds by something that doesn't ask any more of us than our undivided attention.

Are we beyond being able to validate one of the oldest and most pervasive spiritual ideals of all time as having any real-time value?

A return to unknowing

Mindfulness is aimed at the realisation of the **preconditioned state**. When we come into this world as infants, we are pure intelligence – purely subconscious beings. Mindfulness is an attempt to remember – to recall how it was before all of the programming became embedded, before we inherited the vibration of the disconnected beings around us, and started sticking the knives into ourselves for who we assumed we were. Before our reality became skewed by emotions we never chose. Mindfulness is an attempt to align with the information coming in from the senses before it gets filtered down into our 'story' – our tainted version of how things are. Is this state so frightening to the ego because of its 'departure' from reality? This is how we come to master our reality, and use it as a tool rather than an unflattering image we seem chained to.

What a continued practice of mindfulness enables, is the dilution of the negative emotional responses that result from how convinced and certain we are of an unflattering story we've been telling ourselves. The real shift in practicing mindfulness is the new sense of ease we enjoy from being more conscious. Of being able to turn whatever environment we find ourselves in into something more palatable.

Nothing changes

> "Your happiness cannot come to you, it can only come from you."
>
> Ralph Harston

Higher states of mind exist concurrently with lower states of mind. Higher states are not in a different time frame, or coming soon, they exist on a deeper level of the same experience we are having now. It is a dimensional shift – a deepening sense of the present moment. All we need do to sense this higher vibrational condition is 'slow down' – stop the minds compulsive chatter for a moment, and remind ourselves that beneath any sense of boredom, resentment of how things are, or fear for what may happen there is a waiting dimension that can dissolve everything that is not deeply conducive to peace of mind.

What does this place look like? It is an 'absolute' replica of your current experience – and this is the skill we must now adopt in order to realise our ability to manipulate the material world. The present moment is our clay – however we find it, is what we have to work with.

THE CONTROL CENTRE

Identity – our warden in disguise

Our identity, or the image of self that begins to form as soon as we start to identify patterns in our environment, is something we hold very dear to our heart. Not in a sentimental way, but it is what we assume facilitates our survival. It is our way of connecting to, and knowing ourselves in relation to the world. It is our protector, and what we come to trust in as the most valuable asset we possess in navigating our lives. Without it who are we? All of the other stuff we've accumulated, our family, our friends, our standing in the tribe – everything we have come to know as good in the world, all links back to this egoist version of who we assume we are.

Who'd ever suspect this protector of all we know as valuable to double as the single reason we suffer? That this beautiful 'house' we've built around us (the ego sense of identity) would also be our prison. The reason we can't do things outside of our emotional scope has its roots in this concrete and immovable notion of who we think we are – of the story we tell ourselves about what is 'real' and what is 'difficult'. We are the ones who grant everything its power over us by our resistance to 'what is'. By disliking what is, we push against it, making it ever stronger and more prevalent.

I'll put what I mean by this into context. In our earliest years we might have inherited a 'shy' pattern – a model that dictates to us that our family and our way is to be humble – to be 'showy' is dishonourable, and those who truly know their worth never have to 'prove' anything. What this deep-seated value can translate to is what many people experience as 'nerves'. We get all jittery under pressure but never really know where the cause of the emotions lies. The reasons run deep, beneath our awareness and therefore our ability to deal with or counter. We can't know the reasons we feel the way we do – it is too deep in our consciousness. If we attempt to be 'showy' or attract attention to ourselves, our values 'rescue' us from this 'error'. We are deeply conservative people because of a value system that operates in the sub-terrane of our minds.

Segue to twenty years down the track in our life where we have become an exceptional pianist. We can play anything from a single listen, provided of course we have a **limited audience**. Because the story we run at the depths of our mind is that it's not very honourable to 'show off'. We have become amazing musicians, but are completely unable to share our gift or perform under pressure because of an irrational fear that rises in us. A reasoning so deep we can never make sense of or deal with – it's just how we are. Our abilities are arrested by a story we tell ourselves that is less grounded in truth than it seems. But in our humble nature, we remain completely unaware it is an inappropriate set of values that is robbing the world of this gift we have to share. It may even translate in our conscious minds as a voice telling us something to the effect that we are "not really that good anyway".

The joy we might bring people – our mesmerising connection to our instrument – can never be shared, because of a story whose reasons are both irrational and run deeper than we can touch or know. Are we doing the world a favour by maintaining our humility? Believing our gift is not really worth sharing is a story whose logic doesn't stack up. It is just that we are unable to bring it to the surface and see the unconscious entanglement for what it is. We don't know "what our problem is". And we can't access the places where it twists up our reasoning into what it considers a perfectly sound story.

So many of us are sadly the victims of completely irrational emotional responses, and don't know how easily a more intense awareness can bring them to the surface. Nor do we realise how much these false conclusions screw up many aspects of our lives. We hate it about ourselves – we take it out on others – we don't pursue pastimes that might truly open us to knowing ourselves better.

From inside the story, we never get the sense that it is us who is the staunch defender of our own limitations. We talk ourselves out of 'flying', but don't hear it as **our own voice** – it is rationale talking. As irrational as the fear seems from the outside, we are the ones who defend it as a well-founded 'fact', and never sense it coming from our own misguided and deeply unconscious conclusions. We aren't privy to the realm where we would see it is us who are championing our own limitations.

Why does mindfulness work?

Why are we depressed? Because of this single biased view of how our past went. Too much past, not enough presence. Why are we anxious, overwhelmed, or worried about the future? Maybe we've underestimated our abilities, or we are concerned about how it will all go down. You have heard the clichés – worried about things that will probably never happen. Too much future, not enough presence. We have filled up the one place where our life happens with things that aren't happening. We've drowned out the present moment with all of the things that have no real relevance to it, and don't aid the future or past. We live in our heads, not our bodies and surroundings.

Mindfulness works because it allows a temporary unfiltered experience of the outer world, a preconditioned experience. The subconscious mind has no sense of time. It is immersed in the present moment and the data from the senses. And when we are there too, we create a union with the subconscious mind. We exist as one with it. We humans are so unconsciously convinced it is only our identity that has any value that we have divorced ourselves from the joy only available in presence. The conscious mind's ploy is to distract us from the present in a back and forward seesaw between a regretful past and an anxious future. Distracted from the only place peace exists.

Clearing habit energy

> "Because the Cadillac that's sitting in the back, it isn't me. Oh no it isn't me. I'm more at home in my galaxy."
>
> **Shannon Hoon**

The ego is just a fragile shell. If it no longer serves us, we can outgrow it, but not without breaking the shell, and sometimes this is experienced as pain. In mindfulness, the shell softens. We sense what is beyond identity. We are simultaneously everything and nothing – nobody and everybody. In mindfulness we are now living in our larger body. We have gone beyond the ego and the separated sense of self that is wounded by the attacks on self-image.

In the lyrics above from the song 'Galaxy' by Blind Melon, the 'Cadillac' is his old self image, the old ego self he used to travel in, but he has now entered the larger world of his subconscious mind and home – his galaxy. And all is well – everything is seen for its divine purpose, and the higher sense of order so characteristic of being present in our experience. There is no resistance to 'what is'. Knowing everything as part of a much larger picture – everything is connected and an essential part of universal synchronicity – of the 'dance'. We are a part of everything and everything is a part of us. We become much more accepting of how things are, of how we find the present moment, because we understand our part in its creation.

Mindfulness allows us to cleanse the body of the old energy patterns that no longer serve us. Each time we visit the mindful state, we diminish the effects of our conditioning, and habit energy. We loosen the bindings of who we feel we are forced to be. We are carefree, but not in the nonchalant sense that we are unenthused by anything. We are just not bound to outcomes, having to be a certain way to be acceptable to us. We are not plagued by the need to be recognised and validated in order to know our value. In presence we just are valuable, and it matters so little to us if this is not seen – if people aren't reminding us all the time.

In mindfulness, the present lacks nothing. It is complete and perfect. We find it just as we have made it. Mindfulness is a fundamental 'giving up' of all we've been conditioned to believe as 'real' and valuable. But the prize for this shift – well I think that now speaks for itself.

THE CONTROL CENTRE

Discovering now

It was September 2002, and I had just made the hardest decision of my life to leave my partner at the time and our family home. It tore me up and it still haunts me a bit, that my kids' life might have been so much different. But the situation was killing me from the inside and I felt I had to make myself a better person for them and me. It was a killer period for me though, and I can certainly see why some men fold under those conditions.

For some, it isn't an option to leave, and they suffer in silence, rather than being alone and missing the people they most care for. One of the inspirations for me writing this book was that I wanted to bring awareness to mindfulness, and pay tribute to the book through which this awareness came. And it came at the time when I needed it most – I was lost. I found 'The Power of Now' in perfect time, because honestly, without getting all dramatic, I'm not certain I would have been able to pull through had it not been for the awareness it raised in me. I was at rock bottom but this 'now' thing gave me a second chance – it's never too late. What I have, in having awareness, in presence, wasn't just an opportunity to do better, it's something that was more sacred than I had considered before this. It was a game-changer for me. It was the freedom that the past was completely meaningless. The only thing that mattered I had right here with me now.

My salvation was not a relationship, job or situation, but my willingness to be in this moment just as it was, no illusions, no future, no tormenting people, or past. I was an eternal being and had found my deliverance in an ever-deepening sense of the present moment. No more confusions about where to look. Don't get me wrong – I'm still an overly emotional nerd. I still read self-help books one after the other, because I'm a basket case. Well that is probably a little extreme – I have better control over how I feel than I ever have. But personal development, attraction and mindfulness stuff is all that interests me, because I guess it is what I need to learn the most. I'm certainly a much stronger person than I was, and I have to credit that to my discovery of mindfulness and having improved my ability to concentrate.

It is much clearer where I find my peace now. The only place it ever has been. It's not hiding from anyone anymore, and I think that is largely due to 'The Power of Now' – what I have for a long time regarded as my 'bible'. But it has since astounded me how much this mindfulness and time-free awareness stuff seemed to be dominating all the personal development material I encountered.

Salvation was the next breath I took. The next moment I entered. It was all right here in front of me. I just had to start living my life, moment by moment, dropping ever deeper into my own sense of presence.

And this is not a complete cop out of what's going on around me. The more I could calm myself and be one with whatever the moment held, the more the cosmetic or surface stuff of my life just seemed to take care of itself. I was going to be okay, so were my kids, so was everything.

I can do what I can to improve myself – exercise, eat right, help people when I know how. But there was so much that was out of my control. I was just getting frantic over situations and people that were way beyond my control. Children quite naturally live in the moment – they are so present. We actually started having fun when they came over – something I thought was impossible only weeks before.

I thought I had destroyed everyone's life, mine included. But heart health is as much about getting ourselves out of toxic situations as it is food and exercise. If we can't find a way to change a situation, sometimes we have to go to the extreme and remove ourselves from them. If we have exhausted what is in our power to change. Self-care is about being as present as we can in each moment we enter because that's the only place we can make change. If we are obsessing with what is already going on in our heads, we can only see a pre-written story and aren't open to see any possible solutions that presence might reveal.

Presence appealed to me at the time I read the book because it meant I had another chance and that I wasn't forced to be who I thought I was (particularly the parts I wasn't fond of). It meant that my peace, my salvation was never as far from me as I thought. But at the time I could not have envisaged how the luster of mindfulness would continue to grow and become my 'go-to' priority. The guiding principle of my life.

How do you feel?

In the movie 'After Earth', Will Smith teams up with his son Jada in a sci-fi adventure of a future earth, where they are stranded in a space craft damaged by a crash landing. Will Smith's character, Cypher, is wounded in the accident and so has to rely on his son Kitai to complete a mission to facilitate their rescue. Cypher has a radio communication with his son, and before embarking on his mission asks him several questions to ensure he has his instructions clear. The last of the questions he asks him is, "How do you feel?" and Kitai replies, "I feel with my whole body".

This is the essence of mindfulness – of bodily awareness. The question is no longer an enquiry about how your ego model of the world has been wounded, but about what the vehicle is that you feel through. It is no longer about how has this illusion of the real you been affected by your tortured view of what happened. Not what you feel, but how you feel. I feel through my whole body – every cell and every sense engaged in my experience of the external. I don't even know what all of this sensory data means – I am open to it being what it is. And I just love that I can see, hear, smell and sense the world around me. I have not boxed my experience with meaning, and so I am free to interpret as I think suits my will best. I have, in doing this, gained the power over the physical – I have bent it to my will – made it what it is. And all by the simple enquiry being a question that goes beyond 'how was I affected'.

If we could be fully present in this moment, we would not only be free from our conditioned 'situation', we could turn the way the world seemed, into something that felt truly amazing. The more present we are the less susceptible to the illusions created by conditioning, and the more able we are to allow ourselves a glowing review of any situation. Safe in the knowing that all which has not yet come to pass is on its way.

Mindfulness is a step out of our circumstances and into the awareness that they are a story we are telling ourselves. And for no better reason than they are the ego's version of 'safe'. So do you feel safe? Or do you feel anxious, angry, nervous or depressed? Do you feel mad that you have been fooled by your mind? Imprisoned for all of the wrong reasons?

MINDFULNESS EXERCISE

Mindfulness can be practiced anywhere and at any time. It is very simply the practice of immersing ourselves in the physical senses so strongly that all the mind-made situations go to the background. Stop thinking about everything for a moment and just hear the noises. Feel the temperature and the wind on your skin and the smell, the subtleties in the environment.

What can you see? What are the colours? The contrasts, what are the sounds far from you and then near you? What can you smell? What does the air feel like as it goes into your lungs? What do you feel on your skin? How do your clothes touch you? Do you have a meal you're digesting or are you hungry? How fast is your heart beating? Mindfulness is quite simply increasing our sensitivity to the physical senses and body – the body is the mind.

I hope just from this you get the picture. We are making ourselves more sensitive to our subtle body, our feeling body. To the intuitive and instinctive body that exists in unison

THE CONTROL CENTRE

with the physical body. The more sensitive we become to the physical body, the more aware we are of how we are vibrating. When we have this close sense to the frequency of our heart, we are better able to clear out old habit energy. Mindfulness allows a connection with our innermost being, and an ancient and omnipresent part of us.

Mindfulness cleanses our vibration. It can be done anytime and anywhere. Washing the dishes, mowing the lawn, driving the car. We don't have to be in a meditative position to practice mindfulness – just deeply immersed in the sensory experience. Practice it a few times for as long as you can and see if you notice any difference in how you feel, and how aware you are of the subtleties in your body.

CHAPTER SUMMARY

- Mindfulness is an ancient practice for clearing the mind of situational illusions caused by our clinging to identification with mind and who we think we are forced to be.
- It allows the clearing of habit energy and prejudiced expectations that aren't aligned with who we want to be.
- It is fast gaining popularity as the go-to for all types of mind healing, in both science-based (psychology) and more alternative and spiritual types of treatment.
- It highlights awareness of the self-image being the inadvertent and unexpected cause of our suffering. Something we are conditioned to value and protect can never be recognised to double as our torturer.
- Mindfulness allows us a union with the subconscious, and to experience a preconditioned state of mind. A state of mind widely celebrated as the highest available to human beings.
- The broader implication of mindfulness is that the Promised Land is not a place, nor is it coming in the future. It has been here the whole time waiting for us to adjust our vision. See beyond our pattern of looking for threat and danger in our environment.
- Peace on earth begins with peace within ourselves. We can change the world by changing the condition of our minds. It is not a matter of time; it is a dimensional shift into presence.

CHAPTER 8

Mind Spa

THE CONTROL CENTRE

"Accessing the subconscious is the most direct and powerful way to create real lasting change in your life."

Melanie Tonia Evans

We wake up in the morning and the frantic begins. We are dragged from our slumber into a frenetic state of high alert – a madness everybody experiences and we are so accustomed to, we call it normal life. We are under increasingly more pressure to stand out and prove ourselves. Our perceived value is determined by how many eyes are on us, and how much attention we can attract. Many people are unconsciously elevating their stress levels and tolerance of perceived pressure, because it is what translates to us as success. How much pressure you can take often falsely translates to high achievement.

This rat race we are running in is often counter-intuitive, yet it never occurs to us how far from sane many of the reasonings are that define the terms of the 'race'. We sacrifice our health to make money and then try to buy our health back. Or we work longer hours to buy things that are less important to us than being able to choose how we spend our time, but still never really feel like we are 'getting ahead'. We sometimes make things far more stressful than they probably should be, so we can handle more pressure. We make obstacles tougher than they really need be, never realising how much easier a shift in our perception might make them. We think nothing of burying ourselves in our work, but rarely to never review if this is in alignment with our values, or if where we are heading reflects them.

And I wager it is the same with relaxation. We have this association with relaxation being letting the mind off the leash to wander aimlessly, or going somewhere to break our normal routine, but the same old mind patterns that cause the inner disturbance don't change. The same frustrations that cause the dissatisfaction and turmoil simmer on low heat, but we're not removed from them, they're just put on hold for a bit. True relaxation is something quite foreign to our culture. It is a subject most people know little to nothing about, and have a poor to no idea what it entails. Many of the colourful and creative ways we go about it are neither recuperative or healthy for us. Calming the nervous system deliberately and systematically is the only way to remove the knots and contractions that get stored in the muscles and organs of the body that occur as part of our normal day-to-day encounters. If unchecked our habitual stresses compound on themselves and will almost certainly develop into what we know as illness (dis-ease).

We think leisure activities and breaking our 'normal' routine is all that is needed to relax and revitalise the body, but these activities often bring us home feeling even less rejuvenated than we left. They do nothing to allow the nervous system to let go of stored emotional tension. Worry, stress, and anxieties are all stored in the body, and can only be released via a deep, deliberate and systematic relaxation of the body and mind. Very few people are aware of this need of the nervous system to recoup, or how to do it. As a result, we are left with a very emotionally unwell society. One with poor emotional health due to poor relaxation strategies and practices.

This is a short chapter but, if I'm honest, I think one of the most important ones. For it is because of this lack of awareness of how to apply these relaxation techniques that there is a lot of unnecessary turmoil in our lives, homes, and world at large. And to me the tragedy is these techniques are easy – easy to do and easy to understand why they are effective, but culturally we don't get the value. We get wound up like rubber bands and take a lot of shit out on each other. It pains me to think how different it all might be if we understood and practiced deep relaxations.

In a world where heart disease accounts for more than every other cause of death on earth, we still fail to realise that our hearts are 'broken', or how to fix them. And of course, there is more to fixing them than relaxation alone – we have to fix the skews in perception that lead us to conclusions that we are 'less than' and we need to cultivate a sense of purpose from what we do. But I think the biggest part of achieving this – of it occurring to us – is in calming the hell down. We cannot hear our heart until we can quiet all of the noise of mind.

What our hearts and emotional well-being rely on is connection. Connection to ourselves and to our tribe of like-minded. We need to belong to a group of people who share our philosophies and values, and build on the depth of those connections through time, support and compassion. We need to know there are a group of people we can relax and be ourselves around. This is a chapter about deep relaxations, but I think it is worth mentioning how much our heart health and ability to relax in who we are relies on these close connections. It is not just that we don't know how to calm the nervous system properly that has led to these 'heart' concerns. It seems we have fallen prey to this confusion between attention and connection. And it is our hearts that are the consequential victims.

We don't need more fake news, fake food or fake friends. We need to develop meaningful relationships, both in the work that we do and our friendships. We know social media is partly to blame for this lack of a meaningful relationships. Our Facebook friends aren't exactly the strong, supportive relationships we used to get from our tribal lives, or even life before internet connection, but they could be. Of course, we already know this, but in this age, we are starting to fall prey to this numbers game, where we are confusing quantity with quality. I don't really want to generalise here, because some are well aware of this, and I think they are much happier because of it. But for many we don't get enough 'likes' and we're destroyed by it. Is it any wonder our health isn't good?

The poor kids growing up in this era don't know how to live without their phones. Author and speaker Simon Sinek equates having a mobile phone to a similar type of dopamine hit that we might get from alcohol. In effect it is like we have opened the liquor cabinet up for them – "If things ever get you down, just jump on your phone and post something". And many adults have fallen prey to the same thing. Very few of us value relationships for what they are or know how to connect with each other, and it is crucial to our heart health. We don't experience anything unless we have someone to share it with – who cares about our outcomes? We don't care about people because we can just get on Facebook and connect right? Obviously best we answer that for ourselves. But I think social media has put us even more in the 'fishbowl' than we ever have been before, and it is very detrimental to our health and relationships.

What people think causes depression:

Weakness, laziness. An inability to "Suck it up".

What causes depression:

Trauma, abuse, neglect, bullying, brain chemistry, grief and loss, overworking, excess stress, genetic factors, lack of fulfilment, lifestyle factors, perfectionism, lack of social support.

What also causes depression:

The patriarchy, racism, capitalism, lack of a living wage, societal pressure, body shaming, lack of mental health support, gun violence, discrimination, gender stereotypes.

Depression is not a personal failure.

Depression is one potential consequence of toxic social, cultural, and political systems.

Author Unknown.

THE CONTROL CENTRE

My apologies to the author of the above content in italics. I did search long and hard to find who wrote it, but I thought it was very apt to include it here while I'm having a rant about mental health. Because I think very few people understand how far reaching and multi-dimensional the causes of depression are. As our society becomes ever more connected through social media, we also fail to realise we are moving further away from the sense of belonging that is as vital to our health as food and water.

To our surprise we are feeling remarkably empty from our relationships, and even more judged than ever. We think we have to post this amazing stuff all the time, and we dare not show the slightest sign of vulnerability or anxiety about how things are with us. There are very few genuine relationships anymore and it is our hearts that inadvertently suffer most from this 'evolution' of our times, and the fishbowl we live in. I read in Daniel Goleman's 'Vital Lies Simple Truths' that the root cause of mental illness is a gross over-estimation of other people's concern for what we do. The truth is most people don't mind in the slightest what we do – they're too busy worrying about their own life to even notice you. It is up to us to be clear on what we care about and what's important to us, or we leave ourselves open to ill-conceived criticisms.

> "So much of what we take in is about bigger, better, and more. But for some of us – small, simple, and quiet are all we need. It's ok to be happy with a calm life."
>
> Erica Layne

A nervous system

Human beings are a nervous system – a network of neural pathways, with thousands of tiny reactions going on at a subtle level every second. And for many of us, our nerves are frayed. The system we live in seems overwhelming, and rightly so. We are not evolutionarily equipped to cope with the mind-boggling amount of stresses and inconsistencies that continually press against our ability to calm ourselves. We live with the perceived threats of climate change, war, overpopulation – many of which, rightly or wrongly, are indicative of our species longevity seeming unsustainable and it has put our nerves on a wire. Even if these issues are never given our attention or the time of day there are many stimuli in our environment that have gotten us all a little edgy, to say the least. It is still in the back of our minds that something has got to give.

Highly strung is the norm – even if we've managed to adopt some effective relaxation strategies, in our heart we know we are surrounded by a world gone mad. We've trained ourselves to be less bothered by it all or we risk exploding. Kind of hard to consider what our life's purpose is when our goal is to keep our head above water one more day, hoping the next one won't be a repeat of the last few. Which is even less likely when we become aware that what we thought was our life is little more than a habit that is running itself. Our nerves are fried and I think many people have given up thinking they can do something about what happens, both to them and in the world. There is something we can do, and it starts with learning to relax.

Hopefully I'm not being dramatic here, and the plight of the world doesn't seem too dim to you, but from what I've witnessed many people feel out of control of what is happening to them. Nothing is as out of our control as it might seem if we can just learn to calm down and take heed of our reactions – take some perspective on the changes we would like. And calming down is what this chapter is all about. Incorporating some tried and true relaxation practices into our health routine. The point I'm making is that this is a much more difficult era to live in than has come before. There are many complex and 'global scale' issues that don't seem solvable – all we can control is what goes on inside us. Many people seem convinced that it's irresponsible not to be mad at everything that is wrong and shouting at the multitude of things we have no power to change. But I beg to differ.

The 'Dreaming' still exists

No matter how crazy these times might seem, there is still something deeply primal and calm within us. We are connected to an innate sense of peace that we share with a time long gone. It is a peace that our ancient forefathers knew intimately, and without trying. A peace that existed when the world was quieter. The time when indigenous people roamed in relative peace before the hum of industry, before the apparent chaos we call civilisation. The Dreaming, as the Australian Aboriginal referred to it, is timeless – it is still here. It still exists beneath the madness and the pace of what we've been caught up in. The quiet is beneath the noise. This is still the Dreamtime. It waits quietly in our heart of hearts to wake and bring a new peace to the earth. This seed of peace waits for us to sense it, and our instincts to be restored.

It is very hard for us to fathom what life on earth was like thousands of years ago. How quiet the earth was, and how quiet it was within our own minds before we become madly obsessed with our self-image and the pictures of success that drive what we now refer to as 'normal life'. But imagine it for a moment, what life would have been like before the 'machine' we now call human progress took over. There is an ancient seed in our hearts that has begun to sprout because it represents our future. It is the timeless wisdom of our hearts and can bring us back to calm whenever we remember our connection to this past. It is a peace that has for now been lost to the noise.

We can go to this calm place and awaken the innate timeless wisdom within us. We can frequent this calm place if we wish, but it doesn't happen naturally. It doesn't occur to a mind obsessed with the need to stand out and be seen, heard, liked and 'valued'. It doesn't happen naturally – we have to seek whatever comes to us with intention.

What happens naturally is we are sucked into the frantic pace of modern living. The competition to be noticed, and we have to be playing this game to be considered sane and normal. We are social animals, and are drawn by our nature to the game everyone else is playing, whether it makes sense to us or not. There is a primal magnetism drawing us to abide the 'rules' everyone is playing by. But there is another game we can play, a more conscious game. A more soothing game that actually helps all we wish for fall into place. In our heart of hearts, we are calm and at peace, but it is a peace that has become quite foreign to us. It can barely be sensed beneath all of the noise and flashing neon lights competing for our attention.

When we quiet the mind down, it's not just us who are more at peace, but the rest of the world seems that way too.

Rewiring our brains

Peace is our natural state, the state we were born into, and the 'frantic' is what we have learned. What we've been conditioned by. When we incorporate deep relaxations into our wellness routine, it will lead not just to better health and outcomes – the state of being deeply relaxed is also where we alter our programming. The subconscious mind becomes highly receptive to suggestion when we are in the deeply relaxed state.

Deep relaxation and trance states are a fundamental aspect of hypnosis and all effective reprogramming of the mind. Phobias and habits that have persisted for many years can be altered in a matter of minutes if we are able to access the deep regions of mind where these conclusions are stored. When we enter the trance state, we awaken what is referred to as the relaxation response. A state of mind where we can embed new instructions. The conscious mind stands as the guardian of our beliefs – the protector of what it assumes facilitates our survival. So to interrupt the programming we have to sneak past the guard. To embed new beliefs and suggestions about who we are and how we want things to seem. We have to lull the conscious mind into a state of quiet where it is not needed. We have to get the conscious mind to 'stand down'.

This is why subliminal messaging is so effective. Subliminal messaging flashes pictures or words that are either so fast we can't see them, or so quietly that the conscious mind doesn't hear them. But the subconscious mind that operates many times faster does. The conscious mind doesn't see or hear so therefore can't reject or question the subliminal suggestion, so they directly impact the subconscious program. Hypnotherapists employ a lot of language trickery in a bid to seem like they are allowing us choices when they are not. They will go to lengths trying to make us forget what we have heard in hypnosis. The conscious mind can't reject what it hasn't heard.

I have guided hypnosis recordings that play different messages in each stereo channel at the same time. The conscious can only pay attention to one, so the other must impact directly on the subconscious. Besides deep relaxation states being pivotal in getting suggestions to impact the subconscious, the practice is probably the single healthiest thing you can do to help heal and calm your nervous system. Psychological tension is stored all over the physical body in the organs and tissue of the body/mind. Massage is a good way to release these unconscious stored tensions, but not as effective as deep systematic relaxations. Deep relaxations are far more rejuvenating than sleep, and take a fraction of the time. They do far more to integrate all parts of our body into a single synergistic system than any other practice. They get all of our cells communicating with each other, and our glands or chakras into alignment speaking to each other. They allow the body to fire in harmony as a single, intelligent system.

Add to this that the visualisation exercises we talked about in a previous chapter are far more effective when they are done in the deeply relaxed state. There isn't a more effective means of altering our programming than clear visualisations done in the deeply relaxed state. You want to change how you feel? Deep relaxations are the key.

I'll go through a deep relaxation exercise at the end of this chapter, if you have never been introduced to the idea. But it is basically a systematic shutting down of the nervous system where all parts of the body are integrated into a single living unit.

Meditation

> "If every eight-year-old in the world is taught meditation we will eliminate violence within one generation."
>
> Dalai Lama

I'm not what anyone would consider an expert on meditation, but I am qualified to give this simple overview of how to do it and why it works. In meditation we are quieting the mind to allow the muck to settle. Adjusting the tuning knob of our internal radio so our thoughts become clearer and going in the same direction instead of the usual static, and our thoughts darting in opposing directions. Sometimes the thoughts we have are erratic and counteract each other. So in meditation, we are tuning into our thoughts so we are clear on their effect. Meditation is very simply quieting the mind from its normal habit of chatter, by anchoring ourselves in the core unconscious functions of the body – the heartbeat and the breath.

Meditation can be done sitting or lying, eyes open or closed. I've heard of practices of staring into a naked flame, a single point on the wall, or even a mirror. But generally, meditation is done seated, legs crossed and eyes closed. Some practices include humming a mantra, to help focus the minds natural propensity to dive back into unconscious thinking patterns, and harmonise our vibration. I'm not going to pretend to be an expert in something that I don't believe you have to know lots about to practice and benefit from.

I offered the variations to illustrate that the meditation's effectiveness depends on you. Running can be a very head-clearing meditation, as can sitting in a fishing boat, staring quietly at the ocean. It was a common practice in Eastern traditions to immerse oneself in a repetitive task, to help clear the mind from its habitual chatter and enter a flow state. The conscious mind is typically in a habit of racing from one pointless thought to another diametrically opposed one. It is what is referred to in Eastern traditions as the 'mad monkey' mind, and it can run off with us as the unconscious passengers unless we slow it down occasionally. We have to slow it down sometimes or we become the victims of the nonstop voices, coming from the hundreds of different masks we wear that fire off automatically without pause or reprieve.

The most important aspect of meditation is that we **don't judge how we are doing**. We typically beat ourselves up for how we are going in everything else we do, but for once this is against the rules. If our mind wanders off, it's okay. If we don't think we are 'doing it right' that's okay too. It is one of the very few times in our life where we can't get it wrong. Just keep quieting the mind, and coming back to the heartbeat and the breath. Even if we feel like we didn't shut up in our minds the whole time – it's ok, we'll get better. It is a practice.

I won't go too much into the breathing thing here, but there are many people who are convinced we can transform our life simply by breathing more consciously. By getting into the rhythm of our breathing we can align with the deeper flow of our energy and there are many books devoted to this very subject. The breath is a bridge between the conscious and unconscious worlds – the spiritual and the material. An unconscious function that we can consciously control. It is a core unconscious function of the body that can improve how we think, our metabolism, how we sleep and our nerves in general. Deep rhythmic breathing doesn't just help us think better, it connects us to an older and more peaceful part of the mind.

Sleep. Where the subconscious works its magic

The subconscious mind wakes when we sleep. It goes to work, probably relieved that the pesky voice of the conscious mind has stopped for a period, so it can get to work 'cleaning up' some of the contradicting gunk in our minds. The subconscious goes about its job of rearranging our perception – how we have consciously affirmed we want things to seem. Ensuring that the thing we've noticed and shown interest in becomes a more prevalent part of our experience. It ensures that when we wake our attention is drawn to the markers that define we are in familiar territory. It turns us towards what we've said we'd like to see more of/know more about. We notice more of the things that relate to the goals we set ourselves. It makes the things we were grateful for more prominent. "Simon said he liked this. I'll put it bang in the middle of his experience so he can't miss it."

We can never be consciously aware of all the ways we ask for things, but sleep is the place where the subconscious works its magic. It makes us more like the people we'd rather be, makes what we are grateful for more prevalent, and makes the things we want to learn more about front and centre where we can't miss them.

So that little window we're in before we drop off to sleep, and when we first wake up in the morning, is a particularly powerful opportunity for reshaping how our world seems. This is a period where the subconscious is highly receptive, and we still have some consciousness for which to state preferences. We can send ourselves very clear messages about who we are and how we want things to go when we are in this transitional state. These intermediate states of consciousness are widely utilised in many manifestation techniques. I'll mention them very quickly here – our states range from beta through to delta sates. The beta state is when we are immersed in a task that requires our full attention. The next is alpha – when we are daydreaming or doing something we can do automatically or without very much focus. Theta is the next which can range from partially awake to not conscious to dreaming states, and delta is where we are in deep dreamless sleep.

It is the theta state that we are primarily concerned with in making new and desirable suggestions to the subconscious mind. When we are in the twilight between awake and asleep. Our window is both ends of the sleep cycle – just as we wake, and just before we nod off.

You may have noticed in the visualisation chapter that this was something Michael Phelps utilised - replaying his 'winning stories' in this time before and after sleep. The time when we drop from an alpha into theta state of consciousness is a profound window of opportunity to embed suggestions about the type of feeling states we want to spend our waken life in. Just before you nod off to sleep, get all of the negative stuff out of your mind. Anything that happened in the day that was displeasing, run it back to go as you would have preferred. Be in the state you want to live your whole life in.

Play that favourite song that epitomises abundance for you or whatever you most value. And similarly, when you wake, who are you now? Bring it to mind. Do you feel a little different? What is different about it? Expect the absolute best your day could bring. Expect to be surprised that things really did go your way. If we notice the good, we subconsciously give it permission to keep showing up. Sometimes it's fast, sometimes it's slow, but we always grow. If by some miracle all of your dreams came true while you were sleeping – how would you know? We have to define and be specific about how we want our experience to be different if we are ever going to be able to see it.

PRACTICAL EXERCISE

Dropping into the relaxation response

Relaxation is commonly associated with eating a good meal or having a few too many quiet ones. We don't give a second thought to crossing an ocean so we can break the cycle and get far away from our worries. But this doesn't alter the powerful emotional habits and patterns that run our life. True relaxation is a systematic and deliberate subduing of the nervous system. It is the single healthiest thing we can do to soothe the body/mind, and we don't have to cross an ocean or go on a long drive to do it.

If you are unfamiliar with the relaxation response, there is no shortage of guided meditations and relaxations out there on the net. Find a voice that doesn't annoy you too much. Put some headphones on and lay down in the dark. Make sure you will not be disturbed, the temperature is right, and your clothing is loose.

The guided relaxation will ask you to start with a few deep breaths and systematically work its way around your whole body so that every part of you is chilled and relaxed. Some use strong visual imagery (as we know this is highly effective in moving emotional states). As an example the guide would describe your relaxation in physical terms – picture a warm glaze sliding down over your body. Your body becomes heavy and not so much impossible to move, you just have no inclination to move. Not frozen, just deeply connected and contented. It feels so good, you just want to keep dropping deeper. You can often feel your entire body as one integrated and living system, your heartbeat and blood flow felt in your toes, hands, and face as much as in your chest.

Make deep relaxations a regular part of your health routine. Even if you have a busy family, you will all reap the benefits of you being a more relaxed and whole person. You can do it at night to help send you off to sleep, if that is the only window of opportunity you can find. But the more you implement this practice, the more relaxed you will feel, and the more you will feel your life is under your control.

CHAPTER SUMMARY

- Deep relaxations are the most rejuvenating thing we can do to cleanse ourselves of habit energy and the tension that is stored in the muscles and organs of the body.
- Deep relaxations are the best means of consciously impacting the subconscious mind, and embedding new instructions to the program.
- Before and after sleep are profound windows of opportunity for making suggestions that become embedded directly onto the subconscious mind.
- Meditation doesn't just calm us down, it helps us concentrate, and gets all the unwanted and contradictory messages out of our mind so we are more conscious of thought and aware of their effect on how we feel/attract.

CHAPTER 9

Living by Accident

> "If you don't know where you are going, any road will get you there."
>
> Lewis Carroll

We cannot have a great life without defining what that means for us. Without being clear on the details and some sense of a plan on how to get there. We cannot arrive somewhere if we don't know where it is we want to go. Nothing 'great' can happen 'by accident'. What would be great? What would you love to see happen? Having goals doesn't just pool our energy, it is how we have some semblance of control over the physical conditions we experience. It allows us to bend the world to our will rather than be blown around by 'apparent' conditions.

You did that on purpose

Remember when we were kids and you 'accidentally' knocked someone over and they exclaimed, "You did that on purpose" – meaning of course we did it intentionally. It has been suggested that we either create consciously, or we create unconsciously. We either know what we are asking for and do it intentionally, or we get 'whatever' and consequently have no idea where it came from. We either live intentionally, or our lives happen by accident. I want to make it clear how different a life that is 'on purpose' is. Because unless we have that thing that would make us feel great in our sights, we can never get a sense of how much power we have to bend the world to our will.

Without living intentionally, we can never get to see the higher order at work in the universe. Never be awakened to the magic of meaningful chance, and what the universe can do for us to bring our aims to the table. Living intentionally is both how we **impact the programming**, and bend reality to our will. We change what we look at by what we look for. We make what we desire visible to us by our looking for it.

We bring it out of the 'forest' of possibility. We are looking for and can now see something that **literally didn't exist** for us prior to the intention.

What we universally want

This chapter is about the true value of having goals. Not just because it allows us to pool our energy and resources in a single direction, but also because we are allowing the universe to show us what is possible – how it can bend and change things to suit our need. We are saying, "Here's my goal, now show me how it can all come true". We wake to the expectation that there is more to it than we are conscious of. With our goals, we are 'employing' the universe, and asking it, "What can you do for me?". Rather than it be some cold, grey and hopeless place that is out to get us, our goals and our hopeful expectation allow us to see another side. That is the real value of goals, and it is the only real difference in people – that they have a 'heading' that means something to them. And they enjoy some sense that they will be able to get there. Each step of their journey bringing a little more awareness to their own abilities, and that 'help' and guidance that comes from the outside – the higher order.

But as I say goals are the difference between people – our goals are what allow us to see that things can move in our favour. If we don't want for anything, how do we know what happened is good, or miraculous even? The world moves in relationship to our goals. An event's meaning can only be put into perspective by how it affects/relates to our getting where we want to go. What is the difference in people? What they want and care about, and what they are willing to do to get it. Every box ticked and every mountain we climb just re-enforces, "I know what I can do, and I'll set my sights accordingly".

One part of our mind thinks and decides – and the other supplies meaning, and gives us a sense of identity and direction. But the mind that doesn't think – that controls how the world seems – takes its lead from us. From our conscious decisions on how we want things to be. Give the programming some sense of direction or there is no one at the wheel. In the subconscious mind, there is no decision-making faculty – there is quite literally 'no one home'.

Although we've all had different experiences and have different values there is something we all universally long for:

- To be loved?
- Something sacred?
- To belong?
- A sense of purpose – that we have helped someone?

We want all of these, but they can be summed up by this – **a goal worthy of our life**. Something that is a worthy recipient of all we have to give – all of our energy. What Nietzsche referred to as our **'organising idea'**. A central guiding principle of our life – by which all the events of our life can be brought into context. An organising idea that seemingly develops a life of its own to guide us at our 'forks' in the road and channel all of our energy. It is this 'thing' that allows us to know we are pushing forward in a single and unified direction. And when we have this, we can hit the accelerator sometimes, and we can coast at others, centred in the fact our lives have a sense of direction that we've made a conscious choice in. Our organising idea is more than just a goal, it is a direction by which all of our goals can be joined and oriented. Our lives have a rudder that allows us to navigate through difficult times. Our organising idea is our north star that lights the way home no matter where we find ourselves.

The analogy I like to make is it is our pyramid – this grand sculpture we build on for many of the years of our life. If we are always guided in a single direction we can get further. Life is often tedious, disappointing and we can lose sight of why we are doing something when we don't see results and it is not brought into the context of something larger. Sometimes building the block we are currently working on seems boring and we wonder if it will all come together. When we know that the block we are working on is an important aspect of our pyramid, we can do it with all the care, focus and precision we need to make it right. And we stand back as we progress and know we are always contributing to this grand scheme. To a goal that is bigger than our own needs.

We want to know that it made some difference that we were here – there was a point and meaning to what we tried to accomplish. For many this organising principle is their families, for some it is a moral justice they are lobbying for. It doesn't have to have neon lights attached to have meaning for us, but it is what all of us want, and I wager even more than fame and fortune. If we find that thing that has value for us, we can easily turn our back on the confused and often shallow values of our culture.

The movie **'Mr Holland's Opus'** was a great example of what I'm referring to. He was always neglecting the big opera he was working on because of his commitments as a father, and dedication to his students – only to one day many years later find that his students were his big opera. The influence he had on so many lives had become his swansong. We don't have to be working on some big 'opera' we think everyone is going to be astonished by when we are doing what we care about and what has meaning for us. We just keep working on it every day sensing the part we are doing now in the context of the bigger picture.

What we all want more than anything is a goal worthy of our life that we can keep contributing to – building it into the opus of our lives, or our pyramid. Our grander vision of something beautiful. Our goals are the smaller part of this grander organising principle that helps us remain on the track of where we think we are going. Even if this 'thing' is just a hobby for us at the moment – something we think no one else really appreciates. It has meaning for us, and it's what we love to do. We can handle the setbacks and the impatience, when nothing seems to be happening, when we understand what the piece we are making now is connected to. We are 'watering the bamboo', not seeing immediate results but seeing the big picture even when no one else can.

It is by our goals that we are able to consciously shape what's happening – turn the nature of events to our liking.

> "Three years from now you could have what would be good for you, but you have to figure out what it is and aim for it."
>
> **Jordan Peterson**

I thought you said I was good enough how I was

And of course, we are. But if we are breathing, we want to effect change. We are compelled as human beings to want to improve the conditions of our life. It is in knowing how good we are that we want to open the thrusters. All anyone ever wants, more than anything, is to find that thing they care about so much that it absorbs them. A target so blinding that we can no longer see the 'muck'. All of the BS just fades from our attention because all we see is the bullseye of our target. That is what our goals do for us. We no longer obsess over all the things we can't change because we're focused on the thing that we can. We all want to be useful – we all want to know that we have helped someone do something. That is the meaning of purpose – to help. But finding that purpose that means more to us than our own life is not just for the lucky ones.

'To be or not to be', isn't a valid question. It isn't a question because the answer is always the same – 'be'. Because the slings and arrows we may have feared – the criticisms we might face from showing more of ourselves – don't mean a damn thing if we know what we are 'being' has value for us. We provide the meaning, never anyone else. Besides, criticisms say far more about the critic than they ever do the criticised. The goal means something to us, not anyone else.

It doesn't matter a bit if we are not splitting the atom, or winning the Nobel Prize for our efforts. If the world isn't going, "Wow, look what so and so has done". That isn't even close to what it means to live with intention, as I mentioned in the chapter on the mind's agenda. Our society is diseased because of this agreement on the value of anything only being able to be measured in sales and attention. We can't be stamped with a price tag and told the value of what we add, because it only has value for us. Sure, we can get paid for it, but I think it is an injustice to our worth and creativity to be guided first by dollar signs and only second by what it means to us. Other people don't decide what things mean to you with their opinions. We just shouldn't do things based on how many people will look at it today.

> "The planet does not need more 'successful people'. The planet desperately needs more peacemakers, healers, restorers, storytellers and lovers of all kinds."
>
> Dalia Lama

We shouldn't have the type of goal that, if no one's watching us in a year, we try something else. Our goal should be something more like the bloke who carted buckets of water into the desert for 15 years to start a new wilderness for the teams of wildlife that now call it home. Make it your life's work, not this month's work, and we'll always be building on the skills we gained yesterday, and focusing our energies towards the big picture.

We assume it is the lucky ones who have found their thing – the 'chosen' who are called and unwrapping their gift – but we are all called. We all have that thing – if we don't consider we've found it yet, just keep asking and listening. Keep listening to our heart, and moving forward. It may not be what you are doing now. You may not have a burning desire to do what you believe is just a 'job' and what you are doing 'at the moment' (as so many people say). Most everyone wants to be doing something else for a living – but that doesn't stop us doing what we are doing now with a sense of gusto and purpose. No one else can add that spin on it that is us.

We define success

> "If you're focusing on what everyone else's idea of success is you'll never achieve it. Success, like beauty, starts from the inside out. You have to go deep inside yourself to define your own version of success."
>
> **Chris Dessi**

So few of us live our lives intentionally, because we aren't aware of the depth of value – of how it enables us to take control of our lives, how we feel and what happens to us. Yeah, we get up, and do a job. If we're lucky, we don't even mind what we do, but how many can say they love what they do? How many can say they are living intentionally, with purpose? That they are doing what they do because it is what they have always wanted to do. Earl Nightingale, in his recording 'The Greatest Secret' defines success as, **"The progressive realisation of a worthy ideal"**.

Many people think they have to be reinventing the wheel if they're to consider they are living with a sense of purpose. They think they have to be doing something earth-shattering to have the right to consider a 'job' a vocation.

What if there was nothing wrong with the life and job we have? But we just kept listening to the narrow-minded opinions of others, telling us how far from great our lives were. What if the lives we had now were our purpose, and we could do them with more zest and zeal than we used to, just because we made the decision that it had meaning for us? It is true that in writing this I wanted to increase awareness of our programming, and the benefits of mindfulness, but what I also hoped for was us being able to see these lives of ours that many consider to be 'broken' to be our purpose. That people could do what they've always done, but with a renewed sense of fulfilment. Whatever you are doing now is your purpose.

If we are helping a kid tie their shoelaces, or listening to a friend, in that moment that is our purpose. It doesn't need to be met with a parade. If we've been doing what we have this long, it is very closely tied to our purpose, and many people just never realised how much. How much we were helping people out in giving them a hand with something small - enquiring what they were up to, or lending an ear so that they are heard.

> "Too often we underestimate the power of touch, a smile, a kind word, a listening ear, an honest compliment, or the smallest act of caring, all of which have the potential to turn a life around."
> **Leo Buscaglia**

I've seen so many make the super wise conclusion that they are so small and insignificant that it wouldn't matter what they do. They can act like right fools because 'it doesn't matter'. Well heads up – it does. What we're doing adds to the whole and will have implications around the world and for generations to come. Be conscious, and be considerate of that, and you just might start to get the picture that what you do makes a difference here.

I for one was under this delusion that there weren't enough bells and whistles for me to consider what I did mattered. Yeah, I wanted to make some 'difference' but how could anything I did matter? The illusion lives, because of this idea that 'it has to be huge and noticeable' to be 'a difference'. Well here's the 'down low' on what we do no matter how insignificant it might seem. This is a very different environment we live in to the one that existed 30 or even ten years ago.

Ordinary people are the change-makers of this modern world. We don't have to be fixing the whole world to 'make a difference'. We have to be fixing our world – the people we share our lives with. Work colleagues, family, community. They are all part of the difference we make. And for the best part we are already doing it. I just think if we knew how much difference we are making we might just step with a little more grace and dignity – and do what we are already doing with a renewed sense of pride. Too many people walk around with their heads down with this, "I'm not famous" attitude, and have no idea the difference they're making. And it is a shame.

Ok so I'll get off my soapbox now, but I just think it is worth mentioning here, and it will be re-enforced later, that by our nature we are good and extremely intelligent people. We are compelled to do what is right and it is hard-wired into our DNA. Our species would not have thrived if we didn't care about the welfare of others. We don't have to be doing anything different to what we've been doing – just realise it matters. We are aiding the evolution of the planet by caring what we care about.

> "Each of us is put here in this time and this place to personally decide the future of humankind. Did you think we were put here for something less?"
> Chief Arvol Looking Horse

It's not our status that allows us to connect with our work, but how much we like doing what we do. Doing what most consider a menial task is nothing to be ashamed of, unless we buy into the bullshit that everything has to be done in flashing lights. What if the life we had now was our purpose? And we did it with more intention than we ever had because we recognise it as our piece to a bigger grander puzzle. We started to do it like it mattered to us. Do you think we'd be in a better mood and more tolerant of the trivial BS that goes with every job?

How different our lives will be when we realise the difference we make.

We are the stars in the lives of the people we're close to, and no matter how hopeless we might think we are at times, we're doing the work of angels. And I don't mean that in some rainbows and unicorns sense – we are healing and helping every time we listen to someone's story, or offer any small gesture of goodwill. It is a mistake to think our piece, the part we add in this evolutionary puzzle, doesn't matter to anyone. And it might even seem like what we are doing has no point, but it should matter to us. Our real goal is to extract more meaning from the things we do. And for a lot of it, we don't have to do anything different to what we've been doing – just know that it matters.

Aligned with our purpose

If what we're doing doesn't feel like our purpose and we're desperate to find out what it is we were born for, it will never occur to us until we align with it energetically. Until we think in terms of how happy we will be when we do know. If we are hating life, we can only see more supporting evidence of hate. If we want to know how it would feel to live a life of purpose, we have to act like it is what we are doing now. We can't loathe our job and think somehow it will all just magically change. We have to use our current situation as the stepping stone to knowing what will feel better.

If we ever want to ascend to greater highs of connection to our work, it can only come from being more present, and loving what we do now. It is our right to dream of better things, but they can't occur to us until we lift our head, and appreciate something about the life we have right now. We can only begin to realise a dream by accepting where we are. To get to something better we have to work with the environment we're in right now and make it seem like it's what we dream of. To get to where we want to be, we have to know we are responsible for where we are now. We can turn it around by how we look at it – we might be shocked at how different it seems when we do. And something else might appear as an opportunity when we are energetically in sync.

Oftentimes our 'progress' has as much to do with patience as it does 'getting stuff done'. All of our actions become inspired when we align with the energy of doing our lives on purpose.

The difference a target makes

> "You can't hit a target you can't see, and you cannot see a target you do not have."
>
> Zig Ziglar

If we aren't living our lives on purpose – with intention – we are living by accident. We have deferred to the default settings of the program. And for the most part this is not entirely tragic. It is how human beings were designed to operate – that the program would be on set and forget and carry us through all of the days of our life. But if we don't like how it's going, it's not as difficult to have some control over as I think a lot of people assume. We just have to give ourselves a sense of direction. "This is how I would like my experience to be different." And explain why. Our 'why' gets us through the tougher times. Once we've appealed to our sense of logic, the prescribed change will always make sense. If we don't have that deeper sense of why we do what we do, every moment in our lives will seem like a means to an end, and this becomes our never-ending story. If we don't know where we are going, and why, we can never arrive anywhere desirable, and our lives will always feel like an unwanted accident.

Have you ever heard of 'the Hero's Journey'? It is said to be the baseline for every script ever written. There has to be a hero we are invested in if we are to be bothered watching the movie, or reading the book. There has to be an obstacle to overcome – what seems like impossible odds. And as the story goes, there is a teacher and training, and then the final battle, and victory. The point of the storyline is that we have to be emotionally invested in the heroes outcome if we are to be bothered watching the darn movie. And our lives are no different. We have to be overcoming something that matters to us to overcome, or achieving something that has meaning, or we become disinterested in our lives. And if we are disinterested, how do you think anyone else is going to feel about us?

The meaning goals give

The glory is not in getting to the goal, but having the goal. It changes us, and the way we see the world. The world is always seen in relation to our goal, and our goal puts all things into perspective. The world is our means of getting there, not something that is blowing us all over the ocean. We know what things mean, or that they are of interest by putting them into our 'goal computer' – is this taking me closer or farther away? Whether this is a waste of time can only be known in relationship to our goals. A goal puts events into perspective and allows us to define what things mean.

A goal gives order to what might otherwise seem like a random series of events. Things are considered to be 'synchronistic' because of how our desires are seemingly magically met by fate. There is a higher order to the seemingly chaotic universe. Sometimes what we were asking for or thinking about just uncannily appears in perfect timing. Meaningful chance can only occur when our needs make meaning out of the chaos. The event is judged as 'meaningful chance' because it unlocks something mysteriously helpful about how the universe can bend to serve our need. Without the need, there can be no magic.

When we have a goal, our conversations aren't as random. There is always an underlying interest – not anything you'd consider an ulterior motive, but an open ear for, "How does this connect to my cause or the cause of someone I know?". When we have goals it puts us in the mindset of helping. Not just how we can mutually benefit from the conversation, but how the subject connects with anyone we might know. There is always something about the conversation that is relative – and sometimes indirectly. How we can connect them/recommend them to someone we know in a mutual exchange of value. When we have a goal we enter this now 'connected' world of how we can all benefit one another.

Someone always knows someone, and that becomes the point of conversations – making connections. Not just for the sake of business but to bring the right people together. We operate with a view to help people of similar interests connect – on top of the more general interest of what's going on in people's lives. And that's the real benefit of goals – people's lives matter more to us, because things in general matter more to us. "How can I help?" becomes the pervasive mind-set.

We can easily avoid conflict and time-wasting pursuits by putting them into perspective via our goals – "Does this relate/matter to where I want to be?".

If we aren't asking for a specific need to be met we see the world differently. For example, I have a goal to write a book – and the universe might just decide to plonk me down on the next flight I take in a seat next to the very person who can make that dream a reality. Or might put a magazine article front and centre that is related to my goal. It might even 'throw' a book off the shelf that is the very specific one I need to read. It is a magical universe, but unless it is conspiring to meet our needs, it is just as likely to be a grey, hostile and meaningless place.

Without the dream, who sits next to me on a flight is just some random stranger. But when the universe is seen in its context of bending to meet our needs we can be truly amazed at the weird and wonderful place it is. But we can't be amazed by the connected miracle we live in without having the dream and the cosmos moving to meet it. We can't know how we can bend it to our will if we aren't bending it into something specific. What do we want more of?

Without our dream we can never see that there is a higher order to what would otherwise seem like chaos.

No matter our interest, if we love food, or fishing, or fixing cars, our lives are less like a random and chaotic event when our meetings are seen in the light of helping our goals being fulfilled. Do you want your life to seem like a pointless accident, with no meaning to any event, nothing seen as magical or great? Well, that is an exaggeration, of course, but I think you get my point, that we give the universe the chance to show us what it can do when we have a goal. Events are never random or meaningless. Everything matters in the scheme of things.

Concentration - the only true path to peace

A mind off the leash can no better take us towards peace, than a piece of driftwood can sail us across an ocean.

There seems to be an almost universal association between relaxation, and letting the mind wander. Only a mind that is focused on a task has the ability to snuff out the unwanted. We lose confidence, and let all manner of 'squatters' take up our mind space when we lose focus. Only a concentrated mind can keep the crap out – the rubbish that tells us we can't, and causes unnecessary anxieties. All manner of unwanted states of mind are kept out of the focused mind. Concentrating is the accelerator pedal that speeds us towards anything we want to manifest into our lives. The real muscle we have to flex if we are to feel in control of our lives and minds. I'm convinced that suffering is only ever due to an inability to re-focus the mind. A wandering mind is an unhappy mind. When we allow the mind to 'wander off' into habit, those all-too-familiar patterns of how we are trying not to feel come waltzing back in.

When we've got something better to do and are focused on the task, we are taking charge of where our mind goes.

Anxiety 'happens' when our attention takes its leave – and our mind resorts to its old conditioned habits. The mind wanders into the darkness – off the path and into those old false conclusions of what is going wrong. It only happens because we are not present enough in our minds to take ownership of what is going on within it. The only true path to peace is to be so present in our minds that we can sense and snuff out the deception in the bud. Concentration is how we shrink our demons down to size.

I hazard a guess that a lot of our emotional angst is far more related to our inability to focus and be completely present in our minds than we are comfortable admitting. I know myself, anxiety, insomnia, well pretty much everything that disturbs my peace and ability to control my own mind, stems from a lack of focus. I get tired and lose my focus, and habit takes the wheel. I have too many short, conflicting and unintentional thoughts, flitting around my mind without a 'driver at the wheel'. If I am able to go deeper and focus, I wean back some control, even if it is only to aid me to sleep and get some proper rest. We can't fill our sails with the 'wind' of short, unintentional and meaningless thought. All disturbance in me is a lack of focus, a lack of intentionality – and why? Because I'm not engaged in what I'm doing.

Do we want our mind to be as pristine as an operating theatre, or a ramshackle home full of rubbish? We treat ourselves, and our mind, relative to our purpose, and other people sense it and do the same. If we don't feel our lives matter, we treat ourselves accordingly.

> "I will not let anyone walk through my mind with their dirty feet."
>
> Mahatma Ghandi

I heard Bob Proctor once use the analogy of a candle versus a torch. A candle's light is dispersed. It goes everywhere, in all directions, which is fine if you want to light the whole room evenly, but if you want to see something written on a wall 30 feet away, you need a torch. The torch can have one candle of power, but all of its light is deflected, focused in one single direction, and so we can see clearly, much farther away.

We silence the inner critic if it is getting in the way. We stay up later. We have more energy when we are directed at a single worthwhile purpose. And when we see the results of our concentrated efforts, we always feel more motivated. When we are shown the price we are paid for our efforts we always get a jolt of energy.

Do you want to learn a bit of a song on the piano, and know a couple of martial arts moves, or bake an average sort of cake, or do you want to play a masterpiece, be a Kung Fu master, and make an award-winning cake? We can half-do lots of things, or we can master one. That mastery will then filter into anything else we attempt from that point on, but we have to focus our energy. And that is, I think, one of the greatest benefits of goal-setting. All of our focus and energy into one killer punch. We will never know what we can do until we have that goal, and take the steps towards it. We'll never know what we can do until we do that one thing the best we can.

Looking up at the mountain

> "It is a journey. No one is ahead of you or behind you. You are not more advanced or less enlightened. You are exactly where you need to be. It's not a

> contest…it's life. We are all teachers and we are all students."
>
> **Unknown**

I know of a lot of people who set a huge goal and instead of being inspired they stand at the bottom and think, "God, I am hopeless. Look where I am. How am I ever going to get there? What was I thinking?" The person that we want to be is often the tyrannical judge of who we are now. This greater version of us puts its foot on the throat of who we are now, as if we are some loathsome individual. But the person we want to be has to be the one to praise us and give us a hand up. Be our nurturing mentor if it is to have the desired effect. What is this 'better' version of us if it is not our supportive and loving 'parent'?

Desire rises in us to give us direction, so that we keep paying attention to what will make the best use of our talents, not to highlight how dumb we were for wasting so much of our life, how lacking we are, or what a huge journey we have. Desires rise in us because we want a mindset shift. We are not lacking anything, and we **do know what it would feel like** to have this thing in our hands.

If we didn't know, we wouldn't have had the desire in the first place. That's what the desire is, a first taste of a feeling. We already know what it feels like or we wouldn't want the feeling to be stronger in us – wouldn't want it to become a more dominant part of our experience. It's a misconception in our perception if we allow ourselves to rest to long on our haunches, and say, "I am so far from where I want to be". Because there is nothing more certain in the world than us getting to where we want to be, if we keep moving towards the goal. And we are always closer than we think – we just have to change the story that has been unconsciously playing on repeat. The story we keep repeating out of habit, and never think to scrutinise with questions. What is possible for us cannot occur to us from the conscious level of mind.

What does Winnie the Poo say? "You're smarter than you think, and stronger than you know." That's because the mind we think with cannot know what we are capable of – it is not 'us'. It is not designed to think beyond the parameters of our personal history. We have to understand this so we become mistrusting enough of the nature of the thinking or conscious mind. We need an awareness of the nature of the subconscious mind we are sending instructions to. The part that alters perception – because that is all our goals being realised is – a shift in perception.

If we keep moving in that direction, we must arrive. Sometimes, it feels like the doldrums, and sometimes a slipstream. Sometimes, we even get the smarts to alter our direction because we find a better way or we get clearer on what matters to us. We find the old goal no longer suits us, and that is not the same as giving up. When we try for something better, and more suitable, more inspiring, we've just wised up, not given up.

Desire is so we hang our sails and grab our rudder, not so that we put ourselves behind anyone, or anything else. We are perfect, and we are discovering what we like every day. As Thich Nhat Hạnh says, "The path is the goal". It is not arriving at our goal that makes the world seem different. It is having the goal – it is having a sense of direction that changes the world for us and how we look at it. **We can never be finished – we never arrive.** We just keep striving and becoming more focused and clearer on what we want. Keep building our sense of control over how we are affected.

The will to conform

> "The opposite of courage is not cowardice, it's conformity."
>
> Rollo May

THE CONTROL CENTRE

This quote is also taken from the Earl Nightingale recording of 'The Greatest Secret'. I've listened to it again and again – it's awesome and if you've never heard it and if goal-setting is of interest to you, you'll love it too. Nightingale goes on to say, "And that's the problem with our society, people doing what everyone else is doing, without ever really knowing why".

A good deal of the confusion that exists in our world is because we are unaware of how deeply tribal our will to conform and belong is. Many people get offended by the fact that we are not as far removed from smart animals as we think. We are social and herd creatures – our need to stick together translates to 'following the crowd'. In our heart of hearts we are still driven by very primitive emotional needs. We are tribal people with tribal instincts. This is science, not opinion. We are driven at a deeply unconscious level to want to serve the tribe, something larger than ourselves. We want to belong to a community, and play our part in making that larger body as great as it can be. We all unconsciously look for an authority figure to lead us, steer the greater good and needs of the tribe. We are conditionally bound to look for and find these symbols of authority, and are programmed to 'obey'. Obey something we trust has the greater good in mind.

Even in our modern times, when our leadership seems so misdirected and corrupted, we instinctively entrust the greater needs of the tribe to an authority figure. We believe there is safety is in numbers – in sticking together. I'm not saying we are all mindless sheep, but we do have an unconscious will to belong, to be in the middle of the largest group. It stems back from our caveman days, where the big tribe, the one with the small army and the fortress around it, was either going to be our conqueror, or our leader. If we want to live, we get behind the fortress walls.

Humans are very clever and intuitive people though, and will always rebel against a hierarchy with flawed leadership. But our strongest will is to look for and obey those who give the appearance of authority. To trust that the important stuff is being taken care of by the people who are best qualified. If we sense that our leaders fall well short of this, they will not lead us for long.

We all want and need money for more than just our ability to feed, clothe, and house ourselves. Money is a symbol of power, luxury, and intelligence. The economy is the single unifying enterprise which our entire species agrees upon. Economic growth equates to human advancement. We all want jobs, money, and prosperity, but we are unaware of the inherent consequences of this measure of growth we are unconsciously serving. We are the servants to an unquenchable beast that does little to serve the broader interests of humanity.

There is no end to this measure of growth, just a mindless sense of an unsustainable ideal. Collectively we know this to be the case but individually we all want 'things' and success and so we must unconsciously endorse the system that ensures our own demise. We all want 'growth' and as such are willing to back anyone who provides this promise. The very top of the food chain has got this sweet little system set up, where all spending funnels upwards and makes the overlords richer and us more controllable. We want 'growth' so we must support the machine.

I'm not a conspiracy nut (oh well, I am, but I'm not going to expose myself here), and I'm not all doom and gloom. The reason I make the point about our will to conform is because it is a much stronger and more unconscious force than we are aware. The masses force us to the outer if we do anything unusual, or alternative. By our unconscious compliance to the 'group' we are the ones who are 'doing the bidding of the evil' – forcing anyone on the 'outer' back into the centre of the group. The global elite have us, the people, keeping this system of economic inequality in place, and most don't even know it. This money tree is tall, and we could scarcely ever be aware who is pulling the strings from the top, or the extent of the influence cast on our beliefs.

By our own conformity and the unconscious force we apply to those who live in any way alternatively, we keep the ant mine working. By our very nature we are the ones who unconsciously draw those we care about back into the herd – into the safety of numbers. It is a perfect system for those at the top of this money funnel because we are the ones who unconsciously ensure the compliance and shared values of the majority. That the economy remains our 'sacred lord' can never be bought into question. This is the unquestioned pursuit of what?

> "I'm called the poorest president, but I don't feel poor. Poor people are those who only work to try to keep an expensive lifestyle, and always want more and more."
>
> Jose Mujica, President of Uruguay

Our dreams, and what we add, don't have to, and shouldn't always, be about, "Is there a dollar in it? Can I sell it? Does everyone else think it's amazing?". The struggling artist is a cliché I know, but making something truly beautiful often means we have to be truer to ourselves than most people are.

Fewer people may see the value in the art, but the ones who do will appreciate it at a deeper level. If this isn't your idea of a dream, forgive me, but I had to make the point that the economy isn't some sacred God we all must pray to that is worthy of our undying devotion. Our 'art' doesn't have to be pleasing to everyone, or a bestseller. It has to come from us, not something we think they'll all like, and will sell.

Share your real self, and fewer people may appreciate you, but it reminds me of the meme I saw recently, "Even those who appear to ignore you are secretly inspired by you". Be different, because the world needs the difference you make, and it might just inspire those who thought they couldn't show what they really wanted to because it was too far left of centre.

LIVING BY ACCIDENT

Our society shows no signs that what we aspire to is inspired by wisdom, or sustainability. Do you think we will ever look back upon this time in history as if it was something we were proud of? Are we marching in support of something that resembles justice and equality? Or are our leaders just every man for himself, with us blindly in their wake?

Our world seems insane, and we would do well to not contribute to the insanity, or at least be considerate that what we add has some hallmarks of community. The money machine all filters up, and we feed it by our unconscious conformity. We feed the 'money machine' by believing there is no cause greater than our own needs being met. We all want money, and it would be nice to have lots, and be free to distribute it as we saw justly. But so many of us seem under some spell of having the boat, the house, the six-figure income, and only because it is the A-typical 'vision board' version of success. I think many of us unwittingly comply with this degradation of human values because we don't think to bring what matters to us most to the table. Are we blind in our agreement of what 'success' is measured by?

I am aware I'm not perfect, and I don't hate money, or the people who have it. I'm in absolute agreement with the premise that we don't help the poor by being one of them. I just think there is an underlying blind compliance to money being the central theme of what we all should aim for first, and then some thought given towards what else matters to you. I don't know – I don't have the answers – I just wanted this book to be, above all things, thought-provoking, and to question the status quo. As Gary V says, "How we earn our money, is more important than how much we earn".

> "A lie doesn't become truth, wrong doesn't become right, and evil doesn't become good, just because it is accepted by a majority."
>
> Rick Warren

Anyhow, I'll climb down off my soapbox again and get back to my goal-setting point. Is what we are doing or want to do helping anyone? That what we do helps someone out should be more important than the lifestyle picture we have on our vision board. That we are solving someone's problem should be the most essential aspect of our goal-setting process. When what we do serves something bigger than our own needs and comes from an authentic will to help, I think we are unconsciously fueled by the energy of all those we intend to help.

Buried treasure

> "The purpose of life is not to be happy, but to be useful, to be honourable, to be compassionate, to have it make some difference that you have lived and lived well."
>
> — Ralph Waldo Emerson

I have claimed that our state of mind is our greatest treasure, but here I want to extend on that idea. Because our state of mind is really buoyed by what we want to do – by the relentless pursuit of something that matters deeply to us. Our mood is more valuable than any event or material we can own, but it is 'lit' by the reason we want to be here.

To get to that greater state of mind requires us to go deeper into ourselves than might ordinarily occur to us, but the pay-off is its own reward. Going deeper is not something we're accustomed to – the benefit isn't screamingly obvious. And unless we are the victims of gut-wrenching depression, or have endured a sudden and traumatic life change, it won't occur to us that our only real treasure lies within. Deep within. At the deep bottom of our values ocean lies a treasure unlike any we might have consciously envisioned. To find something that matters to us as much as our own life does is the surest cure to sadness – the only defense to the terror of our own mortality. We can only handle the weight of our own vulnerable existence by this deeper sense of meaning. We are vulnerable to the terror we could soon be gone unless, while we are here, we are working on something that has meaning for us. It is the need of every soul to believe there was a point to our lives – to know we were here for some reason.

Why do you do what you do? We are designed to help each other – we are wired for community. It is said that the only gauge of a soul's development is compassion. And that is because kindness is what it takes for a species to survive. It is deeply embedded into our DNA that doing good for others makes us feel good. Compassion and helping people makes sense to us at a deep level. Even being witness to acts of kindness releases the chemicals in us that are as vital to our health and well-being as a good night's sleep. We are built for it. We get all sorts of feel-good chemicals released in us when we help and touch people (physically and spiritually). It was ingrained in us at an evolutionary level that kindness resonates with us – appeals to our deeper sensibilities. We are made of love so we are born to love, want to witness love and to give love.

It probably does more for us to lift others up and encourage people as it does for them. We receive blasts of oxytocin (the love drug) not just from touch and intimacy, but even if we witness acts of kindness, or if we watch a heartwarming video clip. It was built into our DNA and we would never have thrived to the swelling population we now have if we weren't hardwired to help each other out. It appeals to our deeper sensibilities that it is smarter/in our self-serving interest to care about other people. We thrive on the chemical release that can only come from seeing our efforts make a difference to other people. I'll even go as far as saying that I'm certain it is why even though many religions seemingly contradict the truth of their foundations – of peace, charity and kindness – they remain with us, because the ideals on which they are built resonate with such a deep part of our nature.

The natural highs

A very quick mention about those natural neurotransmitters that make us happy and are so crucial to overall body health. I think it's important to mention because there is far more to our good health than eating the right foods, exercise and sleep. We are designed to feel at our best when we doing good things for people. It is as natural a part of our heart health as any of the physical things we do. We are evolutionarily designed to contribute and help. It is more than just a warm and fuzzy feeling inside. Helping people releases a chemical in us that we crave just as much as any drug or feel good habit.

Endorphins – this is a natural chemical released into our system that helps us overcome the stress and pain associated with strenuous physical activities. A natural pain balm that can last many hours after the actual exercise, relieving pain and producing a natural high that elevates our thinking to coincide with the pain-free and care-free state of the body.

Dopamine – is released when we receive or expect a reward. It is what we get when we complete a task, or reach some sort of goal. So it is very important for us that our goals are measurable – that is, we know when we get there. This chemical being released helps us to understand reward reinforcement and whether what we get is worth going back for more of. It can be associated with everything from praise and recognition to enjoying a good slice of pizza. Even our likes on social media are said to provide a spike in dopamine. Dopamine deficiencies are often associated with people becoming addicted to drugs, as it is a far easier method of getting our fix than having to work for it.

Serotonin – is a key factor in our mood balance, social behavior, appetite and digestion, sleep, memory, and even sexual desire. To increase our serotonin levels we need to eat and sleep properly. Make sure we get our dose of sunshine and take steps to lower stress levels.

Oxytocin – is the bonding hormone, helping us to build and value stronger relationships with people. When a mother breastfeeds her baby, both release high amount of oxytocin, leading to strong bonding between them. It is also the reason for strong bonding between couples, and why we are attracted to people with a good sense of humor. Laughter releases high amounts of oxytocin.

My only real point I wanted to make here was the **oxytocin**. We are wired to build strong bonds with people, and share in their success' and failures. There is a high that we can only get through contributing to, and praising the efforts of, others. It's a chemical that is far more crucial to our health than we think. But because many of us have felt cheated, undervalued and threatened we have closed our bank from making any withdrawals. And it is our health that suffers. We must give for the sake of giving, not for the sake of what is in it for us. And not money, but our sincere concern. Quite selfishly it is good for us, so don't be a stinge. It is a crucial aspect of giving our lives a deeper sense of meaning. It is more valuable to us than the material stuff we accumulate. We need meaning and purpose far more than we do fame or money. And to get that wrong can be far more costly to us emotionally than we know.

More than money, fame or recognition we really all want what only oxytocin can deliver.

Many of the rich and famous are in therapy or rehab because this hasn't yet occurred to them. And this is why many of us in developed countries suffer a range of mental health issues that don't exist in poorer communities. Poorer communities stick together and rely on each other. They get their sustenance from relationships more than all of the other stuff we are chasing. They care about each other – they have to or they probably won't survive on their own. We are spoilt by comparison, but don't sense the true cost of this competitive and comparatively superficial social structure.

Seven levels deep

To get the best feelings available to a human and our fix of feel good chems, we have to go a level deeper within ourselves to find what really matters. I've heard this little exercise a few places now, but I first heard it in Dean Graziosi's book 'Millionaire success habits'. It's an exercise where a coach proceeds to ask you the same question over and over on top of the answer you had just given last time. **"Why is that important to you?"** It's called seven levels deep, and as you might have guessed this same question is asked seven times, requiring you to go deeper within your reasons to get to the heart of why what's important to you, really is important to you. What is it that truly matters most?

I'd like to say a fun little exercise, but for all intents and purpose if it doesn't arouse some tears, you probably haven't been honest enough, or gone deep enough. And that's what is asked for when we want to find this 'treasure' of ours – finding our 'why' that makes us cry. And as Dean suggests, there is a point in the questioning process where we become deeply reflective – maybe even back into our childhood. There comes a point where we are cornered and have to move from our heads and into our hearts, to answer what it is that is most important to us. If the exercise doesn't inspire you to change what you do, I'm certain you'll do whatever it is you were doing with more vigour, and enthusiasm than you used to.

And honestly, I'm not claiming to be some 'Good Samaritan' – I haven't thrown this exercise in to try to make everyone feel like we have to be do-gooders to feel good about ourselves. But if we want something more than the buzz we get from a few coldies, we can only get it from lending someone a hand with something they found really hard. Maybe it's within our own families, and maybe it is wider spread, but it doesn't matter.

That we tried to help when we thought it was needed in the way we could is what matters. When I asked this of myself, it was the frustration I felt when I saw people giving their power away to things out of their control. Unwittingly sacrificing control of their outcomes by leaving their lives up to the programming. Turning their power over by not asking for specifics of how they wanted it to be different, and for whatever reason. Maybe they thought asking for things to be better was pointless, or it did no good to ask. I don't know all of other people's reasons, but I think we have far more power to change our outcomes than we exercise.

> "Who looks outside dreams. Who looks inside awakes."
> Carl Jung

When he is troubled he will marvel

It is our problems that bring us reward – that allow us to know ourselves and go deeper into understanding who we are and what we are like. It is only in having troubles to overcome that we can better know ourselves and what we are capable of. It is only when we have an overwhelming mountain in front of us that we can find our genius – find the lever that will shift the seemingly immovable. There is nothing in this world more worthy of your interest and will to understand than your own subconscious mind. There is no one more deserving of your kindness than you. We have to be our own heroes, and be emotionally invested in our lives, our outcomes.

Without the big issue we can never know ourselves, contemplate our strengths, or know what the 'lever' that lies beside us was ever really for. It is by our troubles that we contemplate the truer nature of ourselves, the universe we are in, and how the two combine into a dance that allow what may seem impossible to be seen and done. Our struggles are there because of us – we made them for us because we knew we had the resources to overcome them. We knew how to take the beast down – to move the mountain. It's all moving for us – so that we would know our power to effect change.

CHAPTER SUMMARY

- We either live with intention – that is ask for specific differences – or we allow our lives to happen by accident. And as you might have guessed it rarely, if ever, feels like something we wanted.
- Living intentionally is how we both impact the life-driving program and how we enable the world to serve our needs.
- We see what we look for, and when we are looking to find something different, we see something that was invisible to us prior to intention. We have literally changed the physical make-up of the world.
- Our lives are either left to the default settings of the program and happen seemingly randomly, or are shaped by our will and happen on purpose.
- We can only know what things mean when put into perspective by our goals.
- The universe can only 'show us the magic' when we ask for something we want.
- The entire universe is all moving for you – in relationship to your vibration and how you have asked for your experience to be different to the one you've been having. The universe wants to show you your ability to effect change. To be in the centre and the cause of what happens.
- It is only by going deeper into ourselves and what we value that we can find the greatest treasure of our lives.

CHAPTER 10
Next Level Living

"What you get by achieving your goals is not as important as what you become by achieving your goals."

Henry David Thoreau

One life – one chance?

We have all heard the saying – we've only got one life – there are no rehearsals. Kind of makes it feel like some scarily finite experience, where something going wrong could haunt us forever, and a missed opportunity might possibly never ever present again in our life. They try to convince us that mistakes can be more or less fatal. That we've got this one shot and then…you blew it – might as well give up. Life's not a rehearsal, and not taking a chance, even before we are properly prepared, could well be the last one you ever get. Sorry, but I just don't think it's like that at all.

I think life is a rehearsal – a chance to get it better and better, where preparation is constantly meeting opportunity, and giving us the chance to get it right, again and again. Like in 'Groundhog Day', where although he keeps finding himself in the same situations, he is always better prepared – he is always getting it closer to perfect. It might not seem like we get every practice perfect, but it is always perfect for where we are at the time. We are always precisely – with inch perfect precision – exactly where we are supposed to be.

I definitely believe we exist on levels in our lives, in accordance with our commitment, focus and our willingness to be vulnerable. Courage is defined by our willingness to be vulnerable – to expose ourselves to risks and judgement. But missing an opportunity needn't be as terminal as we're sometimes lured into thinking it should be. I agree that sometimes we have worked so hard to get to opportunities that we've got a lot on the line, but we do our best – we prepare as best we can and give it our all. The affirmation I prefer is that we either 'win or we learn'. Those 'soul-destroying' last chances are less common than I think we're encouraged to believe.

I'm more from the school of thought that chances always come around, and we are always preparing to better meet them. We see something we think would be great to be able to do and we begin preparing – and we practice until opportunity meets preparation. And if we fall down, an even better opportunity is just on the horizon – an even more suitable one. It might not have the same accolades, but it means more to us.

Why do we doom ourselves to disappointment, believing opportunity is so finite that it might never happen again? I believe we'll get where we are supposed to be. Opportunities circle us until we're ready to take the leap. Till preparation is a perfect match to opportunity. I'm more convinced that opportunities exist in cycles. They circle us – always presenting, always asking us – are you ready to jump yet? Are you ready to play at the next level, where more of you is required? Higher stakes, and greater rewards.

NEXT LEVEL LIVING

A game of levels

We're all familiar with those 'platform' video games. The ones where you either have to jump barrels, or battle monsters or whatever. But the gist is we ascend through levels that require a higher set of skills. We practice on the lower skill levels till we get to the end of the level where that big jump is required – the one that is harder than all we've attempted, but will take us to the next platform of the game. A new level where the required skill level is higher – more is asked of us, and we have to be more focused to get through. It's harder but we learn, and we improve, and we get better.

Do we make the jump? Not always, and we go back to the start of the level and we practice it all over again. Next time we get to the end jump, we're better – we are more prepared, we are wiser and we are, maybe, even a little frustrated with that level so there is more at stake in that final jump.

That's my idea of how our life works. We exist on a level until it bores us and we want something more. And sometimes we have to try many times before we get that break – until we make that jump. Until we learn the skills required to live on the next level. But there's nothing to be ashamed of in where we are, and our life will not feel all that different soon after we achieve our goal. Any form of 'missed' opportunity either wasn't exactly the right one for us, or is coming around again very soon. Coming to meet a wiser and higher skilled version of us. We are never starting from scratch – we're starting from experience.

I think we see something happening, or someone performing, and it raises the desire in us. "I'd love to be able to do that." And then we learn, and we practice – we prepare for that day when we are ready to take a shot. Maybe it's not the first time we've taken that shot, but it won't be the last either, because it's what we want more than anything. We exist on a plateau, until it's our time to rise. But this game is never 'over'. We can never reach our destination. The same motivations that got us to the goal will almost be immediately looking past where we have arrived, and setting the next goal. Our journey is never complete so it is unwise to hang all of our hopes on the illusion of what a dream will bring us. The taste is never as sweet as what we thought it would be, so we must always love the practice as much as the prize.

When we get to the next level it feels uncomfortable for a bit, until it all just starts to feel, well, 'normal'. We arrive, and maybe it's everything we always thought it would be, but more often it is not. Opportunities circle us like sharks – they always come around until we're ready to go 'next level'. Desires are raised in us so that we prepare, and when we're prepared it will happen. The flower comes before the fruit as they say. Nature has to take its course. The very last thing to present on the tree is the fruit. We just have to be patient enough to practice, and resilient enough to pick ourselves up and have another go.

In this age of instant gratification, no one seems willing to stick stuff out long enough to get that greater reward. No one seems prepared to do their life's work because we are so desperate for 'results' and recognition. We get side-tracked and interested in the next thing, and then see some flashing lights, and think, "Oh, what's that over there?" all the while never being able to commit to that thing that matters to us – that might lead to something truly meaningful for us.

We say "I'm **'just'** a blah, blah, blah **at the 'moment'**" – and it never feels like we are good enough. Granted, there may be the insinuation that "it's not my passion" or "it's not what I'm most suited to", but from what I've seen most people treat what they do as if it is something to be ashamed of. The number of people I've met who say with a sense of self-assured pride that they're a 'whatever', like it is enough, are few and far between. And sure, we'd rather talk about what interests us, but for the majority, what we are doing is a means to an end. And why? We want more accolades, no one cares about what we do – there is a lack of status and we don't feel we are making an impact. We get that feeling because we can't see the big picture. Can't see how the moment we're in relates to the bigger picture. I think very few people 'get it' – as in, realise that to do something 'better', we have to lift our chin up every now and again.

Very few people like what they do and I think it has a lot to do with society's version of what success means. Success is, "Hey look at me and what I'm doing?". If no one's watching what we're doing then it is only 'right' that we should be ashamed of ourselves – right?

I confess that I'm not really one to preach – I'm often guilty of feeling like I'm not able to give all of me to the job I do – that it's not what I prefer to be doing. But within the job there is still a lot about it that I like doing. Mine is probably the type of job lots of people would love to have – I do like my job, but every chance I get, I'm watering my bamboo. Watering the bamboo is a metaphor that is often used when we undertake work that may take a long period to see any results from. I know I'll get there because it is what I love doing. I'd do it if I thought I'd never make a living out of it, because writing helps me get clearer. Helps me focus and keeps the unwanted from my mind. It's my form of puzzle-solving. Joining words and sentences together to try to get them to mean something.

And everyone's got their thing, I think we just have to stop caring if anyone is watching, because it saps the life right out of our work. Lots of people are depressed because they have no connection to what they're doing, and they don't have the time or energy after work to put into their 'passion project'. They can't see the big picture of the puzzle piece they're doing now. Lots of people are carried along by meaningless distractions because they can't put in time without a result. They can never build the 'pyramid' or 'water the bamboo', because they either lack the discipline to see longer term outcomes, or they listen to the BS other people feed them about what they are doing. We have to pay the price in our effort for anything ever to pay us back.

THE CONTROL CENTRE

We can do anything?

We've been told we can do anything we set our mind to. And while I agree, we also have to understand something of the nature of the conscious mind. We have to lead it little by little into believing the things that are at first difficult for it to believe. We either wade the mind into deeper waters, or we somehow manage to trick it into believing we've been here many times before – as in the acting 'as if' strategy. We can't do anything – we can do anything that falls within our scope of believable. Granted we can work towards things – we can build on the skills we learnt yesterday – we can continue to ascend towards a longer-term vision for our life, but 'we can do anything'?

We can't do anything; we can do anything that feels familiar. The subconscious is like a big scared elephant – we have to coax it little by little into the unknown, encouraging it as we go. We may consciously know how much better our proposals will make our life, but we have to work with this cumbersome and shy 'giant'. The subconscious mind needs to be led – never forced or hated on. The subconscious always fears we are setting ourselves up for a fall, and even if those fears are seen to be completely irrational to us, it still holds the power. It holds that little remote-control device of our emotions. We can do anything, but we have to understand and appeal to the sceptical-seeming nature of the heart's frequency and work with it.

We have to make the changes we want incrementally, break the big goal into smaller steps until they seem familiar. And before we know it, we might be doing something completely different and yet it all feels completely normal. We cannot just quit our current life and walk into an entirely new venture with a seamless segue, with no stress at all. We cannot jump having never even flapped our wings.

Similarly, it is why affirmations are so effective. They don't change anything immediately, because at first it is just words – the effect is ever so faint. But the mind can never ignore anything that is repeated – the words we use have to become integrated into our reality. The sub-mind is bound by its nature to affiliate any suggestion made to it repeatedly as a fact – as taken for granted that this is true, this is how things are. It is now no longer something that has to be forced – it becomes a natural part of our experience. Our perception has shifted.

I like the smoking example because I know it is something lots of people find difficult. But it is impossible to repeat to yourself 100 times a day that "I am a non-smoker" without it starting to infect your program. And what happens when your program becomes infected? Your cigarettes start to taste awful. You will get halfway through one and find you can't finish it – or you'll find yourself sticking one in your mouth to light up and thinking, "What the hell am I doing. I don't even smoke". It just won't feel right to you anymore to live with the conflict. But if being smoke-free is something that appeals to you – keep repeating the affirmation. Eventually it just won't make sense to put one in your mouth. I admit this is probably a little bit of a torturous way to go about quitting – always having it on your mind.

I've just used this example to illustrate something of the nature of mind. It is probably far better to not have the smoking thing on your mind at all if you can manage. It can be made all the easier if any thought of smoking is replaced by another preference. Another means to satisfy the need that smoking filled. An affirmation stated in the future place of "Now that I am smoke free," or, "Back before I kicked the habit". The thought of cigarettes will eventually enter our mind less and less, but it would be wise to begin any program as difficult as a quit smoking one with support and mindset guides in place. But affirmations work. It is not a question of might work, it is how the mind works.

Trusting in the process

Whenever we have an idea of something we like, or something we'd like to do, we get all excited, and then the reality sets in and our enthusiasm starts to wane. If we really believe in its value, and want it

THE CONTROL CENTRE

to come true we have to be patient, and follow through with practice – probably hours of practice. We have to take that step we know as forwards, and take it now. We have to trust in the process – we don't know how long it will take. It will sometimes be fast and sometimes slow, but we are moving in an intentional direction – that's all that matters. Because when we do this, we mould the world to suit our outcomes. Trust in the plan, and that the universe wants this for us too. Everything grows from a seed and our idea is no different. We can only take the action in front of us. Getting frustrated or overwhelmed will only breed events and evidence that match the feeling.

We have to accept where we are with humility, and take the first steps, always believing in our ability and being our own encourager – sometimes we will be the only one we have. Opportunities come, allowing us to be wiser and better prepared for the next assault, or find what suits us better. Make it your life's work instead of this year's work and you will always have a steadier rudder. You will always be building on those previously acquired skills, instead of half starting things and never finishing them. We have to finish something if we are ever able to feel like we can do anything. We are then adding to something monumental – every little step is a block in our pyramid. So no matter how boring or pointless or disheartened we feel in the step we are taking at the moment, we see the big picture of what we are adding to.

I recall the story where there were three bricklayers working on the same site. Each was asked what they were doing, and the first replied, "I'm earning my quid to put food on the table". The second said, "I'm laying blocks – what does it look like I'm doing?" But the third exclaimed, "I am building the grandest cathedral in the land". All were working on the same project but only the last was engaged in the grand vision of his work and the big picture of what he was a part of. Needless to say it changed how he went about his day. When we know what the small pieces are adding to, none of it can seem boring, and it can make the largest of pains seem a little more tolerable.

NEXT LEVEL LIVING

Are you building a cathedral, or just laying blocks? When what we do is part of the big picture of our life we do each 'boring' task with precision and patience. You will get to the next level – there is nothing more certain if we keep moving in one direction, but it probably won't feel all that different to where you imagine you are now. We will have those small victories but it will eventually all just feel 'normal'. Wherever we find ourselves – no matter the level we reach – there will always be another level.

We have to trust in the process – it will sometimes evolve in ways that don't resemble our plan. But most importantly, never forget the power of taking a leg up. If we have a desire, a dream – there is always someone who's done it who would like nothing more than to help us avoid the pitfalls they made. Most of the time we'll have to pay them, but what is the price you would pay to skip time, and heartache, and frustration. Take the help – there is nothing like 'paying' to get us to pay attention, and it can save us years of wasted time. To be guided by someone who is where you want to be, and take those enviable shortcuts – well only we can decide for ourselves what it is worth.

It seems we're happy to spend a lot of money on how we look and what we wear etc., but it rarely occurs to us how much we would gain from the investment in our growth and emotional wellness.

> "If one advances confidently in the direction of his dreams, and endeavours to live the life he has imagined, he will meet with a success unexpected in common hours."
>
> **Henry David Thoreau**

Effective affirmations – it has already happened

It is recommended when we are constructing any affirmations that they be spoken in a language that doesn't resemble the want but rather the state of already having. This will be explored in more detail in the next chapter, but as I've made some reference to the effectiveness of affirmations, I wanted to make mention of how to construct effective ones here. Imagining the state of already having the thing we want is the most effective use of our time and energy towards getting the results we want. So it's useful to remember this tactic when we are crafting our affirmations.

I've mentioned that our goals should always be stated in the affirmative – never say I don't want, but that I want its opposite. And the same goes for our affirmations. If we are to affirm that I am rich, confident and successful, this carries the suggestion to mind that we know that **we are not this yet** (or why would we be repeating it to ourselves?). Repeating this type of affirmation carries the implication it is something we want, but don't yet have.

The aim is to suggest to the mind the reality we want to be in is already here. Using the above affirmation will result in the outcome eventuating, but it is a slower boat to where we want to be. Speak as if it has already happened. Better to make the suggestion to mind something along the lines of us already being rich and successful. "Now that I have all the money and time I want, I will devote myself to…". Speak as if it has already happened and the mind has no ability to dispute what we tell it is true. It is compelled to make our reality 'seem' that way.

CHAPTER SUMMARY

- Opportunities circle us until we have built the skills to live on the next level. Desires are launched in us and we begin to prepare.
- Never fret that it is too late, or that there will never be another chance, or that missed opportunities are fatal in achieving our goals – we are always where we are supposed to be, with pin-point accuracy.
- Life won't automatically seem 'better' when we do leap. In fact, it won't be long before everything will seem just as boringly normal as it was before. It is just how the mind works. Our dreams coming true won't solve all our problems. There is always another level.
- We can do anything when we understand the reluctant and stubborn nature of mind and work with it to encourage ourselves towards new landscapes.
- Everything is learnable when broken into a series of measurable and repeatable steps.
- Let everything add to your life's goal, and you will never feel bored by the step you are taking in the moment.

CHAPTER 11
How Would it Feel?

> "It is not what you want that you attract; you attract what you believe to be true."
>
> **Neville Goddard**

This chapter is about validating the power and effect of imagined emotional states as a very real and tangible manifestation tool. Not just a 'real' tool – the most effective use of our mind and energy there is in allowing favourable conditions into our life. If we want something, we only have to feel like we have it and persist in the re-creation of that feeling. If thoughts are things, as suggested in the movie 'The Secret', then feelings are a force. There is nothing more 'real' than the effect of being able to imagine ourselves to already be in the situations we desire. The true meaning of prayer is to embody the emotion – to live in the faith of the thing being here already. We sense/know in our hearts what it would feel like. Our ability to live in the feeling, and validate it as a usable force, opens doorways in our perception and our 'way of seeing' that we can never fully appreciate from a conscious level.

In order to fully appreciate the power of imagined feeling states, let's recap a quick definition of what attraction is and how it works. The principle of attraction effectively suggests that our state of mind skews our perception of what is real – what seems to be true. We only see in the world – our attention is drawn towards – events and opportunities that match/support how we feel. The only things that become 'real' for us are the things that match our vibration, and confirm what we believe to be true.

Who are we Being?

> "Don't dream it, be it."
> Frank N Furter – The Rocky Horror Picture Show

It is our ability to imagine ourselves to already 'be' the person whose dream has come true that allows the supporting evidence to mount in our favour. We don't 'want' to be because we already are. We don't attract what we want, we attract what we are – what we feel like we already have. To want for something is to suggest to the mind that we don't yet have it, and forms an emotionally suggestive pattern that is always pushing the desire away from us. The program makes the assumption that we want to keep wanting – to continue wanting and the 'carrot' continues to dangle just beyond our reach. Our 'genie' is not a dream-granting super being but an emotional state – the state of knowing precisely what it would feel like to be in possession of our desire, and living in the trust of its arrival.

When we be it, then we can do it

I'm sure most are familiar with the Be, Do, Have philosophy. That first we must 'be' it, then we can do it, and then we will have it. We have to start from the place of being the person who has the thing we want.

The feeling of having changes our perception and what we expect to find in the world at a subconscious level. It turns us away, or 'blinds from our view', what we no longer wish to automatically see. What first requires vigilance, and conscious effort, soon becomes effortless, automatic and 'normal'. To consider this to be 'effort' is to lose sight of this being the simplest way to get a pay-off. To move from the state of wanting to the state of having only requires our imagination, and the commitment to keep it on our mind. 'This is real and it feels great'. This is the most effective game we can play. "What would it feel like?" is not a question but a subconscious command – a set of clear instructions. The imagining is inherent in the question.

It has been suggested that it is just as easy to create a castle as it is a button. It just depends on what is believable for us, which will obviously continue to grow when we task the universe with showing us what is possible.

The dark side of attraction

We don't mind being cranky, worried, or unhappy. Being any way we have become accustomed to. That is until we realise the full consequences of how we are being – the circumstances they give life to.

When a desire is first born in us it is but a tiny strand of a wish. It must be consistently fed with the confidence that "whatever I desire is within my reach". The first instance of desire is flimsy and unsupported – it is up against the powerful momentum of 'how things have been'. As stated in the chapter titled 'The secret agenda of mind', we must remain mindful of the gravitation towards the old patterns. The world we see will still come from the strength of the pattern we lived in before the desire was born in us. We see through the filter of how we currently feel, so these changes are often gradual. And we only thwart their ability to surprise us by our continued insistence that "nothing has changed – nothing is happening". The new feeling states must be nurtured and protected like a young sapling. We have to be vigilant and faithful to keep the feeling alive – keep working on the feeling. Keep making the suggestion of the new reality we now live in. We are constantly shifting how we feel to entertain a new reality. And it is our only job is to look for the differences we want to see and to 'look away' from the old.

The gravity towards the old patterns, and the instinct to keep those old and 'trusted' patterns in place, is also attraction. Attraction is how the mind skews perception to maintain the current vibration. Our persistence is what keeps us on the track of noticing the changes we asked for – of things changing for the better. We are in a trade-off with the mind. We are always in a negotiation – convincing 'big mind' this is not as dangerous as it seems – that there are countless benefits of the 'new'. The old patterns are always sceptical of the new, insisting, "Just shut up, it is a stupid idea". And it is what we hear as our voice of reason. This is the real travesty of our lives – we are listening to a mind that is 99%+ driven by habitual thought, and have come to trust in it as truth. We are relying on a mind that is almost exclusively driven by unquestioned habit to tell us how the world is. Yet we think we are in control.

We are stuck wondering why we are so bored and frustrated with how things are. And it is because we can't tell the difference between the two opposing voices in our heads. We don't know which one to trust – it sounds like the same voice whether it comes from the truth-teller or the liar. The one that knows our abilities and the truth to be an invention, and the one that so reasonably talks us out of the changes that would be good for us and that we are quite capable of. We listen to the conscious mind as if it is an authority on 'what is', unaware it is running off our own preconceived limitations. Beliefs are weightless, but they are mighty heavy in how they restrict us and limit our ability to feel as we wish we could.

It is this 'evil' voice of reason that puts the so called 'obstacles' in our way. It puts stuff in our way as a means of testing us – to get our

HOW WOULD IT FEEL?

reassurance that this is still what I really want. Change makes no sense to the old pattern, and it will do everything it can at a subconscious level to distract and discourage us. It will sometimes come as a frustration, and it will sometimes appear as a perceived failure. As that all too reasonable voice that says, "It is just not possible for us", or, "It would not be at all stupid if we just gave up".

> "I'm sorry for how I made you feel. That you thought it wasn't possible for you. It was just a cycle that I thought was working."
>
> **The Devil**

We don't get that this voice of reason is coming from inside us, or see that its rationale doesn't resemble truth. It doesn't make any sense, yet we are all ears. We don't recognise it as our pattern regulator. It comes across as making perfect sense. The dream killer is the old pattern, and it has come in through the 'back door' as that voice that says, "Things are fine just the way they are". Our world exists in a state of impermanence – in a state of constant flux and change, and we'd be crazy not to make those changes move in our favour. The old patterns are strong and their job is to talk us out of change, making it sound perfectly logical to quit, and disguise the fact of the voice coming from us. The old patterns manufacture all sorts of stories up that aren't true in the name of keeping the old pattern alive. Stories like, "It will upset the dynamics of the tribe", or, "People won't like it", most of which are the very definition of BS.

Are people incorrect in their assumptions of what is true? No, they are not. Because truth is relative to what we have experienced – "It is true in my experience". And they will fight to defend what they believe to be true. We will fight to defend our own limitations like our life depends on it. But don't worry, no one's going to take them off you. But when we are ready, we will realise – we don't need the safety blanket of our limitations anymore, and they aren't keeping us safe.

The old patterns have a 'job' to make sure we don't entertain change and see it as a much higher risk than it truly is. Convince us that an expanding universe is actually contracting and getting worse. But things are getting better and they always will. Sometimes things must seem like they are getting worse in order to get better, but we are always being called – being drawn towards higher states. We get wiser, we improve, we get clearer on what we like and that is the definition of 'smarter', or growth. Often our growth happens without us even realising, we just look up one day and acknowledge, "I'm a different person because that kind of stuff just doesn't bother me anymore" or whatever the case may be. But we can play a much more conscious role in this process when we are aware of it. Aware both of the natural expansion, and the old pattern trying desperately to preserve itself and convince us nothing has changed – and that change is risky.

Validating emotional states

If we are going to devote any time to this wishy-washy practice – if we are to elevate it in the list of our priorities – we must first convince ourselves of the real and transformative effect of these 'daydreams with a purpose'. We have to shift the perception towards the idea that these 'daydreams' are the most credible and valid use of our time. Yes, it requires some 'faith' – some belief in the forces unseen. In the supernatural ability of how we feel to shift our perception and with it the physical universe. **I don't believe that realising emotion as a force is something that should in anyway be considered to be 'based in faith'.** We are moving into a dimensional awareness where we must understand our state of mind to be a reality-altering force. How we feel moves the physical world – and it is what religions have always been tasked to inform us.

Religions brought our species from infancy to adolescence, but we are grown-ups now. It is no longer sufficient to regard emotional states as ineffectual, based on faith, or the 'result' of the conditions we live in. Or that they are out of our control, because emotions are how we control the world.

HOW WOULD IT FEEL?

To take the wheel of our 'life', meaning to be in better control of how we feel, we have to know what we are driving. We have to be able to validate the power of imagined emotional states. Imagining we already are in the type of world we would like to be in is hands down the single greatest skill worthy of our time and learning. In order for us to change our life, this shift in awareness has to become rooted in our beliefs.

Karma is instant

Karma is not some divine system of punishment. Certainly, if we lack empathy of how we have made others feel, it is very likely we will one day be reminded. As a prerequisite to our expansion, we must become ever more aware of our effect on others. But karma is not some tally we keep of good deeds so that no harm will ever come to us – it is the energy we send out and the nature of how it returns to us. Karma is our energy – karma is our state of mind – the effects of which are instant. We don't have to wait for the physical evidence of our dreams coming true to live in a pleasing state of mind. When we can imagine something as real, we are already there in our hearts and will immediately sense the shift in the way the world responds to us. It is not a matter of time but clarity of what defines the dream, and a commitment to imagining the feeling.

The circumstance we think/perceive/imagine we are in now is a direct reflection of our dominant vibration. If we have not manifested the life we want yet, it's because we are not a match to those things. We are living more in conditioning than consciousness, but our feelings can't be forced. They have to be persuaded – they have to be patiently courted. We must become one with the new vibration. We cannot make a harmonious home by aggressive demands, but by being at harmony ourselves. The subconscious mind is our heart - we don't say to it, "Do what I say" – we say, "Wouldn't it be nice?". That is the art of negotiation.

We cannot persuade others to our way of thinking until we understand theirs. And we can neither make those same demands on ourselves, "I want you to be happier" – we have to give ourselves over to the greater part of mind, by passively asking, "What would it take? What would you most like to be doing to feel happier?". We are not the tyrannical leaders of our minds; we are working in unison with them.

> "Happy people like what's happening."
> — Michael Bell

Our challenge is to notice the small changes and keep the faith that what we want is coming. To place our order and not keep 'checking the letterbox' asking where it is and putting the same order in again, or our faith becomes weakened. It is by saying, "I can already feel it now" – "I'm not concerned for how things seem". I am one with them, and at peace with how things are. When we are okay with how things are, we are free to direct the energy flow more easily than if we reject or resist the situation we 'seem' to be in. It's not as real as we think, and we have come to these conclusions for reasons far beyond our range of knowing. Make your peace with however you find your present, if you want to be able to re-mould reality to a chosen form.

I am a student

So, if this stuff truly works, then why don't I have millions of dollars and live on a yacht? Like most people, I'm a student, not a master. These are the conclusions I've borrowed from extensive reading on the subject that appears to be common across the board in all of the material I've encountered. But this makes a lot of sense to me – it resonates with me. It has existed throughout history and come full circle, to the forefront of our experience. I cannot 'prove' the reality of attraction; I just believe it. Attraction is based on insight. It requires a leap of faith. Am I, in my position, qualified to tell you this works and you should do it? Am I the living proof of how powerful imagined emotional states are? For a lot of people, probably not, but that certainly won't change my enthusiasm for sharing this, because of the inherent healing capacity I believe it carries.

I know what I want and I'm working towards it. I am miles ahead of how I felt just ten short years ago. I am secure and happy in my relationship, health, work, and family life. I am more financially secure than I ever really thought was possible. Ten years ago, I had nothing. But with the values I've come to nurture, the truth I've come to realise. I have no desire to impress people with 'things' either. I think all that 'six and seven figure income' hype, and our model for success itself, is a shallow bunch of bullshit. I have a six-figure income, but I'd rather you were impressed by my sense of empathy, purpose, and commitment. And in those, I've improved dramatically.

I'm relatively new at putting these principles into practice, but I am more than just a little inspired at how far I believe this will take me. My work, family life and health all need work and are improving, but I can imagine how good it will feel, and I keep that feeling as a strong focus at the forefront of my life.

> "If people looked at the stars each night, they'd live a lot differently. When you look into infinity, you realise that there are more important things than what people do all day."
> — Bill Watterson

The New Thought movement

You won't find anyone in the personal development field who doesn't use the principles of attraction as a baseline ingrained in every aspect of their work – we have to know how it would feel for it to become our reality. To act as though we already have what we used to want. Convincing ourselves that we already are who we want to become is the common thread connecting all of these ideas. Fake it till you make it, or rather, till you 'become it'. When we be it, then we can do it, then we can have it. We are not tricking our brain as much as we are introducing it to new ideas; trying on a new suit that we think will suit us better. We are not lying to ourselves when we live with intention. We are 'inventing' who we want to be, and are vigilant in our description of who that person is.

The 'Law of Attraction' is the buzz of this era, and as I've suggested it is an idea that runs deep into human history. What was once cryptically hidden in scripture and sacred teachings has now entered the mainstream. It is a global shift in awareness. The gurus, prophets and seers of old all offered us a similar insight into how the mysteries of perception work. Imagining feeling states is the unifying core in all personal development work, and the common theme of religions as well. The segue between ancient teachings and what we are using now as a 'less cryptic' version of the Law of Attraction began as what is referred to as the New Thought, or Mind Cure movement.

The New Thought movement began in the 1830s by a man by the name of Phineas Quimby, an American mesmerist and healer, who noticed the curative effects of riding his horse. How the elation and adrenaline rush of riding his horse suppressed some of the symptoms of his illness.

He spent a lifetime investigating the connection between mind and body, our mental state's effect on outcomes. He was an early mentor of Mary Baker Eddy who founded Christian Science movement. New Thought grew into what we now know of as the Law of Attraction. It was the bridge between scripture, or the more traditional religious versions of attraction, and what we now have today as personal development and Law of Attraction material. The idea that emotional states have a marked effect on real-time outcomes, and that our conditions are a projection of our state of mind, is more of a fact now than it ever has been (depending of course on how you define 'factual').

HOW WOULD IT FEEL?

Quimby's idea was that illness originated in the mind as a consequence of beliefs, and a mind open to God's wisdom or our 'innate health' could overcome any illness. There has since been an evolution of these ideas through more modern New Thought authors such as Joseph Murphy, Jones Ellen, and Charles Fillmore. I won't attempt to list them all, but I am a staunch advocate of the work of Neville Goddard, who worked to uncover the hidden esoteric meaning in scripture. He dealt exclusively with what he referred to as 'The Law', which he later refined into 'The Promise'.

'The Promise' was that if we could imagine the feeling associated with our desires, through all of the senses, we could trust at a deep level that this would soon be our 'real' physical experience (or reality). One could reliably use the power of imagination to change our circumstances. This of course is not dissimilar to what has become more popularly known as the Law of Attraction, which, thankfully for us, has been updated and improved upon in more recent times by Goddard's predecessors.

It is difficult not to draw the line between these earlier ideas and what we now have as the more modern versions of attraction, given to us through the work of Esther Hicks, and in Ronda Byrne's hugely popular 'The Secret'. Most everyone is trying to sell a version of attraction these days. There is no one in the personal development field who is not pedalling an improved awareness of the subconscious mind as the foundation to change, healing and how we can 'reinvent' reality. The 'fact' has carried though – feeling better improves our physical conditions.

Today, with all the awareness we have been granted, we should be no longer guessing about the truth of attraction, or remaining so narrow-minded in our regard for these ideas to be too 'watery' to be considered credible, valid and effective. Law of Attraction is real – this is the reality of the times we now live in. We have been given the insight, an insight that has pervaded throughout time and is now more clearly understood than ever – albeit not 'proved'. Why are we so reluctant to validate attraction as an effective mode of healing? I mean, we can measure thought waves, take photos of the body's electro-magnetic field, but we are reluctant to validate the effectiveness of imagined emotional states, or to use this insight in mainstream healing? Why can't we integrate what we know to be effective into how we treat the body/mind dis-eases?

With all of the breakthroughs in quantum science, and the apparent 'field of potentiality', that the ideas associated with emotions effect on perception (attraction) is still considered a 'leap of faith' astounds me. This is what is missing from modern healing. These insights could cure people's misunderstandings about what seems real. What's real is an invention - same now as it ever has been. But what may have once been cloaked in mystery, skewed by opinion, and greeted with skepticism, is now? Well you tell me. This would seem a commonly known aspect of reality's creation. While the Law of Attraction remains some new age mumbo, it remains unutilised. We are fettering human development by our dismissiveness. The Law of Attraction is an idea that has carried through thousands of years, yet we still don't buy it enough to use it in the mainstream.

Our species' level of collective awareness has been steadily building throughout our history, but made a marked leap with the advent of the New Thought movement. It was the beginning of a shift that has laid the groundwork for the awareness we benefit from today. The Law of Attraction and how state of mind shifts what seems real for us is now clearer than ever. I believe it has the potential to relieve a lot of the stresses of our world, and make us much more patient and contented beings. I mean it is happening – we are becoming more conscious, and more aware of the reality of attraction. So what is the key that can open this to the wider world?

> "The whole of creation is asleep within the deep of men and is awakened by his subconscious assumptions."
>
> Neville Goddard

The value of emotions?

We only want the 'things' for the feelings we assume they will bring.

We could do anything if it wasn't for feelings, right? If we didn't feel so scared, guilty, unsure of ourselves. Emotions are the only real obstacle we face in having our dreams come true, and they are treated with an equal dose of contempt. But emotions are the rocket fuel that can take us to worlds beyond – to improved stratospheres of living. But we experience them more like jail wardens. We are not using emotions as a tool to take us to new realities – we are numbing ourselves to them with medications, because we don't know how to use and create them. They are using us.

We misread the signals of emotion and place ourselves in deeper waters than we are really in. How often do we misinterpret the signals of emotion and allow a bad day to compound on itself because we are not sensitive to the signs, or the cycle perception remains in? How often are we telling ourselves that something is going on that is more imaginary than we realise? That is not as 'real' as we are making it – and we have no awareness, ours is an optional view.

When we are in a positive mental state it affects our world. For most this is child's play, right? It is hardly questionable. But how much effort do we put into 'artificially' elevating our state? Imagining good feelings, good things happening, changes the way we see the world. But very few engage in it.

To attract anything into our lives we must know what it feels like to have it.

Not a matter of time

> "To desire a state is to already have it."
> **Neville Goddard**

We can feel like we have what we want right now. It is not a matter of time or conditions being met that allows us to imagine the feeling – to be in the state of having. It is by the clarity of our imagination that the feeling becomes real – so how well can we imagine? In our validation of the effectiveness of these states, we make them seem more realistic. Being in the state of having is never a matter of time, but clarity, concentration, and how realistic we can make the 'full sensory' visual in our minds.

Can we imagine how it would feel? The desire would never have been born in us if we had not already had a taste of the experience. We liked it and that is why we want more of it. We can imagine it, or we wouldn't desire it in the first place. Us feeling the way we want to is never a matter of time or the 'perfect conditions' being met – they will never be met, from inside the illusion of what the conditioned or conscious mind suffers. Expectations can never be met until the emotional state precedes the perception of conditions. Conditions are always seen through an emotional filter of 'how' things currently are. An emotionally manufactured illusion.

It is not that we have no imaginations or are somehow emotionally flawed. Most have never realised the power they have in their imaginations – it's not 'real' – it is not effective (doesn't change anything) so we never give it a run.

> "Change your conception of yourself and you will automatically change the world in which you live."
> **Neville Goddard**

HOW WOULD IT FEEL?

For many of us the problem is the same – we wait for permission or have been convinced by others who we are, and start acting that way. We fit into the mould others made for us, not unlike kids who were told they were bad. This is an 'act' that doesn't go down well with that all-knowing part of ourselves, and it's what we may experience as resistance – not liking what is happening. We sadly trust what others say more than we trust our inner voice. We can only ever feel unworthy if we allow ourselves to trust what other people say more than the strength of their connection to self. That intense pain we experience is not the subconscious mind torturing us, it is the amount we have distanced ourselves from what we should be trusting in.

When we understand the creative effect (reality-altering effect) of emotions, and that they are the attractive energy we live our lives in, we start to value emotions more than the things we used to think validated/enabled or allowed them. And when we do, the outside world (conditions) start to lose its power over us. We are no longer handing over our control to situations. We can put ourselves in a great state with relaxation exercises and visualisations, but also by a deep sense of appreciation of what we have.

When we can fully appreciate our ability to feel like we have something without the need of the physical evidence, the object of desire not only moves more quickly towards us, but we don't feel like we have to wait anymore. The feeling of having was the thing we really wanted, and we can have it now. We are no longer plagued by the sense of lacking that does more to repel the said object than to bring it to us. The feeling is what holds the real power, more so than the actual object. How many times have we got something we had long desired and didn't feel like we thought we would, or the feeling quickly faded in the wake of our next desire? This happens because the wanting state became our pattern. And it is a pattern no desire can satisfy. We just keep wanting the next and the next and the next thing, none of which can fill us like the power to consciously shift our own state to one of having.

When we learn to value and know our ability to create emotional states, the world outside falls under our spell instead of the other way around. We are the ones who make what happens great, or at least as good as it can be. Altering our state consciously is a skill and, like any, takes practice. But there is no more a rewarding skill that we can learn, nothing more needed on earth than for us to feel great about who we are, and our ability to consciously shift our state. And it doesn't take time, or money, or things to be going right, or people to say so, it takes us. It takes us to be fully present and imagine how good things can be that becomes our present, and becomes our future.

It's not what we do

Getting to where we want to go often has far more to do with us letting go of old ways and ideas of how we go about getting there. 'Getting there' often has much less to do with the 'grinding' and our conditioned way of believing we arrive at our pre-conceived destination. We think there is only one way towards getting what we want, and we only have one perspective of things going 'right' in that story of ours. Giving up our idea of how they will come to pass, and letting go of the results of our efforts is often the very best thing we can do towards getting to this illusive result. It often takes far less of our effort than we are putting in.

This idea was perfectly illustrated in a story about an experiment I once read in the book 'Relationship Breakthrough' by Cloé Madanes. The experiment consists of a number of rats being let into a cage where there is an empty feed tray one at a time. The feed tray still smelling of the remnants of food quickly attracts the rat, who wait in the tray for a fresh food supply. But the food won't be dropped into the feed tray from the above feeder while the rat remains in the food tray. The object of the experiment is to see how long it takes the rat to work out that in order for the food to be released from the feeder, the rat must be out of the food tray for a period.

HOW WOULD IT FEEL?

Rats, being very clever animals, quickly work out that shortly after they exist the food tray, the prize is delivered. So now when the rat enters the cage with the empty food tray it never goes straight to the food tray, but waits outside of it until the food is supplied. Very clever animals, right? But something additional is noticed. The rat goes into its memory of what it was doing just prior to the food being distributed and concludes it was something additional about its behaviour that caused the food to come. The only real requirement was that the rat not be in the actual food tray, and to wait outside of it for a period for the food to enter. But the rat makes an additional conclusion – that it is also something else about its behaviour aside from not being in the food tray that it has linked to the food coming in.

All of the rats were doing something extra aside from not being in the food tray. And this behaviour was linked in their brains as what was needed for the result. One may have been quietly waiting in the corner, facing away from the food tray. Another may have been circling the food tray, and yet another stood on its hind legs. As I say, the only requirement for the food to enter was that the rats weren't in the food tray, but each of the rats made an additional assumption about what they were doing prior to the food coming in that became linked to them getting their reward. And much of what we do in our conditioned behaviours falls under the same flawed pretence.

We are convinced it is our behaviours that are the cause of everything that happens. That it is what we do – the grinding, the hard work that is the ultimate outcome of everything. And sometimes we are right – when we go for a jog or do some exercise, we feel better – when we drink too much our wife gets angry. Sometimes we get the action/ conclusions, the cause and effect right. But more often than we realise, we don't. We live by a dramatic exaggeration that if we do this or don't do that, chaos will occur.

It's not always the things we do that lead to our outcomes, or we would always get it perfect. It is not what we do that most influences outcomes, **but how we 'be'**. Less of the hard work and toil, and more of the positive expectation. We keep working hard and pushing on and aren't getting the same result we once did and don't know why, so we just do it some more – we just work even harder at it. We live by false conclusions about the power of our actions to bring about desired effect.

I guess the point I make is very similar to the message of the movie 'Silver Lining Playbook', where Robert De Niro's character compiles a long list of superstitions contributing to his team winning, none of which make the slightest difference to the actual outcome. We live by these superstitions, both consciously and unconsciously, often working 'harder' but getting less for our efforts. Often the best thing we can do is to start from the state of having. How do we want to feel when it is done? And our actions will come from inspiration rather than struggling towards a result. When we are working towards a peaceful outcome, our actions will always be peaceful. But from the state of not having – coming from frustration, panic and lacking, only breeds more of the same. More supporting evidence – more reasons in our environment to feel the same.

As ironic as it may sound, sometimes the very best thing we can do is nothing. To just wait for the grass to grow, without keeping on tugging it from its roots to see if it has grown. We have to let go of the outcomes. Do our best and leave the result to the universe. As Winnie the Pooh says, *"Sometimes when I'm going somewhere, I wait. And then somewhere comes to me."* How will you feel when it is done? When it is in your hand, or you have just finished? This is the language the universe speaks in – the language of emotion. **How would it feel?**

HOW WOULD IT FEEL?

PRACTICAL EXERCISE

Smile and the world smiles back

Can imagining good feelings effect our outcomes? When we are in a good place in our heads it is always reflected in the world we see. So, can imagining good things change your day and your life?

As an exercise spend just ten minutes of your morning imagining that every interaction in your day goes perfectly to plan. You get the assignments you want, there's lots of laughter and good vibes and no hiccups. Imagine yourself at the end of the day, undressing from your work attire and thinking to yourself, "Damn, that went well. How could it possibly be better?". For the sake of simplicity, **anchor** this perfect workday represented as a single simple image that embodies all of the meanings associated with that perfect day.

It's up to you – a golden mallet snapping down, a bag of money slapping in front of you, whatever works for you. Rope all of that 'great' day routine into a single simple image or GIF that represents "That was nearly the perfect day". Anchoring is an NLP tool where we can associate a complex of ideas, a longer story into a single, 'easy to bring to mind' image. The single image represents a longer story, but is much easier to bring to mind. Anchors are often used to put ourselves into good states quickly without going through all of the lengthy story telling rigmarole.

Whenever something great happens throughout the course of that day, replay your GIF or image. "Boom, what a perfect day." Or when there is a lapse, nothing happening, a bit of a quiet time. Boom, it's all coming true. We are going to have hiccups. Shit just happens sometimes, but I guarantee that

THE CONTROL CENTRE

if we're in the habit of practicing positive states, we'll deal with them better, their impact will be short-lived, and we'll attract to ourselves more scenarios that match our state. Try it for one day anyway and ask yourself if you honestly think it made any difference. For some it is a no-brainer that when we are in a good place, things just 'go better'. But how many make the conscious effort to improve their chances of the world shifting in their favour?

Playing the day back with everything going as planned is another favoured exercise of Neville Goddard. Rewinding it as if the things that didn't go super are re-configured to be more to our liking. What would have we preferred happened? This gives our mind a clear map of the preferred experience and a much better chance of outcomes improving in the future.

CHAPTER SUMMARY

- Being able to imagine feeling states has a real-time effect on the physical universe. How we feel changes reality.
- Perception is a function of the subconscious mind – our 'way of seeing' is such that we can only see what supports how we feel.
- We want things for the feelings we assume they will bring. Imagining the feeling of having is how we take the power back from the situation we assume we are in. If we already have the feeling, the situation we assume we are in loses its power to keep what we want from us.
- Imagining emotional states being seen as effective and a real and valid use of our attention/awareness holds the key to curing the human condition more so than any drug or therapy.
- The New Thought movement provided a bridge between what was cryptically hidden in the meaning of scripture, and what we now know as the Law of Attraction.
- Getting what we want is never a matter of time or conditions being met, but our clarity on how it will feel, and commitment to the feeling of having.

CHAPTER 12

The Return of Alchemy

THE CONTROL CENTRE

> "Everything exists solely for man to become angel."
>
> — Arthur Versluis

As this book has evolved, I guess I have failed in my original intent of making something concise and short. And as such I was left with a dilemma as to whether to include this chapter on alchemy. Was it crucial to the grand scheme of things and the core of the message? I think so – because the aim of the alchemist is one in the same as the spiritual seeker – to realise we can change the world from the inside out. To realise that although perception is a subconscious function, the more conscious we become the more we are able to turn the way the world seems to our choosing. The goal of the alchemist, or magician, is in realising their power to turn the ordinary into the extraordinary. That in yielding to our eternal natures, we can move the physical conditions of the world.

What could be more interesting to us than setting up a pattern where everything started to go our way all the time? Where we understood our power to change the world from within. That what is happening becomes a conscious choice, rather than something beyond our control – sacrificed, as it were, to the operating mode. The alchemist was obsessively committed to understanding the plight of his own energy, and how this changed the world around him. We change the real physical conditions of the world by our way of seeing. So the alchemist becomes ever more careful how the world is seen.

Alchemy is the path to enlightenment – understanding the power we possess to turn the world to what it is. What may have previously seemed a grey, hopeless and hostile environment, becomes transmuted into one of hope, support and opportunity. It happens not in the world – it happens within. It is a practicable skill – an evolution of 'looking on the bright side'. We could learn to turn an ordinary seeming world into the miraculous, and without putting ourselves through hell – through a simple appreciation of what our mind was capable of. Using our 'view' to change how we feel about the world isn't just worthy of us better understanding, it is how we could mould the nature of the physical world into any form we chose.

The beginning is the surrendering to however we find the world – we are ok with however we find it – with 'what is'. This is the start of turning the world – turning what seems like hell into heaven begins with a silent reservation of our habitual judgement. We can turn a difficult situation into a much better one by how we look at it – by our choice to see. The idea of the alchemical practice suggests that we could one day realise how to make heaven seem real on earth. By the proper use of perspective, we could turn the world around.

Forgive the fanciful language Versluis uses in the above quote – man becoming 'angel' was quite simply meaning that everything exists for humanity to realise a higher condition of mind. This was a light bulb moment for me, and the reason I chose to include this chapter. Was it true that the governing enterprise of all human endeavour was for us to 'wake up'? That peace on earth was what we were all really aimed towards at a deeper level. Could it be simpler than we were making it?

It was more than just interesting to me – I was excited by it. Could self-discovery be the route to ending the pain we feel within ourselves, and occur to many in one fowl swoop? Even though humankind seems preoccupied with killing each other, flying to Mars and making smarter phones, we are actually collectively aimed towards lifting the illusion of separation and the suffering this misunderstanding causes. We could, one day in the future, sense the grandeur, the enormity of what we are connected to, and feel guided by it. And by all reports this is not a matter of time, but a way of seeing. All human enterprise is geared towards this end – the evolution of consciousness, and an end to the suffering experienced as a result of us believing we are separate beings. Of us realising what we are connected to through presence of mind.

And it is not as hard for us to realise as we might have made it. We apparently come into this power by relinquishing our ego form. Turn it in like we would a suit at the dry cleaners. "Here you go, I'm turning this ego thing in, so that I will be able to realise my own eternal nature - my connection to everything." And this is not us turning over everything we own and giving up our livelihoods. It is surrendering to the battle within ourselves to be somebody we think we have to be. Someone who 'stands out' more than we do. And breaking our hearts so much of the time, because we don't seem like who we want to be yet.

Surrender is not giving up on ourselves – it is giving way to ourselves. Realising our connection to something larger and our ability to see the world in the image of our making. It is giving up our need to prove ourselves, and we might just become something so much richer in the process. This book was about bringing those fanciful terms down a notch so we could understand how normal and 'realistic' they truly were. Bringing more down to earth terms for God, enlightenment and 'heaven' to our table. They are not some far off, hand-in-the-sky type imaginings. They are real, and things we deal with on the daily. The Promised Land is here waiting for us to adjust our vision. To 'see' by using new eyes – not by trying to change all of things that are beyond our scope of control. To turn the hopeless into the hopeful can begin so simply when we suggest to ourselves – "This is not so bad".

And this is what I hope this chapter can bring us to – the awareness that we change the physical world with 'our eyes'.

The ordinary into the extraordinary

> "Our daily existence itself is necessarily the highest manifestation of the spiritual, if only we could see it so, and it is this kind of healing – the uniting of the spiritual and the mundane, the celestial and the quotidian. That is ultimately the highest task of the Magus."
>
> **Arthur Versluis**

THE RETURN OF ALCHEMY

The spiritual quest was once a marriage of magic ritual and religious doctrine. The use of our daily mundane tasks as a means to transmute consciousness and realise our celestial origins. Magic and religion existed side by side, hand in hand as a vehicle to turning our daily existence itself into the profound. Without magic, religion becomes sterile and void of the amazing, and without religion magic is just as fanciful and unpractical. Neither has any real benefit to us without the ideals of both being realised. Both were designed to complement each other in serving the same end, that being the realisation of mind and our 'otherworldly' origins. But what we are left with now, with the two being divorced from each other, means we have never been further from benefitting from either magic (alchemy) or religion.

What we have now as religion has been drained of any meaning or congruence. We are not closer as a species because of religion, and we are no closer to understanding ourselves or self-actualisation. We are not united in a common cause – if anything we are further than we might ever have been. Religion does more to cause conflict and elitism than it does to lead us towards self-realisation. And magic, it seems, is just the stuff of fairytales, not something we are encouraged to incorporate into our perception and way of seeing the world for our betterment. Alchemy is of no real benefit to the uninitiated. Neither alchemy or religion serves to improve the conditions anyone lives in.

Both magic and religion were designed to inspire in us a sense of the supernatural being alive within us, and that we could use this understanding to enhance the conditions that everyone lived in. What once sparked people to the power of our own imaginations is now lost to the obsession of the material world. The early Christian Church banned the practice of alchemy and witchcraft, murdering many thousands who were found guilty. But for the early pagans, alchemy was the sole means of healing the body/mind and the skews in perception that resulted in illness and dis-ease. Through natural remedies and shifting expectations (adjusting our view), many people were cured through the use of alchemical practice. Alchemy was the 'medicine' of the time.

THE CONTROL CENTRE

One has to think it is our society at large that still suffers from this misunderstanding of the purpose of alchemy, and of religion, not to mention how misconstrued both elements have become in the estrangement from each other. I have heard no one make this point so poignantly than Arthur Versluis in his book 'The Philosophy of Magic'. The 'global awakening' will rely on us once again being able to understand what we can accomplish with perspective.

Our 'portal' to accessing this higher condition of mind is so ordinary we usually dismiss it. Our 'clay', or what we have to work with, is our normal ordinary lives. It is our ability to make it into something more than ordinary that is the essence of alchemy. We all retort, and it is an all too common agreement that our life, and the world, is what we make it. But how many are in the moment to moment practice of bending how things seem to their favour? Making the ordinary into something slightly more pleasing. Is this deluding ourselves about reality, or the real and proper use of perspective and imagination? Of course, only we can answer that for ourselves, but the implication is that we are the beneficiaries. We are the ones who live in a seemingly better world. Of anything we manage to convince ourselves is 'real'.

It is our normal everyday moments that are our tool for turning the world into something more. The mundane into the mystical – the ordinary into synchronicity. We don't always 'pull it off', in an endless stream of feeling like we are in paradise all the time, but it is worth keeping in mind. This is a practicable skill.

What is now judged to be strange occult practices, with weird rituals only understood by the initiated, once served very practical purposes in disclosing the laws of the natural world, the supernatural aspects of mind, and how to realise it was our view that lay at the heart of any illness. If these practices can ever be restored to their original place of understanding they may well give a new life to the more traditional religions that most have lost faith in for having any practical benefit.

The highest goal

The highest goal of the magician or 'wizard' is learning the art of transmuting base metal into gold, which can be seen as a metaphor for turning our ordinary daily existence into something seemingly miraculous. The ordinary into the extraordinary. It was an expansion of the 'normal' and mediocre into something more. Alchemy was practicing the ability to transcend the normal into something 'great' or something better than it 'seemed'. It represents the fullest and proper use of mind and imagination – the highest learning on earth. It is the residue of our habit energy that has us convinced that this existence is anything but amazing.

Alchemy is the waking to a higher level of awareness. Without it, our lives can seem 'artificially' uninteresting and subdued, but it only seems that way because of our own lack of input into how we make it. We are the passengers instead of the drivers. With our use of perspective, our conscious input, we can turn the ordinary into something more. And that is not to say jumping around like idiots saying, "How good is this?" all the time. But a quiet relaxed appreciation of how content we can be with the 'normal'. If our life is nothing to write home about – get out your pad and paper and make something up. You have the world outside of you to work with.

We are so conditioned to believe it is only the super-rich and the famous who are afforded a life of wonder, but fail to realise that behind closed doors, their lives are so similar to us. They might be drinking a finer wine and eating caviar, but that's precisely what we can turn our ordinary meal into. This is the magic the alchemist speaks of. We all experience the world through an identical set of senses, so waking up to them is exactly how we turn the world into something more than we thought it was.

The wealthy suffer the same curses of unease, a lack of meaning and insignificance that we mortals do. Many in fact suffer even more exhausting battles with the very same demons we face. The feelings of unworthiness, and being out of control of their situations. The famous are even more controlled by their situations than we who have less to lose are. Their sales or following slips, and they crumble just like we, the 'ordinary' and vulnerable do. The 'stage' they live on is an illusion of the highest form and an inflation of their value that tortures as much as it soothes – just as our mind tricks us we are 'nobodies', so too does theirs. Wealth never equates to being free from the illusion.

Much as in the advice of the mindfulness chapter, it is up to us to extract more pleasure from each moment by becoming more and more present to the senses. By turning ordinary-seeming moments into pleasing ones, by the power of our perception and will to make the best of things. By us noticing the beauty that once may have just flashed past us. This may seem like an ineffectual and pointless game until we see it in the context of our transformation of the world. Until we see it as how we evolve into something more than we may have thought we were. Someone who can bend the world to our liking. And this is the promise of alchemy – the ability to turn our world into something more than it first appeared. Alchemy was an opening of the doorways of perception itself.

> "If the doors of perception were cleansed everything would appear to man as it is: infinite. For man has closed himself up, till he sees all things thro' narrow chinks of his cavern."
>
> William Blake

It should not be considered some playful game when we have nothing better to do – this is the evolving of our mind and senses, to see beyond the veil. To begin seeing what was once disguised by our habit energy. We are so used to being constantly entertained now that we are dismissive of the ordinary. We have paid a higher price for this than we know. We have become desensitised to the ordinary – the one place we will now never think to look is where our salvation lies. We instead quickly turn to the next brightest sign or piece of 'entertainment'. "Look over here people" – like we are puppets being diverted from one circus big top to the next, and away from the cure.

It is an increasingly more difficult time to live in because we are the targets for these clever and emotionally savvy advertisers. Our strings are being pulled in ways we are hardly even aware. All marketers are experts on the psychology that drives human behaviour, and influences our decision making, and we are the moving targets. It makes it increasingly more difficult for us to realise that our salvation lies in the small and mediocre, when the sensational is thrust in front of us continually in shiny gold wrappers.

Nevertheless, the saving is up to us – up to us to realise how magical these 'normal' lives and bodies truly are. Heaven, for want of a better word is just as much in the scent of a flower, than it is at the helm of our brand-new boat. Our awakening comes by way of that bird that lands close to us with its song, or the smile of a child that fills our heart, as much as it does by having our senses moved by the sensational. Heaven is alive in the ordinary and it is we who must extract the juice in the pursuit of our own will to see joy – to see magic, where there was once nothing – to see colour, in what was once grey.

And this follows from the earlier ideas of our confirmation bias. We can only see that to which we are emotionally aligned. When we wake up to the signs, they begin to show up out of the 'woodwork' of the forest. Where there was only a bland and hopeless world, we have created something else. When we are looking to purchase a new car we begin to see them everywhere. The fact is they were always there we just didn't notice them until we were emotionally invested. And this is an identical principle – the same law applies – we are the ones who turn the normal into something more profound by a practiced way of seeing. A new habit we form in our minds.

I love this little verse I saw on Facebook taken from 'The Parents Tao Te Ching' by William Martin that says all of this so beautifully.

Don't ask your children to strive for extraordinary lives.

Such striving may seem admirable, but it is a way of foolishness.

Help them instead find the wonder and the marvel of an ordinary life.

Show them the joy of tasting tomatoes, apples and pears.

Show them how to cry when pets and people die.

Show them the infinite pleasure in the touch of a hand.

And make the ordinary come alive for them. The extraordinary will take care of itself.

Normalising higher states of mind

I think human beings regularly experience higher states of consciousness, but our habit is to dismiss them, not knowing how 'normal' it is to have these 'glimpses' into consciousness. We have these moments of emptiness, and they feel so alien to us that we want to race to the next 'what's happening' moment. We aren't comfortable with bliss because we don't know or aren't conditioned to sense it when it looks us square in the face. We often experience these moments of 'no thought' in our everyday lives. When we are immersed in repetitive tasks, or staring out across an endless ocean. I think we experience them frequently, but have no reference point for which to gauge the experience and so we rush to fill up our minds with 'more important stuff'.

Our instinct is to fleet by that moment and into the next, scarcely noticing that what just happened was a glimpse of what the meditating monks all seek from their practice. We disregard the normal ability, the human instinct of mind to be at peace. It is not miles from where we spend the bulk of our time. It is right there just beneath the surface of the normal.

We feel it, but have never been interested or aren't 'familiar', so often it is just experienced as a burst of laughter, or our heart melting when we witness something beautiful. Sometimes it is those chills that come when we have a thought aligned with the pure truth of our being. It runs through our body like a stream of light that feels sensational, and we just shrug and go "Oouh – that felt nice". We touch the void, and we touch it much more often than we think, but we're in a pattern of dismissing it. I'm certain that once we know these feelings, and associate them with higher mind and our evolution, we will not only notice them more but we will seek to expand them. We will be able to accelerate their effect and occurrence. We will get a sense for when they are happening and how to conjure them up. We will make a concerted effort to litter our experience with these connections – these windows into our own divine remembering.

My partner found an article that said a lot of this stuff perfectly, so I want to share some of the content here, but the original source also comes with a commentated video explainer that I think is definitely worth a watch.

The Article is called **"On Higher Consciousness"** from the School of Life website, and although I've extracted some of what's pertinent to my point, I recommend reading it all or at least watching the explainer that plays at the bottom of the article.

> *The term 'higher consciousness' is often used by spiritually minded people to describe important but hard to reach mental states…*
>
> *Unfortunately, the way in which these spiritual people discuss their states of higher consciousness has a tendency to put a lot of secular types on edge. It can seem maddeningly vague, wishy washy,*

touchy-feely – and for want of a better word annoying. What on earth do these gurus really mean?

This is how we see it: as human beings, we spend most of our lives functioning in lower states of consciousness, where what we are principally concerned with is ourselves, our survival and our own success, narrowly defined.

Ordinary life rewards practical, introspective, self-justifying outlooks that are the hallmarks of what we would call 'lower' consciousness. Neuroscientists speak of a 'lower' part of the brain they term the reptilian mind and tell us that under its sway, we strike back when we are hit, blame others, quell at any stray questions that lack immediate relevance, fail to free-associate and stick closely to a flattering image of who we are and where we are heading.

However, at rare moments, when there are no threats or demands upon us, perhaps late at night or early in the morning, when our bodies and passions are comfortable and quiescent, we have the privilege of being able to access the higher mind – what neuroscientists call our neocortex, the seat of imagination, empathy and impartial judgement. We loosen our hold on our own egos and ascend to a less biased and more universal perspective, casting off a little of the customary anxious self-justification and brittle pride.

In such states, the mind moves beyond its particular self-interests and cravings. We start to think of other people in a more imaginative way. Rather than criticise and attack, we are free to imagine that their behaviour is driven by pressures derived from their own more primitive minds, which they are generally in no position to tell us about. Their temper or viciousness are, we now see, symptoms of hurt rather than of 'evil'.

It is an astonishingly gradual evolution to develop the ability to explain others' actions by their distress, rather than simply in terms of how it affects us.

Higher consciousness is a huge triumph over the primitive mind which cannot envisage any such possibilities. Ideally, we would be a little more alive to the advantages of this higher mind and strive to make our oceanic experiences somewhat less random and less clothed in unnecessary mystery.

I've shamelessly included a good deal of the content here, but I thought I really had to in order to capture the essence. I think it makes some amazing points which not only allow us to recognise higher states of mind as normal and achievable, but grant us an ability to see other people's behaviour in the light of a defensive mechanism, and not always designed to wound us. I included so much of this article because I wanted this book to be about healing in general, and these points go a long way towards being more tolerant, understanding and not so reactive – it is a practice.

What if to feel enlightened was what we experienced as 'normal', and we just never recognised it – largely because we were so convinced that to be enlightened must be characterised by being recognised?

The Promised Land is here

> "It will not come by you waiting for it. It will not be a matter of saying 'here it is' or 'there it is'. Rather the kingdom of the father is spread out upon the earth and men do not see it."
>
> **Jesus – from the Gospel of Thomas**

As peculiar as this quote may sound its truth has never changed. Christ, the Buddha and other enlightened masters had realised mind. They had realised that the outside world was built by an internal state – and so always found themselves in favourable conditions. Conditions were made in their own minds so what's not to like? Enlightenment was the

THE CONTROL CENTRE

acknowledgment that the outer conditions didn't need to change for us to be able to change them with our perspective. The world can be transformed without anything in the outside changing. But humans have always been steadied by the prophecy of the Promised Land – of a time to come of peace and harmony, where "the lion will lay down with the lamb".

So when will it come and how will we know it is here? It is the promise not just of religions but science too. Darwin and Wallace – both credited with aspects of the evolutionary theory, were in agreement that the ultimate outcome of the evolutionary process would be a **"more spiritual form of existence"** – whatever you take that to mean. Humanity has always been buoyed by the hope of this greater time that would come in our future. But if we are to talk of this promise being characterised by the absence of emotional suffering, it rings true of the same timeless precepts of mindfulness. If the absence of suffering is synonymous with the absence of time, it must stand to reason that this time is here now, not coming in the future. It is we who must adjust our view to see the world in the manner it was created. The Promised Land is not lost but exists here behind a thin veil of our conditioned values. It is not a future event. This 'land' that was promised is not coming, it is here now and we aren't present enough to notice it.

It reveals itself by us looking for it – noticing it. By us becoming skilled at 'seeing' the beauty, and becoming ever more present to mind and the senses. So present that the old ego suffering 'self' fades to the background. It is not a physical place we are moving towards but an inner dimension. And not one that requires years of initiation or a sparkling intellect – it takes us to understand the value of presence. Full awareness or realisation of mind. We can shift the way the world seems with a focused appreciation of the present. I completely understand that this may sound too far-fetched, and an oversimplification of what must surely be earth-shatteringly difficult. But everything that I've read and come to understand is that this age that was promised is not a time or a place but a deepening sense of presence.

THE RETURN OF ALCHEMY

More present to the senses equals more conscious of mind.

Does the world want peace? I think by far the majority do, but very few realise it is by taking on the force of our own habit thinking that we can create a greater sense of peace in our lives. We want peace on earth, but we have concluded that it is out of their hands and has absolutely nothing to do with what we do. It is a gross misconception that the things we do are so insignificant that they don't make a lick of difference. For there to be peace on earth we have to have peace in ourselves – it is absolutely us that is making the difference – an enormous difference. And it is the very best we can do to practice presence. Let's be clear – world peace doesn't matter as much as your peace. Your peace is something you can do something about, whether that also includes doing something about something you think is wrong or not. What you do adds to the 'whole' and is an example to all.

It is not our world leaders that are guiding us to a new and better world, it's you. It is ordinary, everyday people who are shifting the balance and realising every small difference is a momentum shift that will be multiplied by time, and strengthened by our numbers.

The Promised Land is here – we have arrived. It is not some coming time in the future, it exists beneath the thin veil of what we call 'normal' life and waits for the critical mass tipping point to notice it. And when they do it won't just be transformed for you – it will be transformed for the many. I'm not claiming that I know all of the details of this global shift in awakening. I don't know what will go down, and how things will seem. The best I think we can know is that something amazing is coming. Something that will defy our current ability to imagine. Peace on earth? An end to death, suffering and ageing? I understand how defiant of logic this is for most people, **but this is what is written.** My only point is that it is probably far closer than we may think, and we have been left the crumbs – some clear directions as to where to find this peace. A clear map of where it is and how to get there.

THE CONTROL CENTRE

The media and the agenda of the global elite to create a state of panic is only further evidence that they fear the shift in power that this 'event' represents. Us coming back into our strength. They will clamp more and more controls on our freedoms and covertly sell our rights from under us, in a bid to contain the flow of new awareness. But we are in charge of what matters most – our attention and our intention. Those in apparent 'positions' of 'power' fear this coming change and the strength of our numbers. But change it will and strange as it seems it starts with us being able to quiet our minds. When we do, a whole new world will begin to reveal itself.

Consider it like the analogy of a rabbit hiding in its hole – it is just waiting for the coast to be clear so it can stick its head out a little bit. And the same is true of this sacred promise – it waits in our consciousness – it waits for us to still our minds and make time stand still. The more moments of peace we experience the more this shift will be apparent, and the beauty will be revealed. When the mind is quiet the 'rabbit' will begin to show itself.

It will begin to show itself in many forms of good fortune. We will get what we want faster – these are the gifts to aid our evolution. Meaningful chance, or what we call synchronicity will become ever more apparent. And we will individually get a sense that the universe is moving for us. Because it is. This might surprise us because we don't know what we are. We would be astonished if we realised our creative power. But it is all moving for you – to wake us to our ability to see the changes we have defined. How do you want it to be different? We can only see the changes we define, and soon our practice will blind us to all contrary evidence. We are being woken to the wonder.

This is the astounding truth of our times – 7 billion different and interwoven stories meshing perfectly into the final dance of consciousness. The whole universe is there for you – is there to wake you to the ascension. Everything moves in relationship to you. It is our minds that have made everything the way it seems. Nothing would exist without us being here. We are a much larger and more integral part of this whole than we realise. This cosmic dance is for us – so we can know ourselves as a part of the shared and single source of energy that runs through all things. When we sense this, it will be like no sensation we have ever felt or imagined we could feel – it is not as far from you as you think.

> "There is no world. There is only mind."
> Arthur Versluis

Programmed for danger

We are programmed to look for, and inevitably find, danger. We are designed to find what is threatening in our environment – this slant on our view effects the nature of what we find. And in the absence of any 'real' threat we make one up. We 'find' what amount to trivial annoyances that threaten little more than our peace of mind. We are programmed to turn 'what is' (how we find the world) into something that creates panic in us. Panic is the long lineage of the energy we carry. Remember we can only see what we are looking for evidence of. By our conditioning, we are on the lookout for threats that literally don't really exist – we make them up out of what we look at. We are blind to a whole other world. Anything in our world has been invented by our own need, and for reasons we can only scarcely fathom (but mainly so we feel like we know where we are). By our natures, we are only interested in what can harm us, or what can elevate our status.

There is much going on in our environment that we aren't aware of/isn't on our radar, because we aren't emotionally aligned to it. We are designed to see threats, danger and scarcity, and are only in very recent times waking to realise we can turn 'what is' into something other than a force of habit. We make the world seem more dangerous and hostile than it really needs to be. There is nothing there until we make it so by our own creation. We are not running a beauty and peace on earth program – that's not our operating system. But we are waking to our ability to change this. That we literally have the potential to change our world by what we are looking for. By 'brainwashing' ourselves to see evidence of the new. This 'brainwashing' is really a re-washing of our minds.

Benefits of being the alchemist

Alchemy is waking to our minds ability to turn a 'normal' experience into any we please. This is a skill of the highest order, and there is nothing more worthy of our time and effort to learn and practice. Particularly in this age of extreme sensory overload – of the enormous competition for our attention.

We are being bedazzled by the enormous volume of advertising, and they are ever more covert in their methods. Many people are at a loss – not knowing which way to look, what ranks as important, or what are sound lifestyle choices. We are so pummelled by advertising that we are always looking to be excited, rather than quiet our minds. And don't even get me started on our little pocket dopamine fixes (mobile phones) that we can't live an hour without. Human beings are suffering under the sheer volume of competition for our attention, and it has devalued the introspection that would heal us. That would reassure us we are heading towards something that has meaning and real value for us.

We just have to pay attention and care about what we are doing. We rarely to never reflect or ask ourselves those big questions. There is little need to when the next distraction is never far away. We have lost all ability to trust in ourselves, and that is the only place our future lies – trusting in the wisdom of our own sacred instincts.

THE RETURN OF ALCHEMY

CHAPTER SUMMARY

- Alchemy is the 'old' religion of magic and ritual with the goal of turning the world to our favour. We make it what it is – and we can fashion it to our pleasing with continued practice.
- The 'clay' of the alchemist is our routine daily tasks – and our hands are our eyes – or rather our perception. We can change anything into the form of our will, when we know the power we wield in our 'way of seeing'.
- The Promised Land is already here waiting for us to be able to 'see'.
- The beauty waits for us to notice. By quieting the mind, we will begin to see what has been hidden.
- Becoming more conscious is a dimensional journey – it is not a matter of time but presence of mind.
- We will begin to see more synchronistic consequences and things going our way as we make the peaceful space for this energy to enter – when we align and connect with our deep instincts.
- Sensing higher aspects of mind is a normal part of our daily experience, but we don't know it when we feel it so are often dismissive of this change in us.
- As we move towards this shift you will start to get the feeling the entire universe is moving in relationship to you. It wants to wake us to our ability to see the changes we define. And the speed at which this will happen will increase exponentially as we move closer to ourselves.

CHAPTER 13
Through the Looking Glass

"Some believe it is only great power that can hold evil in check, but that is not what I have found. I found that it is the small everyday deeds of ordinary folk that keep the darkness at bay. Small acts of kindness and love."

Gandalf

What would you do?

How would your life look if emotions weren't an obstacle?

If you were able to feel like you wanted to in every moment, what would you do? If you felt bolder, more self-assured, and resilient to everything thrown at you? If people just couldn't get to you the way they once used to? What would you do? Start that new business venture? Record that song? What would you do if you 'felt' like it? Get to the gym? Would you take on that nagging bad habit if it didn't seem so hard? If it didn't feel like something you were uncontrollably forced to do? Would you have better relationships, and worry far less for the opinions of others who really have no idea who you are – nor do they care? What would you do if in every moment you could feel as you pleased?

Because that is the promise of a more conscious and intentional life. In every moment asking ourselves, "How would I like my experience to be different to the one I'm having now, if I had a choice?". And it is not that we are always unfavourable to what is going on, but how could it be better? What truly exhausts us is not our intense focus but our resistance to 'what is'. It is that we always seem to be fighting against a situation that was created by another level of our own awareness. Our constant resistance to how it seems, never feeling like we can do anything 'real' about it, and never realising it was us that made it as it is.

We don't feel like we can do anything about it because our 'way of seeing' is a subconscious function of mind. But in this awareness alone, we become more conscious of what previously seemed out of our control – that how we see the world is not a choice we were making. What is 'going on' is completely relative to what we have consciously declared we want. What's going on is not a decision we're making, but is entirely relative to what we have asked for, both by our emotional state, and by our declarations of – "This is how it is".

We are the cause of our lives. And in a world that seems to be increasingly pushing us to the outer, where we have less and less ability to know our value, we must return to the centre. This world seemingly forces us to the outer of control. That we have to prove ourselves – that we are less than – that we have to buy our happiness, and happiness is always in that next thing. It is up to us to reclaim what has been lost by connecting to ourselves – not anything that can come from the outside world. That it is ok to be contented with who we are. That it is ok to do something different to what everybody else sees as worthwhile. We are the cause of what makes us react. We have the power to change how things seem, by our way of seeing. When we are in the centre, we are not blown about by the circumstances that we ourselves have created. We know ourselves as the creator of what we are experiencing.

We crave human contact like we do air. An infant can be fed till its belly bursts but if it is not touched by human hands – if it is not nurtured with kindness – it will die. We have a need to find our tribe – the like-minded – those whose values we share, and they are out there. The ones who accept us for what we are, and believe in the same value of human connection above all else. They are out there – find them and nurture those relationships. When we know what is important to us, we don't have to chase it anymore – it will find us. When we align with the energy of intention it will be evident in everything we see and do. Being focused in every moment on how we want to feel may seem like hard work and require strength, only until we realise what is on offer.

What is it that they now use as the cruellest form of torture? Sensory deprivation. That's right, the opposite of mindfulness. Because without the sensory input of each moment we can go completely nuts – losing all sense of who we are. Without a moment-to-moment sensory experience we lose all sense of reality – we can actually forget who we are. We lose our direction, and without it who we are doesn't exist anymore. This is more terrifying to us than any form of physical pain.

Mindfulness is ours, yet we relinquish it for what?? Goods and services? Because we think we aren't getting attention? Because we are convinced of how 'wrong' things are going? Mindfulness, we throw away like it comes second, third or fourth to everything else and how good are our lives because of it? For many our lives are torturous – unnecessarily torturous. We are unheard, untouched and invisible and it is all in our own perception. Because we have failed to care about our lives and failed to prioritise simple 'free' pleasures. We've turned whatever we have into something less valuable than it truly is. My motto – don't turn nothing into something when you can turn it into anything.

Very few people are able to be happy because we've been fooled into thinking that what we want is something other than what we have now. We can shift 'what is' with presence of mind.

THE CONTROL CENTRE

And that is what this age of us becoming more conscious truly offers. A more conscious and intentional life means what we want will happen faster, and we will understand the relationship between our intentions and what seems to be happening. We understand our power to turn what is happening to our favour. We are always turning the 'chaos', or the infinite, into the definable – into what it is. There are many who acknowledge that, as bad and panic-stricken as the world might seem, **this is the best time we have ever lived in.** And why? Because of the realisation we can turn whatever we find into something more palatable. Because we are becoming more conscious. This is what an appreciation of mind grants us. Mind is a reality-forming mechanism. And whatever we appreciate can do more for us, and we are coming into the awareness of the control we have over our perception. In knowing it to be a subconscious function, we are more conscious and in control of it. We have been handed the remote to our minds – a mind that turns nothing into something.

It is a neon jungle out there – an advertising minefield all designed to make us feel like we are less than happy without their product. And for this reason, the hardest to navigate in human history, but navigate we can, when we are intentional and connect with who we are. The vibration in our atmosphere often makes us feel like we have something to prove. That in order to sustain our self-worth we must be acknowledged by everyone. To consider ourselves valuable and contributing, it must be agreed on by many. In mindfulness we are 'nobodies'. But it is in being nobodies that we become anybody – we become everybody. Who we are is enough.

So my question to you again – **what would you do if you could control how you felt in every moment?** And I'm not asking people to jump off a cliff into the unknown. To leave their jobs and livelihoods. But to claw back the power we have unwittingly sacrificed by not nipping unwanted experiences in the bud. Not breaking the link in our programmed chain of reactions. To create some elasticity – some emotional agility, and gain the control of what is happening. To do the small things we can to help people, knowing who is truly the beneficiary. To do good is good for us, not just in some sense of karmic justice – it's how we grow as people. We need to nurture meaningful relationships. Our lives are nothing without having someone to share our experiences with – people who rejoice in our successes with us.

Personal development has been so centred on getting richer and status elevation that it is hardly surprising lots of people aren't benefiting from the treasures it offers. The greater emotional control, and understanding our subconscious mind and programming so we can live more satisfied lives no matter where we stand on the totem pole. Building rapport with people isn't just some sales tactic – it is how we better connect with other human beings.

It is great to reach and have goals, but we should never let them become our master. Never let them own us, or be crushed because we are without something in the moment. We are bigger than any situation, and if it doesn't go to plan, we are still floating – still in charge of the emotional control panel. What do we gain in being less bothered by situations and people? The power to turn nature to our hand – "Come with me circumstance – I'm going to make you into something". Steps towards control/awareness are irreversible, and can never be taken from us. Once our eyes are opened, they can never again be closed. We have the power to alter the nature of the physical world with our intention. To mould it into our image of preferences. And when this becomes our practice the 'real' world will match the one in our minds.

There are better times coming for us when we realise this power of living with intention. A world that will possibly blow our minds. But we have to get out of this need to be entertained and pleasured by what the world can do for us. Sitting in the grandstands as mesmerised spectators. We are the controllers of our experience. It takes practice and exercise to shape the world as we know it into our image of pleasure. Never rely on what others are able to do for you in creating a great experience. We need to get back to the basics, of simpler pleasures and not having to have everything in our life come in flashing lights and the promise of an upgraded status. In this coming age, torturing ourselves will be seen for how counterproductive and unnecessary it truly is.

There are better times coming – more conscious and intentional times where people will be turning the world not just into their own versions of paradise but a shared version. A world that will be better for everyone. If this book helps you understand this process of becoming more conscious better, I am happy. If whatever it is you already believe serves you better, I am even happier for you. Take from this what works, and leave what doesn't, because no one else can point the way for us – no one has had our experiences. Align with the energy of your desires, and you will see the evidence everywhere and in everything you do. The greatest 'possession' of our lives is our perspective. Use it to turn your world around. The mind will do whatever you assign it.

What went wrong is we unknowingly turned our outcomes over to the program, and didn't realise we were no longer driving what happens to us. What may have felt like free will wasn't – our experience was coming purely from the program. Our reactions happen in a never-ending cycle, finding perfectly good reasons for their existence in any and every environment we enter. No input from us – and no control over outcomes. So no matter how hard we pushed, we were always pushing against walls we had built ourselves and didn't know it. No matter how hard we worked, we were working to resist a world we had created in mind. A mind-made situation that can't be moved by force – only by surrender.

We have to turn in our egos for the oversized armour they represent – and in exchange we will inherit something far more profound. It is our identity itself that seemingly forces our single and only 'way of seeing'. The very thing that causes the angst operates incognito – undetected, and pulling our strings. It is not **giving up** a sense of identity but **giving way** to something greater.

We have to be looking for something in order for it to show up. We are now looking for something that wasn't visible before. We have, by our asking for something specific, turned the world into something it wasn't prior to the intention – something that was previously not visible to us. We have changed the nature of the world by our intention – by what we are now looking for. Once this makes sense to us, we start to understand there are no limits to what we can turn the world into. To the future we can invent. There are no situations, but the one we have created by defining by our preference.

We have to define how we want our experience to be different. And if we make it a habit to do this in every moment, we will cease to ever be in conditions we find displeasing. We will stop resisting however we find the now. For that is what this age of awareness has brought us. We don't need conditions to change for us to change how we feel.

Our success equates to our emotional agility – which translates to 'did they get to me'?

Two phrasings to avoid

There are two phrasings we use that unknowingly cause resistance, and sacrifice our control of our results. **"I don't like"**. Saying we don't like something is a one-way street. We push against something and offer no solution, so the thing we push against gets increasingly bigger. We have given it life and size and push against it. It is counter-intuitive because we aren't doing 'nothing' – we make it worse by our resistance, and offer no solution. Asking the question, "How would I like it to be different?" offers up its opposite – leads to a solution. "I don't like" pushes against something, and that resistance makes the problem worse.

And **"This is wrong"**. "This is wrong" again offers no solution, and no hope of improvement. "This is wrong" disengages the mind – embedded in this statement is the sneaky unconscious suggestion that "I can't do anything about it". It is better for us to say what we don't like about it, so we can engage in what can be done. In both cases we are thinking more in terms of solutions, rather than pushing against, or being powerless to change it, respectively. "I don't like" means we tie it to our experience – "This is wrong" means there's nothing we can do about it.

The turning point

> "Thousands of years before Christ, someone measured the earth with extreme precision and recorded this information in the dimensions of the Great Pyramid."
>
> William A Fix – Pyramid Odyssey

As I have said I have always had an interest in self-improvement and the belief that when we live with intention, we can be the drivers of our destiny. That in itself is the most appealing aspect of any material on the market in my opinion. If it doesn't improve my ability to control how I feel, what is its value? If it doesn't allow me to improve the likelihood of favourable results, it is neither valuable, nor interesting to me.

If I'm to say there were turning points in my life, they were always books that introduced me to a new paradigm of thinking – that uprooted my old-world view. 'The Power of Now' was certainly one of them, because it gave me a clear and defined place to dwell that was free of any confusions and the subject matter was not steeped in confusing dogma. The 'now' didn't require me to obey anything higher than myself, and was always available to all people equally. But my eyes were first opened in another direction – one that persists to this day and allows me to trust in my own instincts above all things, and I'll explain why.

If I was to pinpoint where my road first forked – where my model of looking at the world first shifted – it was when I read a book I came

THROUGH THE LOOKING GLASS

across nearly thirty years ago called 'Pyramid Odyssey' by William R Fix. I couldn't possibly do Fix the justice his book deserves in the short space I have here, but I can explain the main points and what they meant to me. If you are at all interested in Egyptology, or exploring the evolution of our species, you could do yourself no harm to find yourself a copy of the original text – it was a game changer for how I began to look at the world, and the fundamental inadequacy of our model of history to explain with any accuracy where we have come from, and hence where we are going.

Fix constructs a more than compelling argument of 'The Great Pyramid' being the first of the pyramids (and probably the first of the sacred monuments in Egypt) as it is unique in having **ascending passageways**. The upper chambers of The Great Pyramid were blocked at the completion of construction, so there was no knowledge of them being there until they were discovered late in the 18th century by a traveller named Davison. It would hardly seem coincidental or an insignificant fact that all of Egypt's pyramids have descending passageways, but only one has anything built into the middle of it. Nor were the pyramids tombs. There has never been a body or sarcophagus found in any of the pyramids. The theory that they were tombs is long outdated.

My intention in mentioning 'Pyramid Odyssey' is not to construct a 'belief worthy' case. I believe Fix has done this already – if you don't believe me, or want to prove or disprove it for yourself, read his book. But as I stated in the beginning of the book, I'm not here to try and 'prove' anything, because for many I don't think proof is even possible – if people have already made up their minds, they can only hear and acknowledge evidence that supports their own personal theories. If you doubt what I am claiming here, or are at all interested, I would encourage you to find the book, and I'm certain you will also come to the same conclusions the author has.

And that is that The Great Pyramid was the first of Egypt's ancient monoliths. That the builders knew precisely where the Pyramid was

THE CONTROL CENTRE

situated on the earth, being the exact centre of the earth's land mass. That they knew the dimensions of the earth, not just that it was round, many thousands of years prior to when the flat earth believers lived. The pyramid builders managed to demonstrate superior masonry abilities, and needle-point accuracy that could scarcely be matched today with every piece of technology at our disposal. The Great Pyramid consists of an estimated 2.3 million precision cut stone blocks that have been intricately placed together without the use of mortar.

In Fix's words, "They built a man-made mountain with the accuracy we cut gems". I honestly have to laugh at some of the feeble attempts of our modern scientists to 'explain away' the construction. That they floated the blocks down the river – that they slid blocks weighing as much as 300 tonnes by using water to reduce the friction. It really doesn't explain how they hoisted these blocks 150 metres in the air and placed them without any scratch or discrepancy in the construction. You cannot get a razorblade between these stones – seemingly cut with a laser-like precision. It has been estimated that, if the pyramid was built in the twenty-year period theorised, and they worked 12-hour days, it would mean a perfectly symmetrical block would be masoned, carted and placed every two and a half minutes.

There is very close to 6 million tonnes of precision placed stone in The Great Pyramid. A monumental achievement for people of any age, leave out that our beloved 'science' would have us believe the people of this era (if a construction date could even be agreed upon) were using crude tools and had just begun to discover agriculture. I'm certainly not trying to construct an airtight case here, nor have I any interest in debating the facts of The Great Pyramid – to me the giant 'work of art' speaks volumes in itself. But the reason I mentioned the 'date debate' is the stark evidence of hundreds of years of alluvial erosion on the Sphinx. The erosion on the Sphinx dates it to be many thousands of years older than most scientific models of Egyptian history.

Why I mention The Great Pyramid, and then only skim over a few of the facts in Fix's book, is that I'm only highlighting what the book and

THROUGH THE LOOKING GLASS

The Great Pyramid meant for me. And that is that how we evolved and the nature of our origins seems to have been conveniently overlooked, when science tries to 'explain away' how our race began. There was more than obviously some form of unearthly intervention in how we came to be. We didn't just grow into really smart chimps. There is evidence in our prehistory, long before the flat earth believers, that we knew where we were in the universe, and were capable of mind-boggling architectural feats. We have been lied to about the nature of how we evolved.

The books that we are still taught from to this day in our schools and our model for interpreting our origins is conveniently and systematically flawed. The world at large is in denial of the evidence that presents on our planet that deep in our history a highly capable and advanced race of human-looking creatures existed. Deep in our history, a highly advanced race looking very much like us (going by the art work) left evidence of the advanced knowledge and capabilities that existed at the time.

The very assumptions that science is based in – that knowledge has been a progression, and that we are as far advanced now as we ever have been – is contradicted by the stark reminders of an ancient and advanced past. Not just in Egypt and The Great Pyramid, but in all corners of our planet we see evidence of advanced knowledge existing deep in our history.

A small fact that can easily be explained away? An insignificant deletion of how we go about explaining our evolution and origins. Science claims to have a handle on this – an ability to accurately tell us where we are now and where we are going but denies that it didn't all 'go down' as we have been taught. We claim to have this superior dominion of life on earth – a ruling opinion, and power over nature. But we really have no idea through this misleading scientific model of what the future holds.

We're led to believe there is some masterplan and that we should sit tight in the faith that some scientist or world leader will sort it all out.

But it's BS and we know it. This is an every man for himself race to our graves, and hopefully you can extract some meaning from the time you spend here if you are lucky, or wise, or whatever. But it is not the world we have been lulled into the security of. No one knows what is going on and it is unlikely we ever will while working from this flawed model of who we are and our origins. I hold zero confidence in a model of our history that tries to explain The Great Pyramid as a 'mere' anomaly.

> "I used to think that top environmental problems were biodiversity loss, ecosystem collapse and climate change. I thought that thirty years of good science could address these problems. I was wrong. The top environmental problems are selfishness, greed and apathy, and to deal with these we need a cultural and spiritual transformation. And we scientists don't know how to do that."
>
> Gus Speth

Why did they bother?

Of course, there have been countless theories as to who and why they built The Great Pyramid, with varying degrees of believability. That it was some sort of celestial power source, providing a type of electricity for the region is one. But the hypothesis given by Fix does seem to make a lot more sense. The belief that the Pyramid builders had a vested interest in its construction is the only really feasible explanation of why any beings from any age would go to such an enormous amount of trouble.

Fix surmises that the Pyramid was left as a beacon for humanity so that we would, as we came to the end of the next age, have a grasp on the nature of our evolution, and have some understanding of what was to come. That when we were able to 'meet' the builders by understanding their extraordinary abilities, we might rise in our imaginings of what is truly possible for a unified species that realises the power of mind. Fix surmises that it was us – a former more conscious version of us, who had to leave a reminder of what was possible. To awaken in our imaginations the grandeur of what was to come. To light that spark in our minds of how things were before 'the fall'. Before the fall from higher consciousness that is recorded in many ancient texts, not just as it appears as the 'great flood' in the bible. That we were once a far more knowledgeable, capable being of celestial origins is a theme echoed throughout history in countless different accounts of how we came to be.

For me, the message of The Great Pyramid didn't just cause me to be distrusting of the educated authorities and their ability to reasonably guide us, but to view our history and future with more of a sense of wonder. Can you imagine a person of Christ's time stumbling across the desert to see something that must have not just amazed the senses, but awakened a whole new sense of intrigue? Imagine someone who was brought up using crude carpentry tools and seeing very manual methods of construction, coming across something like the Great Pyramid. What in god's name built this? Back at that time all of the limestone casing was still in its pristine state. With the outer walls still intact, The Great Pyramid would have stood as a jaw-dropping, awe-inspiring monument of pure beauty. Beauty in every sense of the word – for the enormity, but also for the effect it would have had on the human senses and imagination.

And that is precisely what this needs to be for us now. A beacon that ignites something in our mind. Something that lights a spark of imagination that has for a long time lay dormant in our minds. A beacon that inspires hope and wonder of the amazing history our planet has witnessed. The Great Pyramid, and any of the amazing feats in our ancient history that call to question the path of our evolution and the possibility of our celestial origins, should inspire hope in us. They should inspire that our history and evolution is profoundly more amazing than the bleak situation that is portrayed by the panic mongers and the daily news. Our 'news' isn't news – it's a clever beat-up of the ordinary to appear 'newsworthy'. But it is neither newsworthy or of any real interest to what should concern our planet's consciousness right now. Our news is like a staged soap opera – and we've been 'convinced' of its high importance.

For me the message of The Great Pyramid opened my mind to a possibly extraordinary future and human potential that was yet to be realised. Our future was more likely going to be an amazing event, the likes of which would never be realised at the hands of a dictatorship type of education of how we have evolved.

"Can you picture what will be, so limitless and free?"

The Doors – Waiting for the Sun

Where do we go now?

Human beings did not evolve the way we have been informed, and any model we work from that claims otherwise, or claims that we can make any sound assumptions, while ignoring the evidence of our pre-history, is flawed. Do we not know enough about it? Is this enough reason to just throw a blanket over it and say 'anomaly' with the attached undercurrent that it doesn't matter? We know enough about these facts that there should be some agreement about man's ancient past, and be able to work from a model that allows us to include available evidence – not just bury it as strange and unimportant. It is a shame we can't benefit from what we know because it is all labelled in the same context. **Unexplained means unimportant.**

We can't have any frank discussion or know where we are heading if we leave it up to the misleading antics of our educators. It will be a case of "Hell, I didn't see that coming". Which leads me to the point I want to make about why this occurs. If I was to have a discussion like this with one of my open-minded friends, we might share ideas and actually benefit from the mutual transfer of perspectives. But what if we were to invite a third party into the discussion – someone from the 'middle ground' that we now have to come to include in the conversation. The momentum has shifted and we can no longer have a frank discussion because the new belief structure has to be the basis for what can be discussed. What is 'believable' has taken a turn and governs the nature of how productive that conversation can be.

We are governed by the lowest common denominator or the most constrictive, or 'traditional', member of the conversation, and their views. This third party may or may not be as open to some of the beliefs that act as a prerequisite or govern the terms of the conversation me and the first friend were speaking from. We are bound by the beliefs of the group if we're to discuss anything, or it just becomes an argument. And the point I make is the larger this group becomes, the more that shared truth becomes diluted to suit everyone.

The dilution of truth

We have to understand that if facts about our evolution and the amazing evidence on earth is to be integrated as mainstream knowing, and included in how we educate our children, it has to suit an enormous number of prudes. You have to think back to when it first became popular to believe the earth was round. What started as laughable soon became common. But now we have become so smart, our minds and the model we work from has become much more rigid and unbendable. For our working model of how we evolved to change and become mainstream, it has to have all the 'facts' suit every flavour of our varied educational groups. Any value that might come from the new ideas becomes buried in conformity. "Oh no, you can't say that because it doesn't suit their model of how things happened." The 'truth' becomes so diluted it has little to no value to anyone. So it becomes more a case, in this modern era, where we must surmise our own ideas, rather than trust such a diluted truth to alert us as to what might be important.

When you consider all of the high educators throwing in their 'two cents' on what is acceptable to feed to the masses – what we can send to print to teach our young – we have to realise it has been sapped of all meaningful life in the bid to appease all models of belief. There is a line ruled through anything that doesn't suit the model of "let's just all be quiet and get behind the system", and the agreed model of success. What comes to the masses as truth is such a watered-down version, and probably tainted by those in power to discourage and subdue any free thinking – labelling anything relating to the truth of our origins as some kind of 'panic-inducing' propaganda. Our education system is designed to churn out worker ants that don't ask too many questions about the system that produced them. "We don't want them to question the slavery of the nine to five life – just let them know enough to do a 'job'."

I'm no expert on 'groupthink' or the broader implications of this truth dilution and the ignorance we consequently suffer under it. I'm certain someone will enlighten me in the future – suffice to say our leaders, and our educators will never be in a position to serve us up truth of any value.

It seems obvious to me that we could never have a frank discussion on, or hypothesise about, our evolution 'gaps', simply because the playing field needs to be an agreed truth. Not all of the facts can ever be brought to the table because, "Oh no, we can't say that for sure". The truth we are comfortable agreeing on will always be a watered down and ineffectual bunch of tripe, devoid of anything that might allow us to accurately see into possible futures. It is all just conveniently flitted aside as unfounded theories – but it annoys me just how unconscious we have made ourselves to our own intuitions. Our own sense of knowing. It seems we are unable to contemplate or benefit from what we do understand about how life on earth occurred. We must be able to construct a better model than the one we are working with. Surely from what we know of early human knowledge and abilities we can make better and more enlightened assumptions about our origins and how we evolved.

There was quite obviously a fall from higher consciousness. This 'secret' history isn't just recorded as the biblical flood, but is documented in large numbers of ancient writings.

It is a pain point for me that we're left in a dark ignorance about our evolution and the ones who try and shed some light on these 'shadows' or gaps in human development are either dismissed, laughed at, or considered some kind of conspiracy nuts. But annoyed or not, the point I really want to make and why I have included this in the book, is because I do think there is someone we can trust. There is someone we can depend on to guide us into the light of new awareness, and that person is us.

Trust your instincts

We are conditioned to dismiss ourselves – that who we are and what we know is not important. We are programmed to believe our leaders and our educators have it all under control. If there was anything we need know or be alarmed about 'they' will let us know. We are conditioned to believe someone more qualified is taking care of all this stuff, but 'news flash' – there's not. No one is at the helm here. And as I hope I have demonstrated, it is our denial of the type of evidence that might allow us to know where we are that blinds us to our 'true' position, or how fortunate we might really be. The smart ones are all stabbing in the dark – and I have to tell you, firstly I would be mildly sceptical of anyone who claimed to have all the answers, but secondly, such a person could never be heard through the rubbish that would be thrown at them.

I have no idea what will happen in the coming years, how this evolutionary event I'm insinuating will come to pass. But I think 'we' do. I think every human has been installed with a divine intelligence and the seed of self-knowing. The seed to self-actualisation and our own evolution. Surely that is all an enlightened being is? A normal person who has realised what mind is – how to use perspective to turn the world into something else. Something we know we have caused – something to our liking. They worked out how to use mind to their advantage – how to get the best out of them.

I believe the seed of this knowing, the potential for self-realisation, was not only left in us all, but has become clearer by the fortune this age of information has delivered us. We have been blessed throughout our history by the beacons of light who founded our religions, but this truth has become much more universal and easier to comprehend in our present age. **We are the living proof of the outcome of the process of consciousness.**

I make no apologies for the insinuation that the realisation of mind is on our doorstep, or what this means in the broader context – an end to religion as we know it? That the realisation of mind occurring on a mass scale only stands to reason in my mind. It is what we have always been designed for – what we have forever been building towards. Like I say, it only stands to reason that one day this will happen, but while our eyes remained closed it has inched ever closer to us. This time is now and it kind of crept up on us while we were sleeping. But it is nevertheless what appears to be happening and what we are racing towards as this era builds towards a momentum of change. Large scale self-realisation is looking more and more feasible, and might possibly represent our only way out.

This is the evolution of our being, and the pointers we have for a long time been waiting for are staring us in the face. This is that time – I don't believe this event is centuries in the future, I think we bring it to life in ourselves when we notice peace, joy and kindness in our environment. When we witness the type of changes that would typify a more spiritually evolved race. This is a change process we will accelerate by our awareness of what is happening.

THROUGH THE LOOKING GLASS

I think all human beings have this sense inside them that something is happening. Yes – 100% we are conditioned to dismiss it and to shut it off – to tell ourselves "yeah right", and in each moment we do that it dissipates. But when we strengthen it with our beliefs and awareness, we'll concrete this into our shared experience. It doesn't diminish my hope for the future that people regularly miss the beauty and opportunity each moment carries. We all have a heart and with it comes a sense for our heritage – of otherworld knowing. A supernatural human instinct is coming to life, and we are starting to realise that peace on earth is a very real possibility for anyone that wants it and believes in our power to create reality. If it is to happen, it is up to us. We alone are responsible to make our 'corner' of the world peaceful.

We can be calm in a storm – we can be at peace amongst chaos. We are aware that we don't need peace on earth for there to be peace within ourselves. Conditions will never be 'right' – change starts as an inner condition. Conditions don't need to be perfect for there to be peace in us. We are our only responsibility. That is our part of peace on earth. There is no "God" coming to save us, and no saviour in a white cloak – it is up to us.

The seed to self-awareness was planted in us – it was left in us to grow and develop, but that seed is flowering in the minds of humans now. I think we all sense it, and I think we all know if something is to happen it's not going to come from some government, or some announced leader. It's going to come from you – from a ground swell of normal people just 'getting it' – of coming to the age-old conclusion that "If it's going to be, it's up to me". And honestly, for the most part this is not a revolution of kindness and 'do-gooders'. I think we all do live fairly conscious lives. Kindness is naturally appealing – it resonates as sensible – that compassion is the seed of our evolution is a no-brainer. If we are going to survive as a species, we have to give a shit about each other. But we always have – it is why we've thrived to become the enormous force on earth we are. Kindness doesn't mean sacrificing ourselves – it means positioning ourselves to help.

This seed of our evolution is in our hearts – we are good people. Why has religion prospered for as long as it has? Because it resonates with a deep sentiment within all human minds, and most people don't ignore this calling whether they are religious or not. Most are naturally empathetic – it appeals to our deepest sensibilities to help people. I often say to myself that no matter what product you are trying to sell, if it comes from a place of genuine concern for the well-being of others it will fly off the shelves. And no matter how crazy a lot of the ideas I've presented here might seem, and how they might be taken, I rest in that fact – that my intent comes from peace, love and understanding. I know that appeals to by far the highest percentage of the population.

But hell – when I started writing this book, I never had the intention of this getting so heavy, and I don't really want it to be seen in this light. I think this is the good news, not a horror story. People say, "Oh yeah – that stuff is so deep" but I never see it this way. I don't think it's 'heavy' or 'deep', I just see it as some common sense observations of where our world is heading, and how we can, in this moment, have better control over our feelings. There is no point I want to highlight more than that we align ourselves with this coming energy by avoiding the panic, the drama, and the 'it's all wrong' mindset. To sense this change we need to 'lighten up'.

Light of heart

I was watching a show on Netflix the other night about the pyramids. The Pyramid Code I think it was called. A great show with some enlightening views, but I have to say I am always a little disappointed if there is no mention of the fact that the ascending passageways are unique to The Great Pyramid. This fact is definitive and highlights something vitally important in my opinion. Nevertheless, the show still made some significant points of interest. In particular one about an Egyptian ceremony that I found fascinating.

It claims that upon their death an Egyptian would face judgement in the form of their **heart being weighed**. If their heart was too heavy, they would be forced to reincarnate once more, but if their heart was light enough on the scale, they could transcend the living cycle and go to the next level. This really struck me for two reasons. Firstly because here is one of the most advanced civilisations on earth, capable of superhuman achievements in every known aspect, but how is their life measured upon death? What do they value more highly than anything? Did you live your life with a light heart? Were you playful, humorous and childlike? Assuming of course that light-hearted carries the same connotations now as it did then.

But secondly because, no matter how advanced our societies become, we seem to struggle to move away from the idea of status being the highest measure of worth a human being can hold. Here is this superior race of beings, and they didn't value success, or how many pyramids were constructed under your rule. They didn't judge their life by their affluence as we so commonly do. They measured it by how light of heart they lived their lives. I thought to myself, that is so profound, and something we can all learn so much from. I've talked so much in here about there being different aspects to heart health. How forgiveness and letting go is even more important to us than sleep, exercise and eating the right foods. And this sums it all up perfectly in my eyes. Don't trouble yourself with standing out and having a sledgehammer impact on the world. There is far more reward in being light-hearted.

Once again here I feel like I am probably preaching to the converted. Many people I know probably understand this better than I do. I know I often take things too seriously and get obsessive about my results. Some people I know are experts at making light of tough situations, and diffusing tension like they are some sort of emotional bomb squad. They live with a high level of humour, and don't let anything petty bother them. And I salute them because they 'get it'. They got something vital long before I did, in all of my arduous 'searching' for wisdom, and peace of mind. And many of them had endured countless hardships, and been dealt a really rough hand by anyone's measure. And they still managed to come out smiling, rather than bitter and broken.

To be honest I think that this 'enlightenment' idea that has endured as some sort of Holy Grail of the ultimate development of the human soul is probably no more complicated than this. To be enlightened is to be light of heart. We don't always pull it off, but if we are aware it is something simple – an easy target – then maybe it's worth aiming for.

How does this help me?

I think the evidence of ancient ruins represents something truly inspiring, particularly in the midst of all the seeming confusion of the human plight. It often looks hopeless and like we have no real common direction. But The Great Pyramid, and the other evidence of a former advanced race existing in our pre-history should offer us some hope. Certainly, a more defined pointer of the possibilities than anything our governments or world leaders might offer. I believe the ancient ruins should inspire a sense of wonder in us. A sense that there is much more to it, with the probability that we will soon find out. The ancient monuments represent something quite beyond the scope of our imagination. And to me should set off some 'fireworks' inside us with regard the human potential.

But we also have to arrive at the conclusion that the current paradigm that guides our path into the future is a long way from being able to integrate what we can definitely assume of our origins. That our story is far more wondrous than we think. That our beginnings can't be 'explained' should in no way insinuate that it doesn't matter, or equate to it being insignificant. I think we could safely assume that if what is coming has any inkling of what is apparent of our beginnings, it will astound us. The implications of our beginnings that must be taken from the accomplishments of these early earthly inhabitants is, in the least, awe-inspiring. And even more than that it accentuates the need for us to be closer to our own hearts and internal compass. The need for peace and self-trust becomes paramount when we understand something is happening – the likes of which nothing outside of us could fully prepare.

> "Do not be dismayed by the brokenness of the world. All things break, and all things can be mended. Not with time, as they say, but with intention. So go. Love intentionally, extravagantly, unconditionally. The broken world waits in the darkness for the light that is you."
>
> L. R. Knost

CHAPTER SUMMARY

- What started as a self-help for those who had no exposure to this type of material, has evolved into something much farther reaching.
- The rise in personal development interest is the satisfying of the eternal human thirst for self-knowing. It signifies our evolution into more spiritual/subconscious beings. Our evolution, and the natural direction of our curiosity being satisfied are one in the same. All rivers flow to the sea. Towards more conscious beings – the outcome of which is of course a mass scale realisation of mind.
- The Great Pyramid, and many of the ancient ruins on earth give rise to the fact that we did not evolve in the manner in which we have been led to believe. These monoliths should ignite in us a sense of hope and wonder that all is not as it seems.
- Our evolution could never be suitably communicated to us via the current paradigm we are educated by.
- Our next leap into a higher appreciation of mind may be a far closer and more amazing event than we know. Not just from the evidence of ancient ruins, but because of the fact that the vibration of self-awareness is being turned to high.
- The human heart is our 'tuning fork' to what is happening to us. We need to become more trusting of ourselves, and closer to our core instincts in order to allow us a sense of trust and connection to what is coming. It is not something we should fear, but something that will enliven the senses. The coming change is the good news worth getting excited about.
- Of all the traits we consider so highly, what we are judged by at the completion of life is the lightness with which we lived. To be light-hearted is eternally ranked as the most favourable of human traits.

Afterword

What we have said we want becomes the foundations of how our life goes. An event's meaning can only be put into context by how it relates to what we have said would be good – what we would like to see. Our intentions change our programming and the nature of the physical world around us. Our intentions make things we couldn't see visible – we couldn't see them because we weren't looking for them. They change what things mean. What I want people to be able to take away from reading this book is how we ask for the things we want. **We ask by the vibrational state we embody.** We ask by the expectation that the things we want can come true.

Practicing mindfulness goes a long way towards freeing us from the habit energy patterns and resistance that bind us into an unconscious expectation of how things will go. Mindfulness helps us understand how imaginary the circumstances that our feelings keep telling us are so real are. Anything is possible for us if we are willing to allow it – willing to **let it be so.** If we are willing to open ourselves to the world being purely a map of what we expect to find, we will begin to expect with imagination.

What would you do if you had a choice? Because it is this general sense of our lack of options that makes us feel unwell. That we are

THE CONTROL CENTRE

chained to our outcomes, in both what is happening and how we see it. I'm all for the simple life and simple pleasures, but we need to feel like we have options. That we are not chained to a life without choice. Getting to where we want to be is about small changes, tiny steps and consistency.

Many of the reasons we think, feel and see the world in the way we do are conditioned. They go deep into our unconscious, run our lives automatically, and are conclusions that were arrived at long before we had any choice or sense of reason. They are illogical, and play havoc with how our lives unfold. The only way to bring these sabotaging beliefs to the surface is via a detached format of questioning. "What makes you think that? Why do you think this is so difficult?" Unquestioned logic can ruin how we feel, and for no good reason.

My reason for writing this was that I wanted people to understand that we can have more control over our way of seeing the world than we think. From awareness that how we see the world comes from the automated aspect of our life, we realise we do still have a choice. Awareness is the universal cure. We have more control over how we feel than most people exercise, because of a lack of awareness of our conditioning and how our programming operates. We can choose and send instructions of how we want to feel that affect real world outcomes. We can picture things in our minds that will come true eventually. How quickly has a lot to do with our commitment to the feeling state of having. To our willingness to trust in the process of creation. To open ourselves to the expectation. I wanted to help people understand how it was we were asking for the things in our life, so that they came more from our choice of preference.

I'm personally less about achievement and success, and more about how I am being. Do I live with a genuine empathy for people, and listen to understand them – am I helping, and committed to what matters and has meaning for me? Does what I'm doing bring me pleasure? I still regularly suffer bouts of depression, but they are shorter-lived than they used to be because, I understand their effect – that they are part

AFTERWORD

of a pattern, and that I have a choice. I wrote this because I think a lot of people experience emotions that they wouldn't choose if they thought they had an option, and understood the true consequences. I wanted to believe there was something I could do about raising awareness., And because I think a lot of people would be surprised to realise that sometimes a life can be saved by a timely conversation, or that someone's day can be changed by the simplest of gestures. And in saying that, I'm not trying to guilt people into becoming an inauthentic world of 'do-gooders', but to consider "what you are getting out of how you are being".

Yes, we need to know where the path we are on is taking us – that we are developing our strengths, and the world will be better off for us being here. But we only ever want what we do because we associate it with a greater sense of peace. Our goals should never be so engulfing that they make our lives miserable if they are not here yet. How ironic would that be? We need to take the foot off our own throat if we are going to add someone who is at peace with who they are. And that is truly our only responsibility.

Our world won't be magically transformed when we reach the goal. It probably won't even seem that different after a short while, and that is because life is a dance. There is no point to it apart from the pleasure it brings us – there is no end to it, just waves of energy. Remembering fond memories, and imagining good things to come changes the physical conditions of the world around us. No matter what we think we are trying to achieve, we are only ever aimed at the greater sense of peace that comes from intimacy with ourselves. By becoming closer, kinder and more accepting of who we are. Changing our life is about appreciating our life – realising the minds power to change our way of seeing.

Intelligence is not outside of us. No one is smarter than us, for us. The only real form of intelligence is being clear on how we want our lives to go. On the type of experience we would prefer, and stepping towards it with a reserved judgement of how it will all happen. We are

THE CONTROL CENTRE

never the slave to it coming true. We are the poised and wise 'boss' of how we feel. Let go of the resistance to how things are, and where we are might just become the thing we wanted, and without anything changing. Own even the parts of ourselves we are not fond of – that is what I think 'intelligence' really is.

Things can, and are getting better. More conscious equates to being more in control of how our world seems – and that is the inevitable momentum of our species. Ask with the expectancy of receiving – relaxed in the knowledge of being on the path. Be more interested in how you are responding than what seems to be going on, and know you are deserving of more than you ever thought was possible. We are living in an improving and evolving world – we know the value of working together – that is inherent in us. Give up the image of self and we will inherit something far more profound. Give up the need to be heard, recognised and approved of – we already are all of those things. Hang up the desire to be elevated by others, and you will experience a freedom very few ever have.

Emotions are not the obstacle they may have appeared to have been. They are the rocket fuel that can take us to worlds beyond when we realise how to use them properly, instead of being used by them. What would you do if you had complete control of how you felt – if you could feel the way you choose in every moment? It is a practice – and something that is gained through awareness. Every step we take towards awareness is an irreversible step towards being more in control of how we feel. Towards a more chosen experience.

This book was just supposed to be an introduction to the idea of mindfulness to people who hadn't heard of it. Who hadn't been introduced to the practice, the theory, and the benefits. Because I believe mindfulness to be the cure to the human condition itself, and that is the good news we've been waiting for. The book is supposed to be no more than some thought-provoking ideas that our evolution may not be as far into the future as we may have thought.

AFTERWORD

I just want people to find their 'True North' – that guiding principle that lights our path and our way out of darkness. The one that helps break down the faulty reasoning that tells us it is hard to get the thing we want. The further in the future our target the sharper our aim, and the more all of the events of our life are brought into the perspective of how they relate to this goal. Our situation doesn't matter – it means nothing where you are in relation to this north star. It is there to guide us and keep us on the track of what has meaning for us – not to beat us up for how far we are from it.

When we understand reality as an unconscious projection – as being made by our expectations, and why – we will come to a place of deep acceptance of however it is we find the present moment. We will accept everything that 'is' as part of our dharma or path. We will know that **reality** is just as it **has been made in mind**. Or, as the old saying goes, it will be on earth as it is in 'heaven'.

All you need is in your soul, and in this moment. Don't ever fear for drowning – nothing can harm you as much as your own thoughts.

About the Author

Simon works part time as a life coach, and has had a thirty-year obsession with personal development, and human potential material. After 20 years working as a landscape gardener and 15 years in mining, he decided it was time for him to do his part towards helping people with personal growth and change.

"Even if there is only one-person suffering, there can never be enough people trying to raise awareness of how to be more in control of how we feel. I felt blessed to have been gifted a very fortunate life, and it became my obligation to give something back. To serve people on a more personal level."

He lives in the small town of Blackwater, Central Queensland, Australia, where he works as a heavy machinery operator.

Notes

www.ingramcontent.com/pod-product-compliance
Lightning Source LLC
Chambersburg PA
CBHW021055080526
44587CB00010B/257